THE SCHWEICH LECTURES ON
BIBLICAL ARCHAEOLOGY, 1940

ISAIAH CHAPTERS XL–LV:
LITERARY CRITICISM AND HISTORY

Photo. F. Stolze

RELIEF OF THE TIME OF CYRUS AT PASARGADAE

ISAIAH CHAPTERS XL–LV

LITERARY CRITICISM AND HISTORY

BY

SIDNEY SMITH, Litt.D., F.B.A., F.S.A.

Keeper of the Egyptian and Assyrian Antiquities
in the British Museum ; Professor of Near Eastern
Archaeology in the University of London;
Hon. Fellow of Queens' College, Cambridge

THE SCHWEICH LECTURES
OF THE BRITISH ACADEMY
1940

LONDON
PUBLISHED FOR THE BRITISH ACADEMY
BY HUMPHREY MILFORD, OXFORD UNIVERSITY PRESS
1944

PRINTED IN GREAT BRITAIN AT THE UNIVERSITY PRESS, OXFORD
BY JOHN JOHNSON, PRINTER TO THE UNIVERSITY

To

ARTHUR BERNARD COOK, Litt.D., F.B.A.

Vice-President of Queens' College, Cambridge

Teacher and Friend

THIRTY YEARS AFTER

Ἐμβλέψατε εἰς τὴν στερεὰν
πέτραν ἣν ἐλατομήσατε

PREFACE

WHEN I was invited, in October of 1940, to act as a substitute in an emergency and to deliver the Schweich Lectures for the year early in 1941, the subject chosen presented itself as a natural development of an historical study published sixteen years before, a development contemplated ever since. The period of history covered by chapters xl–lv of the book of Isaiah has been illuminated by the discoveries of the last twenty years. Literary criticism has followed new courses since the book of Isaiah was last the subject of these lectures. But recently no attempt has been made to combine the two forms of research and to present the main results coherently. The task is necessarily controversial, for nearly every view of these chapters hitherto put forward has been controverted, the meaning of most historical texts disputed word by word. Controversy is not necessarily useless, if argument is allowed to correct statement.

After much hesitation, it has been decided to print the lectures as they were delivered. The lengthy notes on the first two will provide students with a guide to the literature and the details of disputed questions, and justify, or at least explain the reasons for, the statements made. Because the subject involves some acquaintance with specialist studies in various fields, the bibliographical references are more extensive than usual in this series.

The attempt in the third lecture to show that the utterances in these chapters of the book of Isaiah should be treated as a reliable historical source, rather than as subjects for a literary criticism which denies the historical validity of apparent references to contemporary events, may well prove fallible at many points, not because the main argument is unsound, but because the application to the particular instance is wrong, owing to some defect of knowledge or interpretation. This attempt has not been elaborated into a comprehensive treatment of all the historical implications, because the aim has been, not to produce a system, but simply to suggest that, where criticism aims at discovering the original meaning of a prophetic utterance, not all the interpretations that have been presented by modern critics need be considered. The original meaning, as opposed to the meaning which the later theologian may rightly find in these utterances, is likely to be the simplest that an intelligent contemporary of the prophet, living through the events of a stirring period, would place upon the words. The veiled allusions must also be interpreted from the point of view of people for whom there was no liberty of speech. The attempt to recover the original meaning may, of course, prove too ambitious, and impossible of accomplishment, in which case criticism must confine itself to the truth which later ages have found or can find in the words of the prophet. But if the original meaning is the subject of inquiry, then that meaning was conditioned by, and had reference to, specific events. Even should some of the interpretations suggested in the third lecture be thought unproven, the general principle may be worth further examination. But even that general principle can only be considered subsidiary to the themes presented in the first two lectures, the case for clearing away much that is erroneous in literary criticism, and the establishment of the historic facts. Only if the statements of these two themes are accepted need the argument of the third lecture be subjected to criticism.

With great regret a paraphrastic translation of the passages cited has been given, not the familiar cadences of the Authorized or Revised Version, because neither of these, owing to the influence of the Septuagint or of the Christian versions, gives, in doubtful cases, the correct, or the simplest, rendering of the Hebrew. The numbers in the margins opposite translations give the rhythm assumed. The retention of the tetragrammaton as a symbol, not a name, may be allowed as a personal idiosyncrasy, justified by passages in the text (xl. 10; l. 5, 7, 9). Failure to mention foreign publications later than 1939 is due to the circumstances of our time.

.SIDNEY SMITH

7 Fellows Road, Hampstead, N.W. 3
    MAY 30, 1941

ADDENDUM

MY sincere thanks are due to Professor Hooke for his most helpful criticisms and suggestions, and to Mr. H. A. Thompson for his meticulous correction of the proofs of the lectures; they are not, of course, responsible for mistakes or misprints that remain. Professor Hooke suggested the inclusion of a 'Chronological Arrangement', for the sake of clarity; readers will understand how tentative such an arrangement must be, and how doubtful many details are, without constant repetition. It has been possible to include a very few references in the notes to such articles and books published since 1939 as have become available; the bibliographies will, nevertheless, appear regrettably out of date.

S. S.

British Museum
FEBRUARY 1, 1944

CONTENTS

MAPS

LECTURE I

THE chapters of the book of Isaiah which are the subject of these lectures are generally recognized as prophetical utterances delivered between 547 and 538 B.C. If that dating is correct, these documents should be a source for historical study, exceptionally valuable because contemporary. Incidents that occurred during those years, already forgotten by the time of Herodotus in the third quarter of the fifth century, are now known from cuneiform documents; this new knowledge permits a restatement of the history of the reigns of the last king of Babylon and of the founder of the Persian Empire. But before material in the chapters from Isaiah can be used to throw further light on the history, it is essential to examine what the nature of this material is. For that purpose some account must be given of modern criticism, especially of the development due to a particular school, so that, amidst the confusion of conflicting assumptions, deductions and interpretations that have proliferated during the last thirty years, some opinion may be formed of the literary character of Isaiah cc. xl–lv, before the documents are used as an historical source.

The first lecture is, therefore, a brief account of recent criticism. The second will be an outline of the historical facts not to be found in the text-books, for the years 556–538. The third will deal with some unrecognized historical material in these chapters.

RECENT CRITICISM OF ISAIAH cc. XL–LV

It has been wisely said [1] that 'the original sense of a poem which is now in the Psalter need not at all be that which the editor of the collection attributed to it, any more than the sense attributed to it by the editor need be that which the Christian Church connected with it'. This is as true, even more true, of cc. xl–lv of the book of Isaiah. The Christian Church found in these chapters

verses forecasting the coming of Jesus,[2] an interpretation
which must exceed the views of the first editor of the
complete book. Jewish scholars found a mode of interpretation suited to their faith and time, and recorded it in
the Targums; the Septuagint translator found meanings that
deviate from the original.[3] Modern criticism has for over
a century been attempting to discover the sense intended
by the man who first wrote or spoke the words. Linguistic
and literary criticism have been used in the attempt to
determine the original wording, historical and theological
analysis to ascertain the original sense. For use as a source
of history, these chapters must be understood in their
original connexion; critical views on that point have
changed and are much confused.

The separation of these chapters from what precedes
was suggested very early and has not been doubted by
many since Döderlein.[4] Duhm was the first[5] to propound
the arguments for separating them from what follows, on
historical grounds. The references to a return from exile
begin with c. xl; from that point to c. lv no authentic
passage is incompatible with the last days of the exile.
Twice the name Cyrus is mentioned. The chapters which
followed these must be later in date, written at a time
when the Temple had been rebuilt. Duhm regarded
cc. xl–lv as a book, written by one man, but subject to
interpolation and editing. Four passages concerning 'the
servant of YHWH', and other passages concerning the technique of idol-making, or rebuking Israel for sin, he excised,
to conform with a theory of theological development.

The views expressed by the late Professor Kennett in his
Schweich Lectures for 1910[6] marked, perhaps, an extreme
point in the disintegration of cc. xl–lv in authorship and
date, by applying the methods he considered proper for
other books of the Old Testament. He thought only the
passages indubitably concerned with Cyrus and Babylon
belonged to the sixth century;[7] much that concerned the
return from exile and all that refers to the glorious future

for Jerusalem and Israel he assigned to the time of the
Maccabees.[8] In general he was guided, as were many
others, by three principles: in accordance with the school
of Wellhausen he regarded any wording that might be re-
motely connected with Jewish eschatology as late; good
Hebrew untainted by Aramaic was, he thought, used at a
much later date than in fact it was; and any passage that
could possibly be brought into connexion with the history
of the Maccabaean period was so interpreted.[9]

During the last thirty years criticism has always started
with the examination of Duhm's position; it has been
generally recognized that it is impossible to assign any
passages to the Maccabaean period, both because the
chronological assumptions are not soundly based,[10] and
because Kennett's dichotomy is not in accord with the internal evidence provided by subject, style, and language.[11]

Though the Hebrew text is recognized to be in a good
state,[12] very few words being hopelessly corrupt,[13] attempts
to recover an earlier text by applying formal criteria have
led to extensive excision and emendation. One criterion
thus employed is metre; to obtain some regularity one
critic [14] rejected 77 out of a total of 333 verses, introduced
extensive alterations in the remainder, and still admitted
'mixed metres'. Such a method condemns itself; cc. xl–
lv, though, as Lowth proved, they are for the greater part
in verse form, show irregularities that prohibit the application of a formal scheme,[15] and the verse is declamatory,
like Babylonian [16] or Saturnian or some early English. The
other formal criterion is a deliberate structure, called
'structure in strophes', *Strophenbau*. This inaccurate use
of the Greek word strophe leads to much confusion. A
strophe requires the repetitive use of elaborate and specially
contrived combinations of metrical feet, an antistrophe.
There are no such combinations in Hebrew poetry, and
therefore no repetitions. It is not difficult to produce short
periods of 2, 4, 6, 8 lines which might be called stanzas,
because the *parallelismus membrorum* on which rhythm is

based tends to such divisions,[17] but the stanzas can nowhere in these chapters be proved to balance each other artificially.[18] Wherever this criterion is strictly applied, many omissions have to be assumed and frequent excisions made. The historian must abide by the text as it is, with only the minor adjustments ordinarily required.

The only other guides for textual alterations are the manuscripts and the versions. There is a growing tendency to accept the evidence of a few Hebrew manuscripts, or even one, as significant, because any divergence from the normal in the carefully guarded tradition must have sound reason.[19] As to the versions, the major question is the proper use of the Septuagint. There has always been a tendency to use the Greek version of Isaiah, in spite of its frequent divagations, as if it were a literal translation, whenever that is possible.[20] Some scholars have consistently introduced minute alterations into the Masoretic text to secure complete agreement with the Greek; more often the application of the Greek wording has been spasmodic and subjective.[21] Recently, intensive study of the Septuagint version has finally proved that it is not a literal translation; the original intention was not merely to translate, but to interpret, and the interpretation belongs to its own time.[22] It has been well said, quite recently : 'The Septuagint pertains rather to the history of the exegesis of the Old Testament than to the history of the text.'[23] The full effect of a more scholarly treatment of the Septuagint will only be apparent in future commentaries; much lumber should be removed from proposed emendations. But more careful attention is required to the sense of the Greek version, and to the reason why that sense was found in the Hebrew.

The separation of cc. xl–lv from what follows has been much contested. While some regard cc. lvi–lxvi as imitations of the style and adaptations of the themes of cc. xl–lv by later hands at different dates, or by a single author at a later date,[24] others maintain that all cc. xl–lxvi are by

one hand,[25] but that cc. lvi–lxvi were written at a later
date. On either view cc. lvi–lxvi are outside the period
covered by the present inquiry. The separation of this
section of the book at c. xl has also been questioned.[26]
The reason is that c. xxxv deals with the same subject,
the road through the desert, as passages in xl–lv, and
employs much the same language. But the superficial
similarity of vocabulary is due to the subject, the road,
and to natural phenomena ; there is a distinction between
the road of xl–lv which is to run over levelled mountains
and raised valleys, probably a real road, and the road of
holiness, probably eschatological, in c. xxxv.[27] For historical purposes, the interpretation of c. xxxv must not
prejudice the interpretation of cc. xl–lv.

The critic who regards cc. xxxiv–xxxv as an integral
part of the work of the author of xl–lv believes not only
that the Chronicler's account of a return of exiles in the
time of Cyrus was a mistaken deduction and the Aramaic
document embedded in the book of Ezra a forgery, but
also that an editor of the book of Isaiah, misled by the
Chronicler, inserted the name of Cyrus into xlv, 1, and that
consequently he wrote and inserted xliv, 28.[28] The whole
composition is dated to the end of the fifth century.[29] The
weakness of this argument is immediately apparent in the
treatment of the references to Babylon and the Chaldaeans.[30]
These terms are not allowed to mean what they seem to
mean, but become, symbolically, something else, or are
simply excised. Such a system of interpretation is no support for violent excisions. Critics unable to accept it, who
are yet convinced that there was no Edict of Cyrus and
no return from exile, have inverted the basic argument.
The Chronicler's invention, they suppose, is due to the
existence of these prophecies of a return, which were not
in fact realized.[31] There is, however, sound evidence for
the authenticity of the Cyrus Edict, as it is cited in the
Aramaic document, provided by the literary form of
Persian documents and archaeological discoveries of early

buildings,[32] whatever may be thought of the Chronicler's own account.

The principal development of literary criticism has been a radical rejection of the treatment of these chapters as a book. This has resulted from a new system of analysis introduced by Hermann Gunkel.[33] The primary truth which formed the basis of the system, that prophecies were spoken words, had not, before 1914, been allowed to affect interpretation of the book form. Yet obviously, if the original form was that of the spoken, not the written, word, criticism must be affected. This recognition of a simple truth was a great advance, but it was obscured by accretions. Gunkel's methods were elaborated in a study of the Psalter.[34] Now the Psalms are intended for repetition and are public utterances for a community, or for an individual using a common formula; they therefore can be catalogued under 'type' labels. From such cataloguing arose the system, *Gattungsforschung*, research into types. All Hebrew literature, Gunkel said, especially poetry, fell into types, or classes, each clearly distinguished. They were of more importance in Hebrew than they would be in modern literature, because the types conditioned absolutely the possible forms of expression. Each type has three distinguishing characteristics: (1) a common set of thoughts and sentiments, (2) a traditional set of conventional formulae, (3) some function in the life of the people,[35] the origin of both thought and expression. In the case of prophecy, the original function was the oration by an ecstatic[36] in public.

This doctrine was applied to cc. xl–lv by Gressmann,[37] who undertook to show that these chapters were a series of short, independent units and to catalogue these into types. The only specific argument for the independence of the units was an analysis of c. xl,[38] not accepted by other critics of the school. His general arguments were directed against the view that the book was planned as a whole. The various themes in these chapters are announced in the opening sections; the argument is reinforced and repeated with slight changes.   Gressmann said: 'A writer who has thought out his work and formed it as an artistic composition does not repeat himself, unless for some special reason.'   He did not stay to consider whether there might be a special reason in these chapters, whether reversion to, and repetition of, a theme might not occur in long speeches;[39] perhaps his definition of artistic composition excluded long speeches.   Again, Gressmann wrote: 'An author who writes according to a clear plan, conscious of his intention, also has a good arrangement, and in every good arrangement the sections are sharply divided the one from the other.'   Such divisions may be requisite for a university thesis, tiresome in sermons, a complete failure in a speech meant to persuade and convince.[40]   The real aim of *Gattungsforschung* was to secure short units, the reason, analogy; because other, earlier, prophecies fell into short utterances of types that could be labelled, such units should be found in cc. xl–lv.[41]

The principles for delimiting the units were thus defined by Gressmann:

The last, conclusive resort in deciding whether there is a connexion or a fresh commencement lies with logic.   But logical considerations . . . can be the better omitted because it is precisely logic that is supported, and indeed partly replaced by, 'enquiry into types', *Gattungsforschung*.   Criticism that pays attention to style will often be able to say for superficial reasons, such as the occurrence of particular formulae, whether there is a connexion or not.[42]

This statement is not in itself logical.   If logic is the final resort, it cannot be replaced, even partly, by an argument from formulae.   If the formulae alone decide, then logic is not the final resort.   *Gattungsforschung* has in fact rested principally upon the conventional formulae; the underlying doctrine can again be given in Gressmann's words:

As the prophetic types have not been handed on in tradition, they must first be recovered and reconstituted.   A methodical enquiry must start with the introductory and end formulae, because they have formed the germinating cell of each type, and have always remained, in the course of later development, too, characteristic pointers. Where we meet introductory and end formulae, no doubt can exist about the division of literary elements. If we had a collection of fairy stories in which the individual stories were not separated from one another by lines and titles, we should still immediately recognize the beginning and the end of each story by the usual formulae, 'Once upon a time', at the beginning and 'If they have not died, they are still alive' at the end. The task is more difficult where the typical formula is missing in the introduction or at the end, and most difficult where the formula is absent in both places.[43]

Even so, he continued, 'The position in reality is tolerable because the prophetic utterances are very simple in construction. The trained eye can almost always recognize beginning and end at the first glance.'[44]   Not surprisingly, since the task is so easy, scholars of the past, who had failed to recognize the obvious, came in for reproof: 'The way commentators have obstinately misunderstood the meaning of style is almost unintelligible.'[45]

Yet if the formulae on which Gressmann relied[46] be examined, the question inevitably arises whether this confidence is justified. He maintained, for instance, that divine utterances are marked at the beginning by 'Thus saith YHWH', and at the end by 'saith YHWH', or by some slight variation of these formulae; the divine utterance, with clauses attached, is always an independent unit. Subsequent critics have had to recognize that the divine utterances are included in longer units. These formulae do not resemble those of the fairy stories; they are not much more than quotation marks. At most they might be compared to the formulae marking, not the beginnings and ends of stories in the *Arabian Nights*, but the nightly sections, and even that comparison would be inept. When the divine utterances are oracles, one need not be necessarily separated from the other; oracles in sequence, dealing with a series of questions, were well known in ancient practice.[47]   The units proposed by Gressmann,

short as they are, have not been accepted;[48] each new
critical study produces a different set. The differences
in each proposal are significant, in spite of the constant
features. These units overlap in many cases, and are not
so easily distinguished.[48a]

The same fate has befallen the types. Gressmann
divided them into two classes, those originally prophetic
in character and those derived from other literature. The
prophetic types were (1) visions,[49] (2) threats,[50] (3) promises,[51] (4) invective,[52] (5) warnings,[53] (6) words of comfort,[54] (7) court pleadings,[55] (8) words of assurance,[56]
(9) historical reflection.[57] The non-prophetic types were
(1) songs of victory,[58] (2) railing songs,[59] (3) hymns.[60] It
will be immediately apparent that these types are not
dependent on form, as are, for instance, ode and elegy in
classical literature, but simply labels for the content of
units. Are such labels instructive? Why must all the
units belong to one type or the other? Gressmann's own
conclusion justifies these questions, for he said:

If Deutero-Isaiah is to be assigned a place in the literary
history of Israelite prophecy, it may be said to be characteristic
that the dissolution of the prophetic types begins with him. The
fixed forms that had prevailed till then break up. While the
types of speech which had been employed by the prophets before
the exile are mostly quite sharply distinguished from one another,
exact separation is often impossible in the case of Deutero-
Isaiah; the supplementary reflections, with which the oracles are
surrounded, have grown luxuriantly over everything, so that
the lines of division between an utterance of God and an utterance of the prophet cannot always be clearly recognized. Thus
the promises and the words of comfort coalesce. Moreover the
distinctions between warnings and invectives have lost their
meaning. Individual motifs have become independent and found
their expression in poems which cannot be regularly classified
under any heading. Finally, nearly everywhere, constituent
parts of hymns which were originally foreign to prophecy have
been included and burst the framework.[61]

This conclusion is tantamount to a confession that these
chapters are not suitable material for cataloguing into

types.   Yet, as with the units, each new critical study provides a new lot. The latest writer to do so admits the
position freely.

If [says Professor Begrich] it is possible for the text xlv, 9–13
about the limits of which there is, in substance, general agreement, to be treated by Gressmann and Haller as 'double
invective with oracle', by Balla as 'a hymn in the first person',
by Volz as a 'song', then it must be admitted that the comprehension of the literary types of Deutero-Isaiah has clearly not
been successfully achieved yet.[62]

This admission ought to have led to a study of the cause
of this failure; but the doctrine still holds sway. Begrich's
new set of types consists of: (1) the oracle granting salvation or proclaiming the grant of requests,[63] (2) the word
of comfort, (3) the court pleading,[64] (4) the argumenta-
tion,[65] (5) the short injunction,[66] (6) the warning,[67]
(7) the instruction of the herald,[68] (8) the invitation of
personified Wisdom,[69] and these are followed by types
called lyrical, (9) the hymn,[70] (10) the song of lamentation
or thanks by an individual,[71] (11) the national song of
thanks,[72] (12) the eschatological coronation song,[73] (13) the
railing song.[74] After twenty-five years *Gattungsforschung* is
still engaged in changing the labels.

It is therefore proper to ask whether this division into
units, and these labels, which would affect interpretation,
should influence the historian. The God of Israel addresses
His people thus:

3	And I will feed them that oppress you with their own flesh,
+3	and they shall be drunk with their own blood as with sweet wine.
2	And all flesh shall know
+3	that I, YHWH, am your Saviour,
+3	and your Redeemer, the Mighty One of Israel.

(xlix, 26.)

Gressmann called this a 'threat'.[75] It is part invective too,
but largely promise; superficially it is an utterance of God,
in fact it is patently the speech of man. No type label can

adequately describe the passage. Some can see in the words a picture of the 'last day' that is not repeated so elsewhere.[76] Historically, contemporary Israel was promised victory over Babylon at great cost of life to the enemy. This literary analysis has not illuminated the words, but produced an endless controversy about words. The units are no more than paragraphs,[77] the type-names not very reliable headings.

More might have been expected from a study of style, for these chapters are strongly marked by idiosyncrasies. Violent similes, meant only to illustrate a single aspect, are not uncommon. YHWH can be compared to a woman in labour; Israel is a 'little worm'; Jerusalem, addressed as a woman, is to ascend a high hill, perhaps the Mount of Olives; Babylon is to fall from her estate, as a queen might become a prostitute. Allusions to unnamed persons are constant, and general truths are introduced in a way that shows they have a specific application. Though much work has yet to be done in this direction,[78] *Gattungsforschung* has been devoted exclusively to the formal elements, with a tendency not to test, but always to reinforce, the theories of 'unit' and 'type'. An example will illustrate the analytical method employed. The opening verses of c. xl read:

3	¹'Encourage, encourage My people'
+ 2	says your God.
3	²Speak unto the heart of Jerusalem
+ 2	and proclaim to her
2	that her forced service is completed,
+ 2	that her punishment has been accepted,
2	that she has received from the hand of YHWH
+ 2	double for all her transgressions. (xl, 1–2.)

In this utterance each word has its special force, contributing to the whole. But the critic of style, Professor Köhler, says that the sense could have been expressed thus: 'Your God says, "Comfort my people of Jerusalem with the fact that its fault has been removed because it received twofold punishment for its sins from my hand".'[79]

The clause 'that its fault has been removed' is distended by a doublet, 'that her forced service is completed'. 'Completed' in this connection he calls colourless; of the whole, he says, 'a single thought with double the words necessary for it'. The three imperatives at the beginning are due to a desire for 'filling up and rounding out'.[80] Everywhere this critic finds mere verbiage. Thus he writes:

> At the moment when the radiant Persian appears as a victorious hero and Messiah of the Jews on the heights of Iran, all the doors of his [that is, the prophet's] heart spring open for hopes to enter. A whirlwind of ideas, a torrent of declarations pours out. There is no polished unity, and the picture given of individual elements of the argumentative dialogues as consecutive in thought is erroneous, if our view is not concentrated on the fact that these elements whirl here and there in confusion, piling up, hurrying along, changing places, repeating, completing, covering and inter-secting. Everything he says is a great, unique, unified continuity, created suddenly, changing everything, measureless and dis-orderly, a flood, a revolution, corresponding to the whole extent of his doubts and anxieties.[81]

This description seems to achieve the style it is attempting to describe. But before the words of these chapters are dismissed as Asiatic style, their content should be more carefully examined.

Oddly enough, this supposed verbosity does not prevent Professor Köhler from considering the prophet a great stylist. Yet he proceeds to charge him with poverty of vocabulary.[82] The example occurs in xl, 12.

3	Who has measured the waters in the hollow of his hand,
+ 3	and has marked off the heavens with the half-cubit rule,
3	and held in the 'third'-measure[83] the dust of the earth,
+ 3	and weighed mountains on the steelyard[84]
+ 2	and hills in scales?

This passage is so artificially contrived that it is one of many that might convince a critic that, though these words are intended to be spoken, they are not spontaneous. The verbs and the objects are carefully balanced to cover the measurable forms of matter,[85] and all the types of measurement. The mention of the two methods of weighing solids, one suitable for heavier, the other for lighter, objects, has its point and place in these questions, which expect the answer, 'Nobody'.[86] But the critic of style puts the matter otherwise. 'Five clauses with five objects', he comments, 'but for the fifth Deutero-Isaiah seems to have no fifth verb.' It is impossible to trust such criticism.[87]

More importance attaches to a subtle development of the view that the verse is lyric, the independent units by different authors. Critics of the *Gattungsforschung* school regarded unity of authorship as axiomatic, and were inclined to retain some passages excised by Duhm and others. Professor Caspari, dissecting the 'book' form of cc. xl–lv, found that cc. liv–lv were specially composed as the end of the book; c. xl, a patchwork of 'units', had been put together as an introduction. There is no indication of unity, he thinks, in the authorship of the units, merely a unity of purpose, due to the time of writing. There are different uses of the same word in different units, while different words denote the same thing; there are variations in the use of the types, inconsistencies in metrical usage. The phrase 'servant of YHWH' is used both as a collective, for Israel, and also for different individuals. There are inconsistencies of thought. Thus in xliv, 28 the restoration of Jerusalem is imposed on Cyrus as a duty, while in xliii, 3 YHWH rewards him with the richest lands in the world. There is no accord between the severity of reproof and the gentleness of comfort expressed; the lack of a unifying intellect is felt. Caspari's view of the authorship may be summed up in his own words:

A movement in Babylonia demanding the restoration of Jerusalem must have preceded the actual restoration; (that movement must have been) the result of an unintentional co-operation of orators and enthusiasts who formed opinion. Among them Cyrus was called 'the anointed', 'the servant', 'the shepherd', 'God's favourite', perhaps also 'the falcon'. All are mutations of a single basic thought, of an optimistic kind; the proclamation of it came from more than one mouth.[88]

Each proclamation, this critic thinks, took the form of a communal utterance or recitation before a community, with *responsa* by the audience. Mostly the utterances were marching songs for use by the exiles on the way back to Palestine; but pilgrim songs, festival songs, and songs of home are united with these, without any sharp dividing line. An instance of the *responsa* is found in xlvii, 4.[89] The railing song against Babylon is put into the mouth of yhwh, and after the opening verses come words unrelated to the context, 'Our redeemer, *yHWH ṣᵉbā'ōṯ* is His name, Israel's Holy One'. Many commentators have inserted 'thus says', without warrant. Caspari regards this as a communal interruption of the reciter, at an arranged point. But even if this were true, it must still be a late interpolation, used in the synagogues owing to the expressions in the preceding verse.[90] There were no original *responsa*. As to the use of the units as marching songs, the strongest argument put forward is based on the wording of xl, 28–30, a call for confidence in God: 'He does not grow weary or tire . . . (warrior-)lads grow weary and tire . . . those that wait on yhwh . . . run and do not tire, march and do not grow weary.' Of this Caspari says: 'The restless return in this section to the leading idea, the central motif, points to vocal accompaniment of some regular rhythmic action of many people, and from the subject that theme may be recognized as a march.'[91] This is misplaced ingenuity.[92] It is impossible to believe that the sense of reverence and fear would have permitted such use of profoundly religious utterances, or that a collection of marching songs has been mistaken for prophecy for two thousand years.

It is unfortunate, because the question deserves closer consideration than it has received, that the argument against unity of authorship is confounded with this interpretation of the units. Caspari's points against unity of authorship are not so objective as they seem. They are based on too stringent a demand for consistency in the use of words and ideas by an individual,[93] a demand proved erroneous by common experience. If these speeches were delivered on different occasions, there need be no absolute consistency of thought. The same word can, in every language, bear different meanings in one passage. And the assumption of a close, but unintentional, correspondence in thought and in allusive reference by many different authors requires much more faith in the spontaneous origin of the same thought in many persons than the historian will readily feel. But it is perfectly possible for a small body of men, sharing the same views, to use similar language, intentionally.[94] Had Caspari limited his thesis to the demonstration of two or three different authors, some of the arguments used by previous scholars for excising passages would have served him. Such an effort to detect different authors by the examination of the vocabulary and content of excised passages was undertaken by Dr. Elliger, who had no knowledge of Caspari's conclusions. The analysis of vocabulary, which examines a text word by word and judges on the percentage whether a passage containing words not used elsewhere by an author, or only rarely used, is spurious, has been employed in other branches of literature, rarely with complete success, sometimes with disastrous results. Dr. Elliger was faced by an almost impossible task. There is not a sufficient bulk of material in cc. xl–lv for this method. Hebrew of the sixth century is not so well known that it is possible to distinguish the rare use by an author of a common word from a distinctive use peculiar to an individual. Above all, his own conception of cc. lvi–lxvi as a unity, written by a man who had been a disciple of the prophet whose utterances are included in xl–lv, presents an added difficulty, making the task much more complicated than the attempt to distinguish, say, the work of Beaumont and Fletcher in a joint play. Elliger distinguished long passages in xl–lv from the hand of the author of cc. lvi–lxvi, short additions and sutures; the compilation of the original prophecies of the man whom he calls

'Deutero-Isaiah', and the publication of the book, he also assigns to 'Trito-Isaiah'.[95]

This thesis does not affect the consideration of cc. xl–lv as historical material, for Dr. Elliger admits that this compilation, in its present form, was published soon after the death of his 'Deutero-Isaiah'. All these chapters, then, contain prophecies and related utterances contemporary with the events of the latter part of the reign of Nabonidus. The only question of interest is whether the words of rebuke and the words of comfort were really spoken by different persons; if there is a good explanation of the rebukes without accepting the differentiation, it is surely preferable. The principal result of Dr. Elliger's study is to show that it is extremely difficult, in a detailed examination of the text, to give any good reason for assuming that there were two or more authors, apart from interpolations, since by his own admission, if there were two, they were related as master and pupil. Such a division is too theoretical. It reduces a historical figure from the complexity associated with life to the simplicity of a single mood. Moreover the argument in such passages as xliii, 22–28 may have been misunderstood by Elliger.

One feature of Elliger's thesis is welcome, because certainly correct. Though he fully accepted and even accentuated the vagaries of the theory of units and types, he showed conclusively that, as the units stand in the present text, they are not all independent, for there are long sequences knit together by a coherent argument.[96] These sequences were, in his opinion, due to the compiler, in most cases; but occasionally he was forced to admit that the compiler found them already together, in written documents, torn and tattered, that came to his hand.[97] There is in this the germ of an idea that may prove correct.

The contemporaneity of nearly all the units in xl–lv is, then, stoutly maintained by the critics of the *Gattungsforschung* school, including Caspari and Elliger. Four 'servant' passages, which remain the centre of discussion and will probably always be so, are too closely connected in style, thought and theme, it is said, to be separated, in the manner of Duhm, from the rest of the text in authorship.[98]   Some critics maintain that these passages are not to be explained from the context, and attempt to bring all four into combination, as Duhm did.[99]   For those who interpret the 'servant' in the four passages as meaning Israel,[100] the sense generally specified or otherwise indicated in other passages of the text, this particular combination causes no embarrassment.   Yet this general explanation becomes complicated by the assumption that 'Israel My servant ' is sometimes the nation, sometimes the faithful in Israel, once even, in a passage not included in the four, the unfaithful ; it would be better to abandon the assumption that the same meaning was originally intended always to attach to the 'servant'.   But those who think that the wording in these four passages points to an individual have also differed, because of the difficulties that arise from treating the four passages as a coherent whole.   Gressmann, who increased the number of passages to seven, maintained that the 'servant' was the cult-hero of a mystery of the pagan type.[101]   That the pagan story may have been applied to some figure of Hebrew history is an explanation outlined but never fully expounded by Mowinckel,[102] who saw in other sections of these chapters festival songs for the coronation of YHWH developed from the supposed pagan type he found in the Psalms.[103]   But attempts to produce parallels, for instance with the Marduk myth,[104] show differences, not similarities, for no such cult could allow the references in lii, 13–liii, 12 to a resurrection to be so obscure ; indeed it is only by forcing the meaning to fit this exegesis that any reference can be found.[105]   Those who find in the 'servant' a figure of past history, Moses, as Sellin did for a time,[106] have been forced ultimately to admit that there is neither evidence for any identification nor probability in reference to the past.   The language points to a contemporary figure, but attempts to name the one intended,

D

for instance Zerubbabel,[107] have also failed. The alternatives now usually admitted are, a great unknown,[108] or the prophet himself,[109] though some scholars maintain that the 'servant' is a form of the Messiah. But these interpretations are largely influenced by a major problem affecting the interpretation of much else in these chapters. Nearly all critics find eschatological elements in sections which appear to deal with contemporary history.

On this question of eschatology there has been a revolution in the last thirty years. One of the critical activities resulting from Gunkel's views was the search for allusions to myths, popular beliefs and superstitions not recorded in any text.[110] Gressmann pursued this search to combat the dogma of the Wellhausen school that eschatological beliefs were not earlier than the third century B.C.[111] He was able to show that much in earlier books foreshadowed, or might lead to, the later eschatological scheme; but his definition of eschatology is so loose that the term becomes unscientific.[112] The passages he cited from cc. xl–lv had nothing to do with the fixed scheme, and need not be regarded as eschatological at all.[113] His position was as extreme in one direction as Wellhausen's had been in the other. But Gressmann's arguments have been widely accepted, even by scholars once opposed to his conclusion. Thus Volz, who had clearly defined the fixed features of later Jewish belief, now says of these chapters and of the prophets generally : 'The coming of Yahwe in the historical act immediately impending, in the judgement or salvation of Israel, is, however, for the prophets at the same time the last, final advent of Yahwe. The prophets are eschatologists.'[114] This merely obscures the fact that there is nothing to show that this prophet was familiar with the conception of a last advent.

An eschatological, as opposed to an historical, treatment of certain passages leads some critics to find an opposition between two stages in the prophet's career.[115] From the time when Croesus was defeated, it is thought, the impend-

ing fall of Babylon could be foreseen. The prophet believed
that Cyrus would become a worshipper of YHWH,[116] that
the nations would be brought by his own mission to the
God of Jerusalem. When Cyrus did capture Babylon, this
argument runs, he acknowledged himself a worshipper of
Marduk.[117] In his disappointment the prophet turned, it
is supposed, to the eschatological hope in God's advent.
Hempel's special application of this hypothesis postulates a
transference of the expectation of redemption for the exiles
and of glory for Jerusalem from Cyrus to the 'servant'.[118]
This entails the strange view that the original prophecies,
recognized to be erroneous, have been left to stand beside
the corrections.[119] The principal argument is the parallelism
between xlv, 1 ff., the address to Cyrus, and xlii, 5–9, dealing
with the 'servant'; that argument fails if the 'servant' is
not always the same person. This hypothesis has recently
been inverted; Professor Begrich dates passages he considers
eschatological earlier than the Cyrus passages, that is before
547, the year of the fall of Sardis, and assumes that the
future fall of Babylon was obvious, to contemporary ob-
servers, during the campaign against Astyages. This is
impossible as history,[120] and the exegesis which dates references to the fall of Babylon many years before the event
cannot be correct.

The assumption that the 'servant' passages which probably refer to an individual must all refer to the same individual is not warranted by the term 'servant of YHWH';
this means no more than 'one who executes the orders of
God', and is not confined to these chapters.[121] The two
passages where the 'servant' speaks in the first person,
xlix, 1–6 and l, 4–10, can only be referred to the author
himself, or to the person delivering the words, if, as is to
be assumed, these words were meant to be heard by an
audience, not read and interpreted by individuals in
seclusion; any other explanation is complicated and un-
natural.[122] The long lament for the death of a 'servant',
lii, 13–liii, 12, whose sufferings resemble those of the

'servant' of the two passages in the first person, may, then, most probably refer to the prophet too; but in that case this section cannot have been written by him in anticipation of his death, a most unlikely development of the eschatological hypothesis.[123] But the 'servant' of xlii, 1–4, a passage in which the actions attributed to the 'servant' are those of a king, has nothing beyond certain epithets and descriptions in common with the 'servant' who is the prophet, and some of these appellations are also applied to the collective person, Israel; they are characteristic not of the person, but of the relation to God. Several voices have been raised to point out that the contemporary who would fit the description in xlii, 1–4 and 5–9, which may then be taken with 1–4, is Cyrus, without avail.[124] The historian is likely to favour that suggestion.

If it be accepted that cc. xl–lv consist of the speeches of a prophet delivered during a space of five years or more, ending in 538,[125] questions arise as to how they were delivered, when they were written down, in what form the present chapters were first published. That it would be difficult and dangerous, if not impossible, to deliver publicly or to publish many portions of this book during the Babylonian domination is generally recognized.[126] Some have therefore thought that the speeches were delivered in the synagogues of the exiles,[127] or in conclaves of sympathizers;[128] the synagogues seem unlikely, for the subjects do not fit the ritual of worship, in spite of a bold attempt to find ritual elements.[129] Others have thought the utterances were written down separately; the expression 'book-speeches', due to the signs of elaborate artifice in the arrangement and in the expression of thought, is not so out of place as one critic asserts.[130] Earlier commentators had the same intuition; they thought of publication of the sections in fly-sheets, *Flugblätter*,[131] like those that appeared in Germany during the Napoleonic wars. The impossibility of mechanical reproduction has been thought to condemn that suggestion,[132] but it does not. These speeches are more carefully composed than spontaneous delivery would permit.[133]   They vary from very short pieces, only a verse long,[134] to sections that exceed the chapters [135] of the present division.   They are written in verse that is meant to aid memory, intended for declamation.   It is quite possible that messengers, mentioned in the text,[136] were sent round to Jewish communities in Palestine and even among the exiles, each one to several, bearing a written copy of the prophet's latest utterance, to be read with appropriate explanations and expansions when possible.   That would explain the allusive style, the avoidance of names.   Such documents need not be put into the form of a letter, as has been asserted.[137]   In Babylonia a polemic in verse form was circulated shortly after the conquest by Cyrus; it must have been issued to scribes to declaim in various places.[138] It is certainly not an address to the gods, as has been suggested,[139] perhaps in ignorance of the Babylonian style for such addresses.

There is no need, for historical purposes, to examine various theories of compilation, save perhaps to remark on the aberration which sought to show that the independent short units had been arranged on a system of catchwords.[140] Such a system might be used in a late compilation, and this theory is not to be rejected on *a priori* grounds, but because the details in its application seem incredible. Whatever the principle of arrangement may have been, there is nothing to show that chronological sequence was aimed at, though it may have been partly achieved;[141] each logical section must be examined, without prejudice, for dating.[142]   It is of more interest to note that there is no decisive evidence to show that cc. xl–lv ever were a separate book,[143] or that there ever was a roll on which xl–lxvi were put together.[144]   It is possible that the first compilation consisted of two rolls, the book of Isaiah.   For there is a characteristic spirit and tone throughout, well known to readers, too long neglected or not mentioned by the critics, which distinguishes this book from those of

Jeremiah, Ezekiel, or the Twelve Prophets. It is a pleasing development of modern criticism that this truth is at times recognized. A German scholar has recently said :

Justice is not done to the book of Isaiah at all, if it is regarded as a mixture of disparate components, or as a tilt-yard for anonymous prophecies and undisciplined editors. Some things may have been included, which were ascribed to Isaiah in the same way as the Psalms to David, the Laws to Moses, the Proverbs to Solomon, perhaps because he was considered *the* prophet as David was *the* Psalmist; the largest part was certainly included as being overshadowed by his spirit, and said in his way. The latest 'Introduction to the Old Testament', that of Eissfeldt,[145] has rightly stressed the thematic relationship of Deutero-Isaiah and Isaiah.[146]

To that relationship, we may add, and to his attitude as the prophet who carried on a tradition, the author of Isaiah xl–lv probably owed his position, during the critical years 545–538, as a leader in Israel, despised and rejected by some, but ultimately justified.

If, then, it be asked what the nature of Isaiah cc. xl–lv as historical evidence is, the durable results of criticism in all the ebb and flow of opinion during the last thirty years may be summed up briefly. Few doubt that the main bulk of these chapters was written some time in the years 547–538. The tendency has been increasingly to regard interpolations as few and brief, and nothing for which a reasonable historical explanation can be found need be treated as spurious. The chapters were, too, what they appear to be, not a book, but a series of prophetic utterances, and very few critics claim that any are considerably later than the fall of Babylon. Whether all the utterances were necessarily so short, or fell into traditional types, as some critics think, is open to doubt ; but that each complete utterance is logically independent and must be judged by itself, without preconception, is one of the great advances due to recent work. There is, for example, no proof of chronological order in the arrangement of the utterances. Finally, in spite of much emendation and tinkering, the consonantal Hebrew text has been proved exceptionally sound, and there need be no doubt that it provides a reliable basis for historical deductions. It must be a first principle, in using the text as an historical source, to avoid adopting any emendation which alters the sense of the consonantal text, or which avoids a pregnant expression to substitute one less forceful. Any emendation should only be adopted when good reason can be found for the corruption.

The primary intention of these chapters was religious, and their true importance still remains so. For that reason they are an historical source of a remarkably valuable, because rare, kind in the study of ancient Oriental history. The allusions to contemporary events are in most cases oblique, because direct reference would have been dangerous and would have stultified its own object, if it led to suppression and silence. But the knowledge of certain events between 547 and 539 was lost little over a century afterwards, and the clue to some of the allusions has been missing, perhaps, ever since. Historical study has progressed a little [147] towards making good that loss ; a consideration of the results of recent discoveries must, then, follow this summary of critical opinions.

HISTORY OF THE YEARS 556–539 B.C.

NABONIDUS, the last king of an independent Babylon, was a usurper, who was elected to the throne by his fellow-conspirators.[1] He was the son of Nabu-balaṭsu-iqbi, a prince, and possibly a priest of Sin,[2] at Harran. The king's Babylonian name, Nabu-na'id, variously rendered in Greek authors,[3] in Herodotus is given as Labynetus,[4] said to be the son of another Labynetus and of Nitocris. The ingenious suggestion that the name of the father and the son have been assimilated owing to some corrupt rendering of Nabu-balaṭsu, the last element being omitted,[5] seems not impossible. The mother's name, Nitocris, Egyptian in form,[6] may also be a corruption. Herodotus speaks of her as an independent queen, and credits to her the work on fortifications carried out in Nebuchadrezzar's reign.[7] When the mother of Nabonidus died in 547,[8] public mourning was decreed;[9] this must be due to her unusual position in the state, as it was not due to her as mother of the king. Unless Herodotus is to be discarded, the inference would seem to be that the mother of Nabonidus and her son were carried captive from Harran when the town fell and was occupied by the Babylonians and the tribes of the Median confederation in 610, and that the lady rose from a position as concubine to become the favourite wife in the harim of Nebuchadrezzar.[10] His mother's position would not give Nabonidus any claim to the throne, but his experience of public business as an officer of Nebuchadrezzar, and knowledge of the court, would lead the other conspirators to name him king. Nabonidus was no relation of the child Labashi-Marduk,[11] whom the conspirators removed, apparently in reaction against the policy of his father, the usurper Neriglissar, the son-in-law of Nebuchadrezzar.

Nabonidus was the son of a prince living at Harran, but that does not warrant the inference that he was an

Aramaean, sometimes stated as a fact.[12] Harran had been an Assyrian province continuously since the time of Tiglathpileser III, 745–727, and even, perhaps, since the ninth century. Ashurbanipal appointed his younger brother priest of Sin at Harran, and there is no reason, on the evidence at present available, to believe that any but an Assyrian prince or noble would have been allowed to hold high position there. The close supervision of the district in the Assyrian interests is shown in the Harran census. The assertion that Nabu-balaṭsu-iqbi and his son were Aramaeans merely because Harran is in Syria is the result of an apparently simple assumption which is, typically, unhistorical, because based entirely on language. Aramaic was the universal, though not the only, language of all the cities and districts of Syria in the sixth century ; but Syria was not an entity, and its population was not homogeneous. The memorial for a parent of Nabonidus at Harran was inscribed in the cuneiform character, not in Aramaic. In the Assyrian provinces directly subject to Assyrian governors, where there were no local dynasties retaining rights as clients, the Aramaeans were a subject people in the seventh century. The Aramaic-speaking population of Syria, Assyria and Babylonia never developed any sense of corporate nationality, and the assumption that Nabonidus, when he became king, brought the Aramaeans into power as a people [13] is a misinterpretation of the historical position.

At one time it was inferred, though without warrant, from his inscriptions that Nabonidus was a priest.[14] A more reasonable deduction which may be found in modern histories was, that he was a 'religious antiquary',[15] a 'scholar with a most conservative respect for old records and customs . . . never happier than when he could excavate some ancient foundation stone'.[16] This romantic view of the scholar-antiquary, based on passages in the inscriptions which aim at showing Nabonidus's devotion to a very early style of religious building and ritual, though

never compatible with his record as an officer of state in
the time of Nebuchadrezzar and as a conspirator, might
pass for possible, were it not that cuneiform documents
prove that this king was actually engaged in religious conflict. The interpretation of these passages in the building
inscriptions is part of a larger historical question. In the
sixth century B.C. new thoughts were stirring in the ancient
eastern world. A race which did not acknowledge a
plurality of gods, the men of Israel and Judah, had been
scattered over many provinces by the Assyrians and Nebuchadrezzar. Peoples who would not worship figures of gods
in human shape, the Medes and Persians, were impinging
on the civilized world of western Asia from the east.
Babylonian religion was only acceptable in so far as it was
supposed to conduce to individual welfare by the practice
of magic. Some effort at reform and clarification of the
polytheistic chaos was necessary if the ancient religion
was to survive. Nabonidus tried, it would seem, to impose
the worship of Sin as the supreme god of the pantheon.
When possible, he quoted ancient documents to support
his activities, which may, in some respects, be a reversion
to old customs; that did not prevent, but at least answered,
the charge of innovation, of impiety, and of confounding
the ordinances which was raised against him.[17] This king
has, then, been badly misrepresented. He had to deal
with great problems in religious and economic administration, and he found some sort of solution for fifteen years.
This background of his reign is little known and cannot
be dealt with here; the present purpose is to trace his
action in foreign affairs.

In 556, the year of his accession,[18] the position of Babylon
was only in one respect worse than it was in the time of
Nebuchadrezzar. That monarch was the recognized overlord of the middle Euphrates, of Syria, Phoenicia [19] and
Palestine. The north-western border of his empire is
indicated by the conduct of the negotiations for the end
of the war between the Lydians and Medes in 585; the

Syennesis or king of Cilicia, and Labynetus, the representative of Babylon, acted as mediators.[20] That means
that the northern border of Babylonian Syria marched
with Cilicia, and thence with Lydian and Median provinces
along the Taurus. The eastern border must have been
east of Euphrates, for Harran lay in Babylonian territory;[21]
but the temple of Sin was left in ruins from 610 to 555, so
not much attention seems to have been paid to the province east of Euphrates. What happened in the reign of
Evil-Merodach is not known. Neriglissar engaged in a
war in the north-west which was not unsuccessful at first,[22]
but his reign seems to have ended in some disaster. This
was probably due to a breach with the Medes, for by 556
Harran was no longer in Babylonian hands, but was occupied by the Median confederation, the *Umman-manda*,
that acknowledged the Medes as the leading tribe.[50] How
high the hopes of a Jewish prophet were raised at the
time of this disaster may be seen in Isaiah xiv, 1–23. But
Babylon did not fall, and suffered no overwhelming loss,
for the route to Cilicia and the metal mines remained open.
In this direction alone was the situation slightly worse.

The new king saw and seized an opportunity of retriev-
ing what had been lost in Syria. The opportunity was
due to a movement within the Median confederation,
which was only loosely bound. The centripetal force had
been resistance to the Assyrians. The methods by which
Astyages secured the allegiance of the whole confederation
are unknown. The Persians, who called themselves *Parsa*,
dwelling in the province round Pasargadae, had claimed
overlordship in the confederation earlier in the sixth
century. The history of this people, long completely
obscure, is now dimly known or conjectured. The tribe
must have been a linguistic unit, distinct from the Medes,
for many centuries. It is possible[23] that the name, *Parsa*,
is due to residence, during the slow migration southwards,
in the land *Parṣuaš*, which first appears in Assyrian accounts
of campaigns in the time oɪ Shalmaneser III, in the ninth

century, and is last mentioned by Sennacherib at the beginning of the seventh.[24] It lay south of Lake Urmia, and may well have been a stage in a migration from Asia Minor.[25] As a result of the great movements that took place in this part of the world during the time of Esarhaddon the land *Parṣuaš* disappeared. By the time of Ashurbanipal there was a new land *Parsumaš* farther south,[26] and this name alternates with *Anšan* or *Anzan*,[27] known to the Babylonians from early, Sumerian, times. Both *Parsumaš* and *Anšan* designate the province round Pasargadae.[28] The move of the *Parsa* into this area must have taken place before 650; it may have been led by Teispes about 670.[24] Not more than a year or two earlier than 640, and not much later, Cyrus I, king of *Parsumaš*, after the final collapse of Elam before Ashurbanipal's armies, formally recognized the Assyrian as overlord by sending his son[29] with tribute.

In his inscription on the rock at Bisutun, Darius I says: 'Eight of my family were previously kings; I am the ninth. We are nine kings, in two-fold succession.' This family tree commences with the eponymous Achaemenes; the immediate derivation was from Teispes. His sons, Cyrus and Ariaramnes, were both kings, and each was followed by kings in his own line. The older line was Cyrus I, Cambyses I, Cyrus II the Great, Cambyses II; the junior line was Ariaramnes, Arsames, Hystaspes, Darius I. The first of the eight kings preceding Darius was Teispes; Achaemenes was not reckoned.[30] The view has been propounded that these kings ruled in pairs, one of the older and one of the junior line.[31] It is, however, unlikely that Ariaramnes[32] and Cyrus I can have been contemporary kings of *Parsa* and *Parsumaš*, for these lands are indistinguishable. Ariaramnes was 'great king, king of kings' according to his own inscription; it would seem that he was head of a confederation, possibly part of the Median confederation, in which case he must have ruled after the time of Cyaxares.[33] Since the father of Darius was still alive and active when Darius came to the throne,[34] Cyrus II displaced a living

D 50

C

tana

A I *Th*

De

PA

Hidalu

A M

O

RSIAN

GULF

50

A AND BABY

member of the junior line; probably his own father had been similarly displaced or his own succession set aside. It looks as if there was some arrangement which permitted alternation in succession between senior and junior lines. There are many ways of securing such alternation. Nomadic tribes often select kings by election from the royal family, and continue the practice for some little time after settlement. The aim may have been to avoid rule by a minor.

According to Dinon, Cyrus the Great was 40 years old when he came to the throne, and reigned thirty years. Dinon is not reliable, and the round figures are suspicious, but they fit the probabilities. Cyrus died in 529; his reign may well have begun in 558,[35] and he may have been born in 598, for his grandfather was already king of *Parsumaš* in 640. Perhaps there had been a succession something like Cyrus I, Ariaramnes, Cambyses I, Arsames, Hystaspes; the average length of reign would be some sixteen years, which accords very well with historical probabilities.

The sources for the history of the years 556–538 are an odd collection. In cuneiform there are royal building inscriptions, with a few incidental references to events; a broken chronicle which cannot be earlier than the fifth century and may be as late as the third; a fragmentary verse account, composed during the reign of Cyrus, a polemic[36] in which events are related, apparently, without misrepresentation, but in an indignant tone;[37] a part of the historical preamble of a building inscription of Cyrus, written in 538 or shortly after; and two brick inscriptions, from Erech and Ur. The Persian evidence is much less; an Old Persian inscription on columns at Pasargadae, and a tomb and a sculptured relief belonging to the time of Cyrus.[38] In the Old Testament there are references to Cyrus by the Chronicler in his account of the first return of the exiles,[39] to the Edict of Cyrus[40] in the Aramaic memorandum from the Persian imperial records embedded in the book of Ezra, and a date in the book of Daniel.[41]

Incomparably the most important contemporary documents are to be found in the prophecies in cc. xl–lv of the book of Isaiah. Lastly, there is the evidence of the Greek historians, often collected and examined,[42] but not recently studied critically.

The cuneiform documents, if his own inscriptions are excepted, are prejudiced against Nabonidus. This prejudice is often attributed to the priests of Marduk at Babylon. These priests doubtless composed both the verse account and the cylinder inscription; but they wrote under the orders, and in the interests, of Cyrus, to reconcile the Babylonians to the loss of their independence by vilifying their last ruler. These compositions served no immediate purposes of the priesthood, for they were written after the fall of Nabonidus.

The characteristics of the classical sources are generally regarded as due to the individual Greek writers. Xenophon's treatise on ideal kingship, the *Cyropaedia*, has suffered particularly from this specialized criticism. Where the facts in this work agree with Herodotus's account, he is said to have borrowed;[43] if his facts do not appear in any other author, he is accused of invention, deliberate falsification, anything but following a source unknown to us.[44] This criticism does not inspire confidence, for it cannot be reconciled with the character of Xenophon as a gallant and intelligent gentleman, nor with the honesty of his other works. It is quite clear that in Herodotus, Xenophon, Ctesias, the quotations from Berossus, there is much that is erroneous, much that is doubtful. But these sources cannot be inconsiderately repudiated; the cause and nature of the errors need more careful attention. Herodotus knew of several contradictory accounts concerning Cyrus. Xenophon says that Cyrus was spoken of in story and song by barbarians in his own time.[45] This is material like the Alexander legend, and should be so treated, with this difference, that there were several Cyrus legends, never artificially assimilated into one story, each serving its own purpose. In the childhood stories there are elements deliberately introduced from the legend of Sargon of Agade, for Babylonian consumption.[46] The omission of the true story of Astyages from the *Cyropaedia* is due, not to Xenophon, but to his source, the Persian story favoured by the court of Cyrus the Younger, when Medes must not be offended and things best forgotten were avoided; the name of Cyrus the Younger is remarkable for a member of the junior line, the propaganda for him in some parts of the Cyrus legends not to be doubted. The view that Croesus was the victim of *hybris*, implied in the account by Herodotus, may have come primarily from the Greeks of Asia Minor, but ultimately the defamation of the Lydian was due to a Persian source, interested to represent things so. The common description of Cyrus as just, merciful and pleasant in intercourse is legend too, not necessarily untrue in detail, but the result of propaganda when regarded as a whole. Now all these parts of separate and sometimes conflicting legends are only intelligible if they go back to the time of Cyrus himself, as is also true of the Alexander legend. Invention of legends to profit a man ceases with his death; subsequently the stories are twisted to suit others, Ptolemy I for example, or, in this instance, the younger Cyrus.

In the legends there is historical material. It is the duty of the historian, not to discard two stories that seem incompatible, but to discern, if possible, the cause of error in one or the other or both. Two authorities, differing in some details and agreeing in others, are not necessarily borrowing from one another, or even from the same written source. Where Herodotus and Xenophon agree in broad outline, difference in detail does not prove unreliability as to the main facts. Where all classical writers agree in a general statement, though obviously all ignorant of historical events now known, the general statement is still better evidence than *a priori* reconstruction by modern scholars. A new valuation is a desirability for the future.

In 556 Nabonidus was a man of at least 55, Cyrus over 40. The Babylonian king saw hope in a policy which, according to the custom of the time, required oracular confirmation ; for neither the Assyrian nor the Babylonian kingship was absolute,[47] the kings were representatives of the national god, and their policies subject to the divine approval, in a way that meant that certain men of judgement and experience could check any course they disapproved. The method of consulting the oracle chosen in this case was incubation.[48] The question put to Marduk was framed in terms something like these : 'Shall Nabonidus, the king of Babylon, carry up bricks with his horses and chariots, and restore the temple of the moon-god Sin in the city Harran?' The answer came through a dream or some accidental omens attendant on the incubation, the counting of favourable and unfavourable, and the affirmative decision by the favourable majority.[49] In the record the words of the question could be put as statements into the mouth of the god. Then came the sequent question, as commonly in these state oracles : 'O Marduk, that temple is surrounded by the *Umman-manda*, and he is exceeding strong. Can Cyrus, king of Anzan, help me ? When will he help me ?' The answer was again affirmative: 'The *Umman-manda* of whom you spoke, he himself, his land and the kings who march beside him, shall be no more. In the third year, when it arrives, they will have caused Cyrus, king of Anzan, to arise against him, his petty vassal with his small army ; he will overcome the far-flung *Umman-manda*, will capture Astyages, king of the *Umman-manda*, and will take him in bonds to his own land.'[50] The *Umman-manda*, at first spoken of in the singular and at the end as plural, are the tribes of the Median confederation, personified in Astyages himself; the kings marching at his side are the tribal kings in charge of provinces.[51] The 'they' of the second sentence, the active agents in raising up Cyrus, are the gods of the Babylonian pantheon. The verbs here translated as futures are imperfects; but these imperfects are not tenses but states, and translation by the past tense has led to erroneous conclusions.[52] The third year meant, in which the revolt of Cyrus, but not, as some have said, the defeat of the Medes, was to take place, is that of Nabonidus, 553/2. The oracle had the effect of a state decision ; Nabonidus proceeded to act upon it.

Cyrus must already have been in communication with Nabonidus in 556, if this account, which cannot have been written till 553,[53] is correct in reporting the oracle ;[54] it apparently is, for an alliance with Cyrus would explain Nabonidus's actions during the next three years, and the alliance would assist the Persian. In the legends Cyrus always found allies, even in the camp of his opponents, Harpagus the Mede, the Cilician king, Gobryas, the governor of a Babylonian province. His success was due as much to this faculty as to the speedy movement of his armies. The latter had been practised by the Assyrians,[55] the earliest masters in this field. Intrigue on an international scale was well known to the Chaldaeans.[56] But in his intrigues Cyrus was able to claim a righteousness and virtue unknown to his predecessors. Perhaps that was due, as Xenophon thought, to Persian training ; it conforms in any case to Persian views of *rvata*.[57] He inspired trust in his word and confidence in his performance. Hence the Babylonian decision to act in Syria.

In 555 Nabonidus levied an army and marched against an enemy apparently regarded as rebellious,[58] the people of the Harran area who recognized the Median overlord. Whether he had to fight his way to that city or not cannot be said ; the sources do not present a continuous account, and no argument can be drawn from absence of statement. While at Harran, engaged on the restoration of the temple of Sin, Nabonidus says that he 'caused wide-flung troops to advance from Gaza on the border of Egypt, from the upper sea beyond the Euphrates to the lower sea'.[59] The upper sea is the Mediterranean, the lower the Persian Gulf. Two distinct operations are confused, probably, in

F

this sentence. The Babylonian levy had been raised before the march north,[60] the levy of the western provinces was summoned after arrival at Harran.[61] Ostensibly this levy was for the purpose of restoring the temple ;[62] in reality it was preparation for the later campaign. No attack by the Medes developed, and Nabonidus spent part of the year 554 resting in the Lebanon.[63] His stroke had been completely successful, probably because the Medes had other troubles on their hands. Before the summer of 553[64] the work on the building at Harran must have been complete. In the early months of that year Nabonidus fought in Jabal Druz, then went to the Lebanon, where he fell sick, but recovered by Kislev, November/December. Then he summoned the army to southern Syria, and ordered his eldest son, Bel-shar-uṣur, Belshazzar of the book of Daniel, to come from Babylon.[65] By a customary symbolical ceremony,[66] he 'entrusted the kingship' to his son, divided the standing army of Akkad from the levies, and sent the latter under his deputy's command back through the lands to Babylonia.[67] The army of Akkad set out under Nabonidus, now nearly sixty years of age, on a remarkable campaign.

There was, then, no sign whatever between the years 556 and 552 of any imminent change in the balance of power in western Asia, and certainly nothing to point to any imminent catastrophe for Babylon.[68] The western provinces were held in complete subjection. The levy in the west must have imposed great hardship, particularly on the peasant population of Palestine, but no resistance was offered anywhere. The view now often expressed that the fall of Babylon already seemed imminent at this time is fictitious, and any dating of the documents in Isaiah cc. xl–lv based on this misconception must be erroneous.

From the end of 553 onwards there were two developments, one in the east and one in the west. In the east, Cyrus commenced his revolt. He had only his province, Anzan, only his tribesmen, few in number, as Nabonidus remarked. For some time he fared badly. An account of

the course of this war, on the whole reliable, is preserved
in an excerpt from Ctesias ;[69] even the anecdotes are likely
to be true in spirit, and few anecdotes are more than that.
It has been said that Nicolaus Damascenus speaks of the
war between Cyrus and Astyages lasting three years.[70]
The Babylonian chronicle enters the mutiny of the Median
troops, the capture of Astyages, and the sack of Ecbatana
under Nabonidus's 6th year, 550/49. The various sources
are in complete agreement, if properly understood, but
difficulties can be, and have been, created. The mutiny of
the Median troops would not be intelligible without the
Harpagus story, which is true in the main outline but not
necessarily reliable in detail. Cyrus became king of the
Medes and Persians, but only on terms. Harpagus, or
whatever name that form conceals, and the Medes associated with him remained an extremely powerful element
in the state, and would not readily have admitted that
their status was inferior to that of the Persians.

The victory over Astyages did not imply conquest of all
Median territory, and it did not entail immediate recognition by all the other members of the Median confederation.
During 548 Cyrus must have been engaged in dealing with
the other tribes east of Tigris. There was probably no
difficulty in securing adhesion, provided the terms were
not too stiff; the tribes of the Iranian plateau would not
want to lose the position they held westwards, and an
overlord, a 'king of kings', was necessary for the whole
confederation.

In March/April of 547 Cyrus crossed the Tigris below
Arbela, according to the chronicle.[71] That is a curious
expression, for Arbela is east of the Upper Zab. Perhaps
at this time there was no inhabited city on the Tigris above
the junction of that river and the Zab.[72] It seems probable
that, after crossing the river below that junction, Cyrus
marched through the Sinjar region to the Khabur, thus
reducing a Median province that had not yet acknowledged
his overlordship. But the campaign proceeded farther, and

in April/May he marched against a land of which the name
is unfortunately broken. The ingenious conjecture that the
name Lydia once stood in the text[73] has been rejected,
not on good grounds;[74] but the restoration is uncertain,
and the historical consecution of events is sufficiently docu-
mented without it to remove the need for prolonged discussion of the epigraphical merits of a guess. Even if it
be granted that some other name, not Lydia, was that of
the land whose king Cyrus killed in 547, it remains
probable that this land lay in Asia Minor, on Cyrus's route
northwards to the Halys, to deal with some Median provinces east of that river. It is certain from Herodotus's
account[75] that any activity of Cyrus in those provinces
would bring him into conflict with Croesus of Lydia, who
aimed at expanding his power eastwards after the fall of
Astyages; Croesus had been consulting the Greek oracles
for some time, presumably to whip up support for the
enlistment of mercenaries in the Greek cities, whose principal importance in the Oriental world of the sixth century
lay in the supply of that commodity. It is clear from the
account in Herodotus that after the drawn battle of the
Halys, Croesus retired to Sardis so that his army could
depart to winter quarters; Sardis fell immediately after
the departure of the troops, probably then between October
and December 547. The only real uncertainty introduced
by abandoning the proposed restoration is, whether any
province formerly Median in this region could possibly
have resisted Cyrus. It seems so improbable, that the
conjectured restoration is best accepted, with its consequence, that Croesus was executed.[76] The stories of the
invariably merciful treatment of conquered kings by Cyrus
are propaganda material in the legends, and also testimony
to a new conscience in international affairs, for no conqueror
would previously have desired such a reputation.

The fall of Sardis altered the balance of power in western
Asia; but the position of Babylonia, too, had changed
since 553. Early in 552 Nabonidus 'set out on a distant

journey. The forces of Akkad advanced with him. He set his face towards the city Tema' in Amurru.'[77] On the evidence of this passage from the verse account, the identification of Tema' with the Arabian oasis Taima, originally proposed on other grounds, is now generally accepted.[78] The campaign was described in the chronicle in a mutilated passage which yet makes it certain that the Babylonian army on the way besieged and captured a city, the name of which ended in -dummu.[79] There appear to be only two possible restorations. The first, (mat)Udummu, the land of Edom, would require a city name before it. The other, (al)Adummu, is known as the name of a fortress of the Aribi.[80] In the verse account there is no mention of any event on the march; after insisting that the journey was a long one, the goal hitherto never reached, it records that Nabonidus slew the king of Tema' and slaughtered the flocks of both the town-dwellers and the peasants of the surrounding district.[81] The entries in the chronicle prove that Nabonidus continued to reside at Tema' till at least his eleventh year. Since the name of Bel-shar-uṣur was still associated with that of his father in legal oaths sworn in the twelfth year, 544, it is almost certain that Nabonidus had not returned and displaced his deputy in that year.[82] A memorandum of expenditure shows that special food was sent from Babylon by camel for the ageing king.[83] That is the sum total of the recorded facts about this interlude in history, soon forgotten, unknown[84] to Herodotus and Xenophon.

If Tema' is the oasis Taima, the city besieged by Nabonidus must have been on the road there from Syria, and must lie on the trade route through what was later northern Edom,[85] or Ammanitis, for there alone would water be available. Babylonian armies were not mounted on camels.[86] Now Adummu had been the refuge of the king and queen of the Aribi when Sennacherib attacked them. The lengthy account of Ashurbanipal's ninth campaign shows that the main body of the Aribi held Palmyrene, that the affiliated tribe Qedar lay to the south-west, extending perhaps to the northern end of the Wadi Sirḥan, and that the Nabaite, the Nebaioth of the Old Testament, a confederation completely independent of the Aribi, held the southern part of Wadi Sirḥan and the desert east and south.[87] This inference as to the territory of the Aribi precludes the identification of Adummu as Dumat al Jandal, the oasis of Jawf, much favoured by certain Assyriologists. The inclusion of Adummu in the territory of the Aribi shows that the northern border of Edom in the first half of the seventh century was much farther to the south than it was later. The guess may be hazarded that Adummu lay near the modern Azraq.

In the time of Job [88] and of the writer of Isaiah xxi [89] Tema' was a station on the caravan route from Sheba northwards. There is an easier route nearer the coast of the Red Sea, but that was controlled by Egypt. The war between Nebuchadrezzar and Amasis (?) in 568 was a struggle for the control of this coast route ; [90] Nabonidus, posting himself at Tema', was renewing that effort. The very considerable importance attaching to the frankincense trade in the time of Ptolemy II, who thought it worth while to fight for control of the eastern shore of the Red Sea and the Gulf of 'Aqaba, [91] shows the reason for this attention of the kings of Babylon. Circumstances in the Persian Gulf were an immediate cause. One essential fact, which the historians of this period have neglected, is the silting up of the head of that gulf. This is mirrored in the history of Ur. At the time of its greatest material prosperity, about 2400, before the Agade period, the head of the gulf can have been at no great distance. By the time of the Third Dynasty of Ur, about 2132–2016, a carefully constructed canal system enabled boats to bring wares to the quays round the city.[92] By the New Babylonian period, boats from the gulf cannot have reached Ur ; the marshes stretched far to the south, halfway to Basrah.[93] The best ports for transmission of seaborne goods were no longer in Babylonian territory. In the time of Ashurbanipal the chief port on the eastern shore seems to have been *Ḥudimir*,[94] which may have been in the neighbourhood of Bushire.[95] On the western shore Gerrha was probably already the main trade centre. Trade routes from there went northward and westward. The Babylonian kings could not hope to establish overlordship over the eastern shore, as Ashurbanipal did when Elam fell. Conquest of Gerrha would present insuperable difficulties; there is no record of any military campaign by a Babylonian king to the south-west, nor of any invasion thence.[96] At Tema' the route from Gerrha could be controlled.

There is no one clue to historical events; but the common distrust of any explanation by economic causes, justified by excessive reliance on a theory of a particular school, has itself become extreme. The ancient world had economic problems to solve, and one was presented to Babylonian kings of the sixth century by their restricted control of trade routes. The Assyrians by hard fighting kept open the passes into Media, Armenia, and Cappadocia for three centuries. After the fall of Nineveh the eastern and northern passes were held by the Medes, the northwestern were only open by favour of the Cilicians and Lydians, and subject to a treaty. The traffic from the Phoenician ports was interfered with by pirates from the Lydian coast, and by Greeks, the allies of the Egyptians. It was essential for Nabonidus to secure that trade from the Persian Gulf was not diverted westwards; it was desirable to control the increasingly prosperous trade of southern Arabia and the Red Sea. It was not a question of collecting tolls from passing caravans, nor was the task one to be performed by an officer and a detachment of troops.[97] There are, in the verse account, phrases indicating plunder after fighting, and weary troops, in a broken context.[98] One of the charges against Nabonidus in this polemic must have been the conduct of incessant campaigns in southern Arabia. Those campaigns must have been directed at controlling the eastern shore of the Red Sea from 'Aqaba down to the modern Yanbu', the area Ptolemy II tried to control.

Such control implies the use of a fleet, and these ships are mentioned, in a different context, in Isaiah xliii, 14. Nabonidus resided at Tema' for nine years at least, probably more. He made the city in the oasis 'like Babylon'.[99] That points to considerable success.

One interesting result of Nabonidus's residence at Tema' and of his interference in southern Arabian affairs may be traced in the introduction of the worship of Sin in southern Arabia. Miss Caton-Thompson's excavations have uncovered a temple of Sin [100] which, on epigraphical grounds, has been assigned to the end of the sixth century. The worship of a moon-god was endemic in Arabia,[101] and there may have been many names; but Sin ultimately derives from a Sumerian form,[102] and is therefore peculiarly Babylonian. It must have come to Minaeans and Sabaeans from that land. The introduction of Aramaic at Tema', for which the stele of Ṣalm-shuzub is good evidence, even if the date of that stele be later than the sixth century,[103] must similarly be due to Babylonian administration.

Babylon must have seemed much more powerful in 547, just before the fall of Croesus, than it did in 556, on Nabonidus's accession.[104] The overthrow of Astyages by Cyrus was a gain. Previous losses in Syria had been recovered. There was not only a long-standing friendship with the Syennesis of Cilicia, but Nabonidus had also concluded a treaty with Croesus. When the Lydian had returned to Sardis from the inconclusive battle on the Halys, he thought of calling on the Babylonian king for aid in the next spring, but was anticipated by Cyrus's rapid march.[105] The fall of Croesus altered the real position of the Babylonian Empire. It was now surrounded from the Mediterranean to the Persian Gulf by a single Power, which controlled the metal supplies of all Asia Minor and Iran, and was in a position to raise not merely the Persian cavalry and the mixed forces of the Median confederation, but a large and well-equipped army from the Lydian provinces. Syria and the Phoenician ports were bound to

attract attention from the man who was no longer the
petty vassal of the Medes. But Babylon was still apparently
strong; no one could have foretold her downfall with
certainty, just because Croesus had fallen.

Cyrus gained some of his ends without fighting. Cilicia
did not oppose him. The kings in Cyprus went over to
him.[106] Other districts obviously welcomed the conqueror.
The threat to the Babylonian Empire in the west lay, not
so much in what German scholars have called the 'Indo-
German' onslaught,[107] as in Persian policy and practice.
An inscription from Asia Minor[108] informs us what that
policy was. The text dates from the time of the Roman
Empire, perhaps from the reign of Tiberius, when the
revision of the right of asylum made it desirable to record
all documents testifying to ancient privileges. The translation into Greek was probably done from an Aramaic
original, and is not earlier than the inscription itself.
Doubts have been thrown on the authenticity of the inscription, but there is no likelihood that a forger could or
would have produced a document that conforms in significant details to the official Achaemenean style. It reads:

The king of kings, Darius, to Gadatas, his slave, says as follows.
I am informed that you do not obey my instructions altogether.
Because you till my land thoroughly, transplanting the fruits of
Syria to the 'lower regions'[109] of Asia Minor, I praise your undertaking, and for this much gratitude will lie towards you in the
royal house. But in that you obscure my attitude as to the gods,
I shall cause you, unless you change your course, to experience
my anger, as if I were wronged. For you have exacted tribute
from the sacred gardeners of Apollo, and have forced them to
cultivate profane ground, ignoring the intention of my ancestors
towards the god who told the Persians. . . .[110]

The only predecessor of Darius who can have rewarded
the priests of the Apollo whose temple lay near Magnesia
on the Maeander for a favourable oracle was Cyrus. The
procedure is typical, an early instance of the *medismos* the
Greeks knew later. A favourable oracle was worth more
than a battle; rewards lavishly granted and generously

maintained assured more acquisitions than 'Indo-German' onslaughts.

Not every city in Syria would welcome the Persian. Historians who speak of Syria as an entity mistake the situation. Each city, each district, or, in the open country, each enclave, had its own history and went its own way. Neirab remained under Babylonian rule till the fall of Babylon.[111] But in other towns and in the Phoenician cities there would be a disposition to wonder whether change of masters might not prove profitable. In Palestine there were bound to be some who, if encouraged by Cyrus, would willingly throw off the yoke of Babylon. And support of Cyrus there might lead to a special position for Jerusalem among the cities of the west.

The sources available have little to say about the outbreak of the war between Persia and Babylon, and its course between the fall of Sardis and the commencement of the final attack on Babylon, yet what they do say is quite clear. An excerpt from Berossus[112] shows that according to the Babylonian records Cyrus reduced the remainder of Asia in that interval. Herodotus,[113] giving the popular account related to him in the Asia of his own day, says that 'Cyrus attacked the Assyrians when he had made all parts of the continent subject'. Xenophon,[114] giving the story as it was known at the court of the younger Cyrus, says of Cyrus the Great that, prosecuting his plan against Babylon, he subdued the Phrygians in Great Phrygia, subdued also the Cappadocians, and made the Arabs subject. The term 'Arabs' in Xenophon has a very general sense. In the *Anabasis* Arabia is a land of nomad tribesmen lying across the line of march down the Euphrates.[115] The 'Arabs' subjected by Cyrus before the attack on Babylon cannot be these, for the Euphrates cities round to Aleppo held out[116]. They must then be the people of the Damascus area and Palestine, and this usage probably follows the official Achaemenean nomenclature; for, in the list of subject lands in an inscription of Darius from Persepolis, Syria and Palestine seem to be included in the land of Arabia.[117] Similarly, while Cyrus was in Babylon in 538 after the capture of the city, Xenophon states that he sent satraps to different provinces, appointing Megabyzus to Arabia.[118] This is the province known to the Babylonians by an old descriptive term, Ebir Nari, 'beyond the river', renamed by Darius; it must have existed as a separate entity before it was united with the satrapy of Babylonia under Gubaru, in 535.[119] But there are statements that can only apply to Arabs of the desert, and that some of these were made subject by Cyrus is certain, for the historical preamble in the Cyrus cylinder, describing homage paid to Cyrus immediately after the entry into Babylon, mentions, among the kings from all quarters who brought tribute and did obeisance, 'the kings of Amurru, who dwell in tents'.[120] Amurru should, in this case, be used in the same sense as in the verse account, of the desert east and south of Palestine.[121] The tribute was obviously the same 'gift' as received later by Darius, frankincense.[122] Herodotus confirms this inference, if rightly understood. He says of Darius the Great that 'all in Asia were subject to him except the Arabs, Cyrus having subdued them and Cambyses again for the second time'.[123] The Arabs as distinguished from the other Asiatics must be the Arabs of the desert. It is less clear to whom Herodotus referred as twice subjected, once by Cyrus and again by Cambyses. There is little warrant for believing that Cambyses fought anywhere but in Egypt, much less against 'all in Asia'. On the other hand, Herodotus worded the sentence very loosely, if it means no more than that Cyrus and Cambyses gradually brought all the Asiatics into subjection. Perhaps the Egyptians were included, and the 'second time' refers solely to Cambyses as a second conqueror. Apart from this, although the sentence might seem to imply that the Arabs were not subject to Darius, that is not the intention, for they paid a heavy tribute in frankincense. In the next sentence the

meaning is explained: 'The Arabs were never subject to
the Persians on terms of servitude, but were guest-friends,
having let Cambyses pass through to Egypt; for had the
Arabs been unwilling, the Persians would not have invaded
Egypt.' This can only be understood in one way. The
Arabs, here specifically the tribes of the Sinai peninsula,
let Cambyses through because they were already guest-
friends; the act was the result of the relationship.[124]
Herodotus's words do not therefore mean that the Arabs
south of Palestine never obeyed the Persians as subjects,
as has been thought, but only that they were not in the
same category as other subjects; his account is consistent
with Xenophon's and shows that the Arabs became guest-
friends of the Persian kings before the time of Cambyses.

Xenophon indicates that Arabs as well as Phrygians,
Lydians, and Cappadocians helped the Persians to encom-
pass the walls of Babylon. Now when Nabonidus fled
from Sippar before the entry of the Persian troops on the
14th Teshri of 539/8,[125] he did not go to Babylon, which
Gobryas entered on the 16th, but returned there after the
city had surrendered.[126] The incident is only intelligible
if Nabonidus attempted to escape by the desert to the
south-west, the only direction open, across the Euphrates,[127]
and found the road barred by the Arabs. His decision to
avoid them and surrender to Cyrus's representative could
not, in that case, be considered strange.[128] Cuneiform
sources thus supply incidental and valuable corroboration
of Xenophon. Recent attempts to discredit the statements
of the Greek historians entirely do not follow historical
methods in the use of sources.

The reduction of districts in Syria and the establishment
of guest-friendship with some Arabian kingdoms formed
part of the Persian effort which drove Nabonidus out of
Tema' somewhere between 544 and 540. This effort probably was due to co-operation of the local inhabitants;
where such assistance was not forthcoming, as at Neirab
and along the Euphrates, no action was taken. The cutting

of communications by quite a small force would suffice
to make the Babylonian position at Tema' untenable.
A cavalry force would be sufficient, provided it had a good
road, and a supply train. M. Dussaud has suggested that
'the burden of Dumah' and 'the burden upon Arabia' in
Isaiah xxi deal with incidents in this campaign.[129] At
first, probably, Nabonidus was not entirely unsuccessful,
for the verse account records that his inscriptions boasted
of victories and plunder during this period; it also states
that there were no such victories,[130] but that may be due
to a point of view. But his success must have been evanes-
cent, the withdrawal inevitable.

In order to comprehend the course of events after
Nabonidus's return to Babylon, it is essential to understand that in the account of the campaign in Greek
histories Babylon is not always *al Babili* of the cuneiform
documents, the walled city on the Euphrates, but sometimes
a large rectangle enclosing the central part of the ancient
lands Sumer and Akkad. On the east lay defensible lines
west of the marshes, corresponding roughly in direction
to the Shaṭṭ al Hai; the most important point was Erech.
On the north-east the last line of defence would lie along the
Tigris, from near Kut al Amarah northwards to the junction
with the Diyalah. On the north was Nebuchadrezzar's
Median wall, made the stronger by an intricate canal
system which can still be traced and remains partly in use.
On the west lay the fortifications of the western suburb,
the line of the Euphrates and Borsippa. Both Herodotus
and Xenophon give accounts of Cyrus's entry into the
defence system, which can only be understood if the confusion of Euphrates and Tigris in the text of Herodotus,
commonly found elsewhere, be corrected.

The story of the assault in Herodotus [131] is that Cyrus
assembled an army in the north, for he had to cross the
Gyndes; whether that river is to be identified as the
Diyalah or the 'Adhaim,[132] Cyrus need not have crossed
either, if he was marching from Ecbatana. Xenophon

also says that Cyrus marched from the north with a large mixed army.[133] Probably he divided this force ; the main body would be west, another body east, of the Tigris. Herodotus says that a battle was fought outside the walls; the 'Median wall' must be meant. Xenophon has a longish account of the clearing of ground, which can only lie north of the 'Median wall'; subsequently Cyrus withdrew from bowshot.[134] There is indirect confirmation of the state of siege established in the Nabonidus chronicle. Measures affecting southern Babylonia were reported under the year 540.[135] In 539, after Nisan and before Elul, that is, probably during the height of summer, when nothing is done unless urgently necessary, the gods were removed from the principal northern towns which lay east and south of the inner fortification based on Sippar, Kuthah, Babylon and Borsippa.[136] There may be inaccuracies in the Greek sources ; the main facts are, on the evidence, well established.

Then came the draining of a river, named by Herodotus, but not by Xenophon, the Euphrates. Herodotus's error here may be caused, as not infrequently elsewhere, by wrong order of his notes,[137] or by conflation of two different extracts. The river that can be drained is the Tigris; that is possible owing to the 'Aqarquf depression. The place where Cyrus broke into the fortifications was Opis,[138] on the west bank of the Tigris, the site of the later Seleucia.[139] There it would be possible to divert what remained of the current from the river-bed to a channel farther east.[140] Xenophon puts into the mouth of Cyrus before the assault a speech in which he says : 'We have plenty of pitch and tow, that will raise a strong flame, so that the people must of necessity flee from their houses at once, or at once be burnt.' The chronicle says of the battle of Opis that Cyrus 'burnt the people of Akkad with flame'.[141] The two sources do not contradict each other, as is often stated ; they confirm each other, but patience is required in interpretation, not slashing criticism.[142] The fact that pitch is easily accessible ought also to be allowed due weight; Xenophon's speech is not pure fiction, but contains fact.

Once the fortification on the Tigris had been broken through, Cyrus advanced so quickly that resistance could not be organized;[143] Sippar, the north-western corner of the interior fortification, fell without a battle, then Babylon. Herodotus says of the entry of Cyrus's army along the bed of a stream, that, 'owing to the vast size of the place, the inhabitants of the central parts, as the residents of Babylon declare, long after the outer portions of the town were taken, knew nothing of what had chanced, but, as they were engaged in a festival, continued dancing and revelling until they learnt of the capture but too certainly'. Babylon was never so vast as that. What the Babylonians told Herodotus of an assault referred not to *al Babili*, the city of Babylon, but to *Babili KI*, the district of Babylon, or, more precisely, the fortified inner rectangle; what they told him of the ignorance of the success of Cyrus, and of a festival in the city referred to *al Babili*, Babylon on the Euphrates.

The chronicle records the death of Ugbaru, the former governor of Gutium, who corresponds to Xenophon's Gobryas, shortly after his victorious entry into Babylon.[144] The entry confirms Xenophon's account of Gobryas as an old man, and disproves the modern theory which confused him with the Persian Gubaru, who was appointed by Cyrus satrap of Babylon immediately after his own entry into Babylon. It was chiefly to the activity of this former officer of the Babylonians that Cyrus owed the success of his surprise attack. But how many were in his service who might have been expected to resist will never be known. Treachery played a great part in the 'Indo-German onslaught'.

Cyrus's attitude to the pagan gods was illustrated by his treatment of Babylon,[145] as it was by his grant of privileges to the gardeners of Apollo at Magnesia. The satrap Gubaru appointed district governors[146] whose first duty it was to return the gods collected in Babylon to their own cities and temples. Cyrus, unable himself to undertake the ritual duties of king of Babylon at the New Year Festival of 538, perhaps because that would have offended his own Persians, ordered his eldest son, Cambyses, still very young, to perform the ritual.[147] Cambyses accordingly had to be associated with Cyrus in the dating of the first year; Cyrus was 'king of the lands', Cambyses 'king of Babylon'. The arrangement only lasted a year; thereafter Cyrus was 'king of Babylon, king of the lands'. (Modern scholarship has erected on these datings an edifice of theory[148] that requires more criticism than the sources.) The compliment paid to Bel secured a compliment in return. It was announced that the god of Babylon had chosen Cyrus, given him orders to proceed to Babylon, and provided for his peaceful entry into the holy city. And Cyrus had no objection to being described in a Babylonian state document, the cylinder, as a worshipper of Marduk. It did not affect his true religion,[149] nor could it cause any offence to his Persian subjects, for such worship was not personal, but only a formula such as was later used of the Ptolemies in hieroglyphic inscriptions.[150]

So the Persian became the ruler of western Asia, and turned to subdue the northern and eastern tribes of Iran. He was even able to plan the conquest of Egypt. But one of his greatest successes was to leave a reputation for clemency, celebrated in song and legend so persuasively that modern scholars [151] still prefer to believe that he spared the life of Nabonidus, when the Babylonian at the age of over seventy surrendered, and sent him to Carmania; but Xenophon knew that the king of Babylon was killed,[152] for the younger Cyrus had no objection to that.

This, or something like this, is the story of these years. What evidence can Isaiah cc. xl–lv provide to supplement other sources?

LECTURE III

SOME UNRECOGNIZED HISTORICAL MATERIAL IN ISAIAH cc. XL–LV

THOUGH Cyrus is only mentioned twice in these chapters, it is now generally admitted that he is the unnamed person alluded to in several passages.[1] This indirect allusion implies no great obscurity; once the date of these passages is granted as certain, the inference is inevitable, and would have been still more inevitable for a contemporary observer. The first allusion of this kind in the present arrangement of the text contains a reference that can be dated. The words are an utterance attributed to YHWH:

4	[1]'Keep silence before Me, islands and nations.'
+3	They shall renew strength,[2] approach,
2	then they shall speak together:
+2	'Let us draw near for judgement.'
3	[2]'Who raised up from the east
+3	one whom "the right"[3] came to his feet to meet?
3	(Who) both gives nations unto him
+2	and causes him to subdue kings?
3	(Who) makes his sword as dust
+2	and his bow as driven stubble[4]?
3	[3]He pursues them, passes in peace,
+3	he does not advance on foot along the way.[5]
3	[4]Who has wrought and done it?
+3	One summoning the generations from the beginning.[6]
3	I, YHWH, am the First,[7]
+2	I am also He that is with the last.'
3	[5]The isles saw it and feared,
+3	the ends of the earth were afraid,
+2	approached and came.
3	[6]They helped each his neighbour,
+3	and one said to another, 'Be strong';

[7]and the metal-graver encouraged the refiner, the one while making his hammer smooth the metal, the other while pounding the anvil, saying of the scale, 'Ready, that is', and fastened it on with nails, so that there was no slipping.[8]   (xli, 1–7)

H

The unnamed foes must be the Lydians, just as the one
raised up by YHWH must be Cyrus, for the phrase 'he
does not advance on foot along the way' refers to the speed
with which Cyrus marched to Sardis from the Halys, and
'passes in peace' is an allusion to the fact that the Lydian
army did not oppose the advance. The 'isles' here and
throughout these chapters are the coastlands and islands
of the eastern Mediterranean, the 'ends of the earth' seem
to be distant settlements of Jewish exiles. The reaction to
the fall of Sardis is described as anxious fear, which led
to the Syrian and Phoenician cities taking counsel together,
since they had to consider their position if they became
involved in war, and to busy preparation among the
armourers. The Jewish settlements in the north shared
the anxieties of their neighbours. Some time, therefore,
had elapsed since the capture of Sardis. In the next paragraph, which is closely connected, there is a statement that
Israel, already at war, shall seek the oppressor, now confounded (xli 11–12), so that it is probable that the war
between Cyrus and Nabonidus had started when verses
1–7 were spoken, though there was as yet no promise that
Cyrus would free the exiles.

Cyrus is already 'the one whom "the right" came to
his feet to meet', the theme on which the legends lay
so much stress. The Persian must have established his
connections with possible insurgents in the Babylonian
Empire before this. That implies a date not earlier
than 545, perhaps a year later. The passage is good evidence against the view that the activity of the prophet
'possibly . . . ended shortly after 546'.[9] The absence of
any claim that the success of Cyrus had been predicted
shows that this is the earliest of the allusions to the
Persian.

The claim of YHWH to have foretold success appears
in the next allusion that can be dated. It is a summons
addressed by YHWH to the heathen gods to expound the
course of history, or predict future events; if they would

only do something, good or evil, they might have a case, but they cannot. YHWH continues :

2	[25]I have raised up one from the north,
+ 2	and he was coming from the east.[10]
2	He shall summon in My name[11]
+ 2	and advance upon[12] governors;
2	(they shall be) as potter's clay
+ 2	and (he) as the one that models it;
+ 2	he shall trample the brick-dust in.
4	[26]Who has proclaimed from the beginning, so that we might know?
+ 3	or beforehand, so that we might say, 'He (*or*, it) is right'?
2	As there is none that proclaims,
+ 2	as there is none that announces,
+ 3	so there is none that hears your words. (xli, 25–6)

Though the first verse has been variously explained, only one interpretation would have been possible to a contemporary. Cyrus had marched from the east to the north. From the north an attack on the *seǧānim*, the *šakne* or Babylonian governors of the subject provinces, is in preparation ; Cyrus will issue the summons to surrender in the name of YHWH, in accordance, that is, with YHWH's plan. One of two consequences may ensue. The individual governor may surrender, when Cyrus will mould him to his purposes as the potter[13] does levigated clay. If the governor resists, Cyrus will trample him underfoot as the potter does hard dried clay, kneading it in water with his feet to make a paste. The passage might be interpreted as alluding to the attack on Babylonia, were it not for the explicit reference to the provincial governors ; the provinces meant can only be the western provinces. The attack in preparation would fall on Syria. A state of war existed. The date may be 544 or a year later.

The point of the passage is the claim that no heathen god has produced an oracle about the present course of history, not even one that has proved wrong. The gods in question are the gods of Western Asia ; it is not necessary to assume that the prophet was ignorant of Greek oracles, but he had no interest in Greek gods. The pagan gods of Syria and Phoenicia have failed; YHWH alone has announced what is to be the future of Cyrus. This theme constantly appears, not only in the utterances which directly or indirectly allude to Cyrus, but also in the passages which some critics think are purely eschatological, and later (but according to one view are earlier), than the utterances concerning Cyrus. These distinctions are not historically convincing. There is a steady progress in the confidence with which the claim is put forward that the prediction about Cyrus is true, from this passage, 'I have raised up one from the north', to the direct address of YHWH to Cyrus, 'For the sake of My servant, Jacob, and of My chosen, Israel, I have also summoned you by your name, even though you have not known Me . . ., I have girded you, even though you have not known Me . . .' (xlv, 4–5). Within these terminal points, that is between the years 544 or 543 and 539, it is possible to place not merely the claims to have prophesied correctly about Cyrus, but such passages as: 'Behold, the former things are come to pass, and new things do I declare; before they spring forth, I tell you of them' (xlii, 9); 'Let all the nations be gathered together, and let the peoples be assembled. Who among them can declare this thing, or announce the first things? Let them bring their witnesses, so that they may be justified, or else let them listen and say, "True"' (xliii, 9). Even the passage xlv, 18–25, thought to be based entirely on eschatological beliefs, is in the context and in the wording of the claim, 'Who has announced this thing from of old, who proclaimed it from that day? Was it not I, YHWH? So there are no other gods beside Me, the true God and the Saviour; nought except Me', so closely related to the claims in the Cyrus oracles that it is bad criticism and bad history to separate this utterance from them by placing it much earlier or later than the series.

The claims that the oracles of YHWH alone are true, that the heathen gods have no oracles, are addressed first

to the 'isles',[14] then to Israel,[15] finally to Cyrus.[16] All are
steps, not only in the argument, but also in the achieve-
ment of the prophet's purpose and YHWH's plan. The
peoples of the west must learn to look to Jerusalem for
guidance, to Israel's God for the deliverance to be achieved,
to Israel as an instrument in that deliverance. Israel must
not only recognize the power of the Creator as the God of
history controlling current events, but also admit the truth
of the prophet's mission, as the message revealed through
him became fact. Cyrus, too, must recognize that Israel's
God had indeed girded him, xlv, 5, and put a sword at
his side, Jewish support. He had rewarded the priests of
a little temple of Apollo because their god 'had told the
Persians (all the truth)'; now he must execute YHWH's
plan for the return of the exiles and the future of the
western provinces, for YHWH has foretold the truth. It is
not, of course, necessary to assume that the prophet knew
the individual instance; he would know the policy, for
Cyrus would proclaim it.

After the passages in c. xli announcing the forthcoming
attack on Syria and the failure of the heathen gods to pro-
phesy, there is a message indited in the allusive way already
noted as characteristic of the early utterances about Cyrus.
The opening words are in the style of a contemporary Babylonian letter from a superior to an inferior;[17] a substitute
appellation takes the place of the name of God. He is called
'the First', a term immediately intelligible only to those
who had heard, at the end of the announcement of Cyrus's
victory in Lydia,[18] the words, 'I, YHWH, the First'. This
explanation accounts for the laconic address of the message,
which cannot be separated from what precedes :

[27]The First to Zion. 'Behold him,* behold them.[19] Now to
Jerusalem I give a messenger with good tidings. . . .' (xli, 27.)

In the context the unnamed person in 'Behold him'* can
only be Cyrus, and the unnamed in 'Behold them' are the
heathen gods. The two clauses form an announcement of

* 'him' is restored.

the two subjects of the message. They are followed by a sentence accrediting the messenger sent by the prophet. The announcement of the subject in clauses starting 'Behold' can be illustrated from Babylonian letters;[20] the accrediting of the messenger is rare. The treatment of the subjects reverses the order announced. The first paragraph reports the failure of the false gods to answer YHWH's interrogation:

3	[28]Now I beheld, and there was not a man,
+3	and among them there was also not one giving counsel,
+3	so that I might ask and they might answer.
3	[29]Behold, they are all vanity,
+2	their works are nought,
+3	the cast figures of them are wind and confused matter.

(xli, 28–9)

Then comes the other subject announced, Cyrus, servant of YHWH :*

3	[1]Behold My servant, whom I support,[21]
+3	My chosen, so that My soul is content;
3	I have bestowed My spirit on him,
+3	that he may carry forth (or, proclaim) [22] judgement to the nations.
4	[2]He will not cry for help, he will not lift up his voice in lament,
+4	he will not raise his voice to proclaim in the street.
4	[3]He will not tear in pieces a reed already broken,
+4	and he will not extinguish a wick already dim.
3	He will carry forth (or, proclaim) judgement according to truth,[23]
+4	[4]he will not grow dim, he will not run away (or, will not be crushed),
3	till he has established judgement on the earth
+3	and till the isles wait upon his law.[24] (xlii, 1–4)

* It should be remembered that the historical interpretation of this, as of the other 'servant' passages which have, on grounds of subject and treatment, but not of language or style, been considered interpolations, can only be correct if the text is not interpolated. The rejection of the historical interpretation given in these pages will not affect the interpretation of the remainder of cc. xl–lv. The passages have been included because it seemed desirable to show that there is a historical explanation of the allusions, if they were either by the

There are three affirmations about the Persian king. Inspired by the Spirit of YHWH he will impose on the heathen nations *mišpāṭ*, 'judgement'. There are other passages which are closely connected with this, that show the sense of *mišpāṭ* [25] here. Thus Israel says, 'My way (that is, fate) is hidden from YHWH, and my judgement (that is, decision on my plea for justice) passes away from (is passed over at the hands of) my God' (xl, 27). Again, YHWH summons the isles to judgement, that is to decision on the case of the heathen gods (xli, 1). Cyrus, then, is to impose on his realm YHWH's decision on a case. The nature of this decision is given in the words 'he will not tear in pieces a reed already broken, and he will not extinguish a wick already dim'. Israel has been severely punished; that punishment must now cease. But why the figures of the reed and the wick? Are they, in this particular case, vague symbols, drawn from the small change of poetic prophecy, not true gold? It has recently been suggested,[26] with great probability, that they refer to symbolical practices in legal proceedings. Throughout this passage there is continual reference to legal procedure, which renders this suggestion attractive. Thus the transference of land in Babylonia, during the eighteenth and seventeenth centuries, was accompanied by the symbolical handing over of a wooden object, *bukannu*,[27] and similar practices are known elsewhere. The lamp has in many countries been connected with the rights of free men, and it is possible that in Babylonian psalms the charcoal brazier[28] has that significance. Perhaps the broken reed stands for Jewish land rights in Palestine, the lamp for personal freedom, both nearly extinct under the Babylonian government, as is stated so forcibly in xlii, 21–23. Not only will Cyrus not remove what remains of these for Israel; he will impose a 'judgement according to truth', restoring due rights to the Jews

prophet or, in the case of c. liii, by a contemporary. The onus of proof must lie with those who consider these passages interpolations, not with those who accept the text as it stands.

and securing acknowledgement for Israel from the other peoples of the west, as his law.

That is one affirmation. Another is, that 'he will not cry out for help, he will not lift up his voice in lament, he will not raise his voice to proclaim in the street'. These words have been variously interpreted. One critic has thought that all three verbs refer to the proclamation of a legal verdict by a herald;[29] others have said that they allude to the preaching of a prophet,[30] or the summons to surrender by a conqueror without the walls.[31]   In the paraphrase regular meanings[32] of these verbs have been given; it seems clear that each verb can have a distinct meaning and reference, and so it is not necessary to suppose that they refer to one and the same action.   The 'crying for help' may refer to the calling up of levies for military service in the subject provinces.   The 'lifting the voice in lament' may mean constant rebuke addressed to a subject population.   And the 'raising of the voice to proclaim' might well be used of the issuing of edicts.   It will be remembered that Nabonidus did in fact levy troops in the west, and apparently sent them to Babylonia for a long spell of duty.   The other activities are the normal procedure of any imperial government; but they have no part in the *mišpāṭ*, the subject of this utterance.   These things, it is affirmed, Cyrus will not do in Jerusalem; Palestine will be treated in a manner quite different from that accorded to a subject province previously.   Cyrus will gain and maintain power to impose God's judgement otherwise.

The third affirmation is, that 'he will not grow dim, he will not run away (*or*, will not be crushed), till he has established judgement in the land, and till the isles wait upon his law'.   There must have been Jews who doubted whether the king of a distant land like Persia would interest himself in the affairs of Palestine; this affirmation of YHWH by the mouth of His prophet, that Cyrus will not weaken in his effort against Babylon, and will not abandon the western lands, is the answer to such doubts. It must have been spoken before the Persian attack had reached Palestine, but perhaps after the Babylonian governors in Syria had already been summoned to surrender. In the first figure, 'he will not grow dim', a repetition of the previous figure of the wick for a different purpose, a change of metaphor such as sometimes happens in speeches, Cyrus is already compared to a light, meant to illumine God's judgement.

The text continues with an utterance of YHWH addressed directly to His servant. Some critics have admitted that this utterance follows closely upon the previous 'servant passage', but have mutilated it by excising the last two verses; others have treated it as an entirely separate 'unit', and doubt the authenticity of parts of it which appear in other 'servant passages'. For historical purposes it must be taken as it stands; if any part must be rejected, the reliability of the other parts as evidence is affected. It is still part of the message to Zion, a report of an earlier oracle confirming what has already been said:

	⁵The El, YHWH, has spoken as follows:
3	'The One who creates the heavens and stretches them out,
+3	the One who beats out the earth and its [produce?]
4	the One who puts breath into the people thereon,
+3	and spirit into those who walk in it,
4	⁶I, YHWH, have summoned you in 'right'
+2	and have grasped (or, will grasp) your hand.
2	I will both mould you and give you
+2	to be a covenant of the people
+2	and a light of the nations,
3	⁷in order to open blind eyes,
+3	to bring a prisoner from the dungeon,
+3	and men sitting in darkness from the house that is barred.
2+2	⁸I am YHWH. That is My name.'

Then the message to Zion turns to address the Jews:

3	Now I will neither give My 'glory' to another,
+2	nor praise due to Me to cast figures.

I

3   ⁹The first things, behold, they have come;
+3   and now there are new things I am declaring;
+3   before they sprout, I tell you of them.   (xlii, 5–9)

The assurance that YHWH is making no concessions to
other deities, mere idols, was perhaps necessary for the
ignorant or jealous-minded who would oppose any support
of a foreigner. The declaration that, as YHWH has formerly inspired his prophets truly, so this present prophecy
will be realized in fact, contains the main subject of the
message. But the historical evidence in the address to the
servant, Cyrus, is of more interest. The oracle starts with
a description of YHWH as the Creator, a theme much
emphasized in these chapters, where YHWH particularly
appears as the God determining history. The wording is
to be compared with the close of the address to Cyrus:

2   ⁶Nought exists without Me.
+2   I am YHWH;
+2   there is nought else.
4   ⁷I am the One who forms the light and creates the dark-
            ness,
+4   the One who makes weal and creates evil,
+4   I, YHWH, am He who makes all these things.
                                            (xlv, 6–7)

The terms of this description of YHWH as Creator can
be justified within the sphere of Hebrew religion; the
individual phrases in some cases do, and in every case might,
occur elsewhere. But Professor Nyberg,[33] while admitting
this, has remarked that the collocation is unusual, and the
equivalence light–weal as against darkness–evil, and the
verbs 'form' and 'make' applied to the former as against
'create' to the latter, point very strongly to the language
being adapted to suit Cyrus's own religious beliefs. In those
beliefs there must have been included the myth about the
origin of Ahriman and Hormuzd, who issued from the god
of Time, Zurvan. In other passages YHWH is specially
ʏHWH ṣᵉḇāʾōṯ, the Lord of hosts, and it is made clear that
the starry hosts of heaven are intended. Zurvan was the
starry firmament. The inference is clear, that these de-

scriptions of YHWH, consonant with Hebrew faith, were
nevertheless carefully composed for Cyrus to understand.

The actual address to the servant, Cyrus, in xlii, 6, starts
with the affirmation that YHWH's call to him is 'in right';
what is meant is explained in the next clause. Cyrus will
be accepted as the chosen king of Israel, YHWH will grasp
his hand, a formula of a kind known in many lands of the
ancient East[76] indicating divine acceptance. Cyrus was
not to be a foreign conqueror, but a legitimate king,
appointed by YHWH. Then come phrases that have been
the subject of endless discussions. Critics have altered the
words, excised one phrase or the other or both. What can
'covenant of the people' and 'light of the nations' mean?
Some have affirmed [34] that 'light of the nations' can only
denote 'one who brings light to the nations', and therefore
interpret 'covenant of the people' as 'one who negotiated
a covenant for the people'. Yet that is not what the text
says. Cyrus was to be 'the light of the nations', and it is
the function of light to enable men to see, 'to open blind
eyes', a phrase so worded that it is impossible to say
whether YHWH Himself or Cyrus is to do these things,
because it is a matter of indifference, since Cyrus executes
what YHWH wills. What the nations are to see are new
things, the right, the position of Israel. And the position
of Israel will be assured, not by a written, but by a living,
covenant, Cyrus in person, who is to bring men sitting in
darkness from the house without light, the rule of Babylon,
into the light, his own direct rule. The figures are not so
difficult to interpret. Historically, it is important to note
that the oracle does not state that Cyrus is already
'a covenant of the people', but only that God will mould
him (the metaphor of the potter so constantly used in
these chapters) to be so; and though the plan for freeing
the exiles and restoring Israel is already formed, there is
nothing about Jerusalem or the rebuilding of the temple.
The date is still the time when an attack on Palestine was
in preparation.

There is a clear reference to this oracle in a passage of later date:

3	[4]Attend to Me, O My people;
+3	O nations, give ear to Me!
3	For law shall arise from Me
+4	and I will make My judgement to rest on the 'light of the peoples'.
2	[5]My righteousness is near,
+2	My salvation has risen
+3	and My arms shall judge the peoples.
3	The isles shall wait upon Me
+2	and shall hope for My arm.

(li, 4–5)

The reference is emphasized; the judgement that Cyrus was to proclaim, in the words of the message to Jerusalem, is now made to 'rest upon the light of the peoples', so that all may see what that judgement is, as an object above a Palestinian lamp would be seen amidst darkness. When the allusion in this passage was no longer understood, the words were treated as corrupt, and the Septuagint translator emended them. The difficulty lies, however, not in the Hebrew text, but in its interpretation. The law which is to arise from God is the same law as that which Cyrus will proclaim to the islands (xlii, 4). But there is another surrogate for Cyrus. In the clause 'My arms shall judge the peoples' the word 'arms' can only mean 'rulers appointed by Me'; consequently in the clause 'the isles . . . shall hope for My arm', the 'arm' can only be a ruler appointed by YHWH. That ruler must be Cyrus, and the words 'My righteousness is near, my salvation has risen' imply that this prophecy was uttered just after Phoenicia went over to the Persians. The passage is good evidence that Cyrus was acknowledged as overlord of the Mediterranean coast-lands before the fall of Babylon. It is also probable that the 'arms' who were to judge the peoples were governors for Syrian provinces already appointed by Cyrus. The exegesis which fails to distinguish between 'arms' and 'arm' in this passage, and sees in both a cliché meaning the power of God, derives from an age when the words had no immediate application, and a general sense, applicable to the later period, slurred over the distinctions in words or phrasing. This view need not imply that God's arm in these chapters always refers to Cyrus, for it plainly does not (e.g. in xl, 11). Each passage should, however, be interpreted independently (the advance in critical method made possible by *Gattungsforschung*); it is wrong to insist on a mechanical identity of meaning in expressions which bear a different sense in different contexts,[34a] as it would be in languages other than Hebrew.

The meaning of this passage for contemporaries can be confirmed, and another inference is permitted, by a passage that can only be due to exultation over victories gained in a war still in progress:

4 [10]Sing unto YHWH a new song,
+3   His praise from the end of the earth,
2   O you that go down to the sea, and all that occupy it,
+2   the isles and their inhabitants.
3 [11]Let the desert and the cities thereof cry,
+3   the settlements Qedar inhabits.
2   Let the inhabitants of 'the Rock' sing,
+2   let them shout from the top of the mountains.
3 [12]Let them give glory to YHWH,
+3   and declare His praise in the islands.
3 [13]YHWH issues forth as a hero,
+3   as a man of war He rouses zeal:
2   He is sounding the signal for war, yes, and raising the battle-cry,
+2   He will show Himself mighty against His enemies.

(xlii, 10–13)

This passage should mean that the isles and the settlements east of Jordan and in Edom have both cause to rejoice, and that the true followers of the God of Israel are attacking the common enemy; the verbal forms used can be interpreted of an attack still in progress. The attitude of the isles has changed from fear to joy because of the first successes against Babylon. The way this contemporaneity of exultation in the isles and the desert is to be explained is a matter for conjecture; it may be that a campaign in the area of the Qedar tribe had already reached Sela', the Rock,[35] which must lie on a main route to the south, before the submission of Syria and the Phoenician coast, the cause for rejoicing in 'the isles', was complete. That would point to a date nearer to 540 than 544; and no conjectural explanation is likely to alter that approximation much.

YHWH, and therefore His people, are engaged in war. Men listening to these words in 540, or earlier, would think, not of a symbolic war, but of the real war in progress. But it is not merely weapons of war that YHWH employs, for this passage continues:

```
3  14I have been silent for a long time,
+2      while keeping still and refraining.
2   I will groan like a woman in labour,
+3      I will gasp and pant at once.
3  15I will make waste mountains and hills
+2      and dry up all their herbs,
3   and I will make rivers islands
+2      and I will dry up the marshes.
4  16And I will bring the blind by a way they do not know;
+3      on paths they do not know I will lead them on the way;
4   I will make darkness before them into light
+2      and crooked things straight.
3   These things I have brought (or, will bring) about for them,
+2      and I have not forsaken (or, will not forsake) them.
```
                                                    (xlii, 14–16)

The opening lines must refer to the sounds of a wind-storm from the desert, which is to sweep over the heights of Edom, parching all greenstuff, and drying up the beds of the wadis into patches of hard soil. The marsh-lands round the oases will dry up as in summer. This must be aimed at the enemy, the Babylonian army in the south; a severe drought, if the oasis Taima were cut off from communication with the north, would weaken the position of Nabonidus. In addition to the drought following the sand-storm, means are to be provided for men called 'the blind' to march by unknown tracks to achieve their purpose. These 'blind' can only be followers of YHWH, called 'blind eyes' in xlii, 7 ; they are carrying out His plan. They are in fact that part of Israel which is here addressed by God, as is clear from xlii, 18–19, whatever the exact interpretation of those verses may be.

If there was a campaign against the Babylonians at Taima, this is the interpretation that the passage must have had for a contemporary. It can, of course, and in later times did, lose its contemporary meaning ; it might, with good will, be read as a picture of God's advent in the last days. Most modern commentators see a reference to God leading the exiles home, an explanation that is improbable because men returning from exile would not be 'blind', nor would they march by unknown ways. It might be urged that those who were returning were a new generation, who had not travelled that way before; but the expression implies, primarily, a new, or rarely used, route. In a similar passage this question of contemporary, as opposed to later, interpretation arises. It begins with a reference to traditional history:

3	[16]Thus hath YHWH spoken,
+ 3	the maker of a way in the sea
+ 3	and of a track in the mighty waters,
3	[17]bringing out chariot and horse,
+ 3	the army and the strong together:
3	they lie prostrate and shall not rise,
+ 3	they have been extinguished like a wick, they have been quenched. (xliii, 16–17)

This allusion to the former release of Israel from the captivity in Egypt is followed by an address of YHWH :

2	[18]Do not call former things to mind
+ 2	and do not consider what happened previously.
3	[19]Behold Me doing a new thing.
+ 2	It is sprouting already;
+ 2	don't you know it?
3	I am even making a way in the desert,
+ 2	and rivers in the waste land.
2	[20]The wild beasts honour Me,
+ 2	jackals and ostriches,

3   because I have given (*or*, will give) waters in the desert
+ 2   and rivers in the waste land,
+ 3   to give drink to My people, My chosen.
3 [21]This people I have moulded (*or*, will mould);
+ 3   unto Me they shall declare My praise.   (xliii, 18–21)

Some of the audience addressed may not know the 'new thing' that is now happening. There is already a way; the drought has broken, and it is now possible to do work that will secure military success against the oppressor, so that some of YHWH's people have profited. Once again the passage has been explained as an eschatological picture, or alternatively referred to the home-coming of the exiles. Could any man expect that the exiles would march across the Syrian desert from Babylonia? The ancient route was always by the Euphrates, past Aleppo to Damascus or the Orontes. Is not this desert the desert of the wanderings, the waste land in the Dead Sea region? As to the eschatological explanation, that picture cannot include both the drought of xlii, 15–16, and the flowing rivers of xliii, 19–20. For eschatology, if the term is to have any meaning, is a picture of the last things drawn in accordance with a set scheme, a *logos*; the details, however fantastic, cannot vary much. The weakness of this explanation of many features in cc. xl–lv as eschatological is, that they have nothing to do with the fixed conceptions of all the apocalypses of later Judaism.[36] Those who would see in vv. 18–21 a continuation of the past history referred to in vv. 16–17 miss the natural force of 'a new thing'.

In the passages cited there have been references to mountains, presumably those of Edom, to the desert, presumably south of Edom, and to a way. In the opening chapter this way appears in an instructive context. YHWH gave an order to His messengers:[37] 'Encourage,[38] encourage My people.' The prophet adds an injunction:

3 [2]Speak unto the heart of Jerusalem
+ 2   and proclaim to her
2   that her forced service is completed,[39]
+ 2   that her punishment has been accepted,[40]

2 that[41] she has received from the hand of YHWH[42]
+ 2   double[43] for all her transgressions.   (xl, 2)

The punishment has been received not from YHWH but from His 'hand', His agent Babylon. Babylon has doubled the allotted punishment which YHWH had accepted as a sacrifice. That increase was unjust. Then come two paragraphs, the first beginning 'the voice of one proclaiming', the second, 'the voice of one saying'. There is intentional parallelism. The proclaimer communicates an order :

3 [3]In the desert clear the way of YHWH,
+ 4   make straight a high road for your God in the *'arābāh.*
2 [4]Every valley shall[44] be raised
+ 3   and every mountain and hill made low;
3 the crooked shall[44] become straight
+ 2   and the *r'ḳāsīm* a plain.
2 [5]And the praise due to YHWH shall be disclosed,
+ 3   and all flesh shall see together
+ 2   that God's mouth has uttered (it).[44a] (xl, 3–5)

This must be the earliest known allusion to the Persian high roads in any literature. The words used, *derek* and *m'sillāh*,[45] are not new ; but the road raised over the plain, and driven through a cutting in the hills, was unknown till the Achaemenid kings built such for military purposes and regularly employed them as post roads. Where was the *midbār*, the desert where this way was to be prepared, by driving it through hills ? and the *'arābāh* where a straight road raised from the level of a plain was to be constructed ? The *'arābāh* does not lie in the Syrian desert, but is used of the tract east of Jordan, or of the Wadi 'Arabah.[46] The *midbār*, though the word has a general sense, is chiefly used of the wilderness of the wanderings, the mixed desert and bare hill country from the Se'ir range to the Sinai peninsula. In the natural interpretation of the geographical terms lies the forgotten secret of this road ; but the allusion must have been immediately clear to a contemporary. The road was to follow much the same route that Nabonidus had taken, east of Jordan and through Ammanitis, northern and eastern Edom.   But the Persian was making more careful preparations than the Babylonian had done.   The proclaimer, whoever he may have been, was commanding Palestinian peasants to aid the enemy of their overlord. The other voice, that of a 'speaker', delivered a message which must explain the true purpose of the proclamation :

     [6]The voice of one saying 'Proclaim'.   The answer was, 'What shall I proclaim?'

2   'All flesh is grass,

+2   and all its virtue as the wild flower.

2   [7]The grass is dried up,

+2   the flower has dropped,

2   because the wind of YHWH

+2   has blown thereon.*

2   [8]The grass is dried up,

+2   the flower has dropped,

+3   but the utterance of our God shall stand for an age.'[46a]

                                (xl, 6–8)

Proclaiming publicly is a dangerous activity for rebels, but a harmless generalization spoken in public can, if it be interpreted as referring to particular events, bear meanings dangerous to the ruling authority, though not subject to punishment.   Many commentators have remarked on the apparent emptiness of content of this utterance.   But if the figure be applied to contemporary events, as those who heard the words delivered would apply them, it means that Babylon, too, must lose its strength,[46b] and become parched land.   In place of Babylon, God's word will rule mankind, and Babylon will perish[47] through God's action.

This coming rule of the word of God must be announced by Jerusalem :

3   [9]Ascend a high hill

       bearing good tidings, woman of Zion.[48]

3   Raise your voice strongly

       bearing good tidings, woman of Jerusalem.[48]

* A gloss has been inserted in the Hebrew text : 'Surely the people is grass.'

```
  2   Raise it, be not afraid;
+ 2       say to the cities of Judah:
  2   'Behold, your God!
+ 2       ¹⁰Behold, YHWH!*
  2   He will come as a strong one,
+ 2       His arm ruling for Him.
  2   Behold, His wages are with Him,
+ 2       His recompense before Him;
  3   ¹¹As a shepherd He will shepherd His flock,
+ 3       with His arm He will gather the lambs
  2   and in His breast bear;
+ 2       the mothers He will guide.'              (xl, 9–11)
```

One phrase in this passage that has given difficulty becomes clear immediately the use of a surrogate is recognized. 'His arm' is again, as in li, 5, Cyrus, the deputy of God as king. The 'wages' and 'recompense' are the spoils of war,[49] namely the flock, Israel, which will be released as a result of war by YHWH as a war-god; the exiles will be brought home by YHWH as a tender shepherd, in peace. The sequence of this passage in its context is logical. First came the order to encourage Israel, then a proclamation ordering revolt, followed by a command to the prophet to proclaim the imminent fall of Babylon as part of the rule of God for all things natural and human. Then comes the order to Jerusalem itself to spread word that, as the result of the war decreed by YHWH, the exiles will come home.

This is followed by a long argument to show that God is supreme in nature, in wisdom, in execution, with references to the 'isles', 'Lebanon', and the 'nations', which may have a meaning that escapes us. There is no other god, however cunningly the idol-makers[50] may present their work; perhaps the reference to technique is due to the statue of Sin, made by the order of Nabonidus,[51] which roused special comment. God has power over all nature, in heaven and earth; princes have no root when He blows

---

* אֲדֹנָי יהוה: *qᵉrē* and *kᵉṯīḇ* side by side, prior to the Masoretic recension.

upon them, a clear hint that the line of Babylonian kings will disappear. What God has created and appointed, the host of heaven, the stars, will never fail.[52]

On this argument depends the last section of this spirited address, an appeal for courage:

3	[27]Why, Jacob, do you say (thus)?
+2	and Israel, why do you speak (so)?
3	'My way is hidden from YHWH,
+3	and my judgement passes away from my God.'
2	[28]Have you not known,
+2	or have you not heard?
+2	YHWH is God eternal.
2	Creating the ends of the earth,
+2	He does not grow weary or tire,
+2	His understanding is unsearchable,
3	[29]Giving strength to the weary,
+3	so that He increases force for those that have no power.
3	[30]Even (warrior-)lads[53] grow weary and tire;
+3	(fighting-)men[54] stumble overmuch.
3	[31]But they that wait upon YHWH renew their strength;
+3	they mount, wing-wise,[55] like eagles,
3	they run and do not tire,
+3	they march and do not grow weary. (xl, 27–31)

In these lines 'weary' is said of men who have grown disillusioned and are without hope. The words are a call to a supreme undertaking that requires complete confidence in God, the revolt ordered in vv. 3–5. That was the meaning a contemporary would see; subsequent generations have seen other meanings. This chapter is a unity, an appeal to Israel to take action to assist Cyrus.

This subject is mentioned in a previous address, and it is made still more clear that the task set is to labour on the road:

3	[14]'Fear not, little worm, Jacob, men[56] of Israel;
+3	I have helped you' is the oracle of YHWH,
+2	your redeemer, the Holy One of Israel.
2	[15]'Behold, I have made you to be a threshing-sled,[57]
+2	sharp, new, with (many) teeth;
3	you shall thresh and pulverize the mountains,
+3	and render hills chaff:

3   ¹⁶you shall fan them, and the wind will carry them away,
+ 3   and the storm will scatter them.'
3   But you shall rejoice in YHWH,
+ 2   you shall glory in the Holy One of Israel.   (xli, 14–16)

The insignificant, oppressed nation, the 'little worm', has a part to play in history. That task is to work on mountain-tops and hill-sides so that they permit the passage of troops; the reward will be renewed cause to praise God.

There was bound to be faint-heartedness; opposition to such a message was sure to arise. Some passages[58] in these chapters testify to that opposition. The most striking is one of the so-called 'servant' passages, in which the prophet speaks of himself: *

3   ¹Listen, O isles, to me
+ 3   and attend, O peoples from afar.
3   YHWH summoned me from the womb,
+ 3   from my mother's uterus He called my name.
3   ²He has made my mouth as it were a sharp sword,
+ 2   and has hidden me in the shadow of His hand:
3   He has also made me a polished arrow,
+ 2   He has placed me in His quiver as a secret place.
3   ³And He said to me, 'Thou art My servant,†
+ 2   through whom I will show Myself glorious.'
3   ⁴Then I said: 'I have laboured to produce an empty thing;
+ 4   I have exhausted my strength for confusion and wind.
3   Verily, judgement on me lies with YHWH,
+ 2   and my reward with my God.'
3   ⁵But now YHWH hath spoken,
+ 3   Who formed me from the womb to serve Him,
3   to bring back Jacob to Him
+ 3   so that Israel may not be removed,[59]
    [or, so that Israel may be gathered to Him]
2   and I shall be given honour in the eyes of YHWH,
+ 2   and my God, YHWH, will be my strength.
3   ⁶Now He said: 'It is not enough for you
+ 2   that you are My servant,
2   to raise the tribes of Jacob,
+ 2   and to bring back the preserved of Israel.'

    * See note on p. 54.
    † 'Israel' has been inserted into the Hebrew text.

3   I will also make you a light of the nations,

+4   that My salvation may reach the end of the earth.'

(xlix, 1–6)

The career of the prophet was, then, divided into two.
In the early part he thought his task was confined to Israel,
and there again his task was twofold and militant; he must
find means to re-establish the old land arrangements for
the Palestinian peasants,[60] and at the same time prepare
for the release of the exiles. But in both he was frustrated
by opposition to his support of the Persian, and began
to despair. Then came the intimation that to succeed he
must enlarge his views, and become, in the words previously
applied to Cyrus, a 'light of the nations', that is, must
show the pagan peoples of the Babylonian Empire God's
judgement and induce them to accept His law;[61] success
could be achieved by turning to the other peoples in the
western provinces. The utterances in xl–lv belong to this
second phase, and this passage is to justify the appeals to
the 'isles'. The same phrases can be applied both to the
prophet and Cyrus because they indicate God's common
purpose for both.

Even so the prophet still had bitter experiences. In
another passage he speaks of himself: *

[4]YHWH† gave me the tongue of the experienced[62] to know
(how) to twist[63] the word towards the weary one; He rouses
morning by morning, He rouses my ear for me, to hear as do
the experienced.[62]

This passage clearly refers to the allusive manner he was
forced to adopt, in his preaching to his own hopeless people,
because of Babylonian rule. He then continues:

3   [5]YHWH† opened my ear,

+2   and I was not rebellious,

+2   I did not turn myself away.

3   [6]I offered my back to the smiters,

+2   and my cheeks to them that laid them bare;

3   I did not hide my face

+2   from insults and spittle.

* See note on p. 54.   † See note on p. 71.

There has been much discussion as to who these persecutors were. The words themselves are decisive in one sense; these attacks were not punishments inflicted by a regularly constituted authority, but spontaneous actions of individuals or a mob. The passage implies that the persecutors were among those to whom the prophet insisted on delivering God's message. Then comes the expression of confidence in God:

2	[7]Now YHWH* will help me,
+2	for that reason I shall not be ashamed:
4	for that reason I have set my face like a flint
+3	and I know that I shall not be dishonoured.
2	[8]He that justifies me is near,
+2	who will contend with me?
+2	Let us together take our stand.
2	Who is opposing me at law?
+2	Let him approach me.
2	[9]Behold, YHWH* will help me,
+2	Who shall condemn me?
3	Behold, they shall all grow old like a garment.
+2	Moth shall consume them. (l, 4–9)

At this time the prophet was in hiding,[64] but he still issued appeals for more support:

3	Who among you fears YHWH,
+2	obeying the voice of His servant
2	that walketh in darkness,
+2	nought shining for him?
2	Let him trust in the name of YHWH
+2	and lean upon his God. (l, 10)

Success did attend the prophet's main effort, to aid the attack on Nabonidus at Taima, that would drive the Babylonians from the west. There is an isolated verse that is only intelligible in the light of that success:

Thus saith the Lord, your redeemer, the Holy One of Israel: 'For your sake I have sent to Babylon and have brought south all their divining priests,[65] and the Chaldaeans[66] whose cry[67] is in the ships.' (xliii, 14)

* אֲדֹנָי יהוה: q‍e‍rē and k‍e‍t‍īḇ side by side, prior to the Masoretic recension.

The meaning of this oracle was lost so soon as the history of the period was forgotten.   Ships had been brought to the Gulf of 'Aqaba or some port on the eastern shore of the Red Sea to facilitate the Babylonian withdrawal.   No Babylonian army moved unless diviners were present.[68] The adventure at Taima was at an end.

Then the prophet could see trade long interrupted returning to Jerusalem, no longer directed elsewhere.   For in an address to Jerusalem he says :

> [14]YHWH hath spoken thus;
>
> 2   The produce of Egypt and the traffic of Nubia,
> 2   and the Sabaeans, men of stature,[69]
> 2   shall pass over unto you, and shall be yours.
> 2 + 2   They shall follow you, they shall pass over in bonds,[70]
> 2 + 2   and they shall fall down unto you, unto you they shall make supplication, saying:
> 4   'Surely God is in thee, and there is nought else;
> 2   there are no (other) gods.
> 4   Verily, Thou art the Hidden God,
> 2   O God of Israel, the Saviour.'
> 3   They are ashamed and also confounded, all of them,
> 4   all the casters of figures shall go together, with insults.
>
> (xlv, 14–16)

For an Egyptian or a Nubian the Hidden God[70a] was Amen.   So great is the victory gained that the prophet foresees traders from a land not involved in the struggle admitting that the One God is not the supreme deity of their own pantheon, but the God of Jerusalem.   The passage implies that trade between the Delta and Palestine had been interrupted and then renewed, and must refer to the Babylonian withdrawal from Taima.

The prophet lived to see the fall of Babylon, the allusions to which are universally recognized.   The direct mention of Cyrus in xliv, 28, and the address to him, xlv, 1–7, must belong to the days just after the entry.   In the address the prophet not only shows how intimate his knowledge of Babylonian customs was, but seems to describe incidents he himself had witnessed:

3   And I loosen the loins of kings
+ 3   to open before him the double-doors,
+ 3   and no gates shall be shut.   (xlv, 1)

It was an Assyrian, and therefore probably a Babylonian, custom that client kings who had revolted and then been captured, might be punished by being fastened to the bolts of the city gates with chains in such a way that, bound round the middle, they were forced to adopt a sitting posture; this gave rise to ridicule, for they looked like squatting bears.[71] Thus fettered, they were forced to open and shut the great gates as commanded; the prophet seems to have seen them, freed from their bonds by Gobryas, opening the gates to Cyrus voluntarily when he entered in peace. Similarly the 'stores of darkness' and the 'hidden treasures' (xlv, 3) recall the language of Ashurbanipal about the sack at Susa.[72] Where the Persians later expected to find great treasure, owing to their experience in 539, is probably shown by the story of Darius the Great searching the tomb of Nitocris,[73] and the similar story of the entry of Xerxes into the shrine of the dead Bel,[74] that is, probably, an underground sanctuary.[75]

But the most remarkable feature of the address to Cyrus is, of course, the parallelism 'My anointed ... whose right hand I have grasped'.[76] The meaning of the latter would be clear to every contemporary, for in nearly every city-state of the ancient Near East there was some ceremony like that indicated in this clause, a ceremony that established the king as the vicegerent of the city-god. Cyrus was thus proclaimed king of the pagan western provinces by the election of yhwh, according to a pagan custom; he was to be the one king, elected by the One God. But his kingship in Judah depended not on that conception, but on the preceding words, 'My anointed'. This title, used of a foreign king, must have shocked innumerable pious Jews. It even shocks a modern scholar, who, while admitting the prophet's boldness in applying the title to Cyrus at all, attempts to avoid the true implication by

L

denying the immediate significance of the term in favour of an 'eschatological' explanation. Cyrus, it is said, is greeted as 'My anointed' because he is to fulfil the vague expectations of a coming Messiah which may have existed among the exiles.[77] But that is not the meaning the words would have had for a contemporary when he first heard them. The second part of the phrase, applicable to pagan kings, shows that 'My anointed' must refer, not to a Messiah, but to a living king. If Cyrus was the anointed of YHWH, he had taken the place of the line of David, and had become the true king of Judah. Such an announcement was indeed bold, but it was inevitable, the only possible result of the realization of the Persian success that had been prophesied. The consequence, equally inevitable, of this proclamation of Cyrus must have been that the prophet would seem to some of his own people a traitor, worthy of death.

Almost the last message he sent to his followers in Palestine was that which assured them of the return of peace:

3   How welcome on the mountains[78] are the footsteps of one bringing good news,

3   announcing peace, bringing good news, announcing salvation,

2 + 2   saying unto Zion, 'Your God is King'.[79]   (lii, 7)

At last the new things had come; the Persian, summoned 'in right' by YHWH, would rule as His vicegerent in Judah. But if those modern critics are right who see in c. liii a lamentation for the prophet's death, he was condemned and executed as a criminal shortly after. The Babylonian authorities, of course, were no longer in a position to impose such a punishment, and the Persians had no cause. His enemies in Jewry must have fallen upon the prophet. Yet even in death he still served the nation he had tried to lead to freedom, for the very cause of his condemnation must have been the support steadily given to the cause of Cyrus in the face of opposition against which he set his face like

a flint;[80] so he secured recognition for the cause of Israel
from the Persian king. Arrangements were made by Cyrus
for the restoration of the Temple and for the return of the
ritual vessels. The failure of those arrangements was due,
not to the prophet, not to Cyrus, but to want of faith
among the exiles.[81] That lack was ultimately repaired by
a later generation, but the opportunities of Zerubbabel,
Ezra and Nehemiah were created by Cyrus and the records of his time kept in the Persian royal house.

EPILOGUE

This attempt to find in these passages direct references to contemporary events in no way excludes the
deeper meanings that attach to them. It merely serves to
show that the prophet of cc. xl–lv was a man of the same
stature as the Isaiah who prophesied in the time of Heze-
kiah, a religious leader facing the urgent political problems
of his time with greater faith and courage, from a broader,
less national, point of view than the majority in Israel could
understand. This later prophet is anonymous, yet his work
is included with much else in the book attributed to his predecessor. It is strange that those who have understood and
explained the Hebrew use of personal names to represent
communities, and have realized that collective entities are
constantly personified, have not seen that the name 'Isaiah'
came to denote a body which endured in the national life
of Israel and Judah from the seventh century to the fourth,
an order of prophets, producing national leaders at times
of crisis, distinguished in character and teaching from
Jeremiah and Ezekiel.[82] Owing to the traditions of that
order the book of Isaiah contains much that is finest in
Old Testament thought; in that book the section con-
sisting of cc. xl–lv holds the central place by reason of its
supreme confidence in the discernment of God's will as
effective in history, past, present, and to come.

NOTES AND
BIBLIOGRAPHICAL REFERENCES

ABBREVIATIONS

AfO	Archiv für Orientforschung. E. F. Weidner's Selbstverlag. Berlin.
AJSLL	American Journal of Semitic Languages and Literatures. Chicago.
AMI	Archaeologische Mitteilungen aus Iran. Berlin.
AV	Authorized Version.
BHT	Sidney Smith, *Babylonian Historical Texts*. London, 1924.
BWANT	Beiträge zur Wissenschaft vom Alten und Neuen Testament (hrsgg. von A. Alt und G. Kittel). Stuttgart.
BWAT	Beiträge zur Wissenschaft vom Alten Testament (hrsgg. von R. Kittel). Stuttgart.
BZATW	Beihefte zur Zeitschrift für alttestamentliche Wissenschaft.
CAH	Cambridge Ancient History. Cambridge.
FRLANT	Forschungen zur Religion des Alten und Neuen Testaments (hrsgg. von W. Bousset und H. Gunkel). Göttingen.
JA	Journal Asiatique. Paris.
JBL	Journal of Biblical Literature. New Haven, Connecticut.
JEA	Journal of Egyptian Archaeology. London.
JRAS	Journal of the Royal Asiatic Society. London.
JSOR	Journal of the Society of Oriental Research. Chicago.
JTS	Journal of Theological Studies. Oxford.
LAAA	Liverpool Annals of Archaeology and Anthropology. Liverpool.
MVAG	Mitteilungen der vorderasiatischen und ägyptischen Gesellschaft. Leipzig.
NF	Neue Folge.
NTT	Norsk Teologisk Tidskrift. Christiania.
OLZ	Orientalistische Literaturzeitung. Leipzig.
PRE	Pauly's Real-Encyclopädie der classischen Altertumswissenschaft. Neue Bearbeitung begonnen von Georg Wissowa, hrsgg. von Wilhelm Kroll. Stuttgart.
RA	Revue d'Assyriologie. Paris.
RV	Revised Version.
TSBA	Transactions of the Society of Biblical Archaeology. London.
WuW	Wesen und Werden des Alten Testaments, hrsgg. von Paul Volz, Friedrich Stummer und Johannes Hempel. (BZATW, no. 66.) Berlin, 1936.
ZA	Zeitschrift für Assyriologie. Leipzig.
ZATW	Zeitschrift für die alttestamentliche Wissenschaft. Giessen: Berlin.
ZDMG	Zeitschrift der deutschen morgenländischen Gesellschaft. Leipzig.

LECTURE I

SELECTED BIBLIOGRAPHY

In the notes, apart from the abbreviations, references to the names of authors refer to books or articles in the following list; different contributions of the same author are numbered. The list only includes works in French, German, or English published in the years 1910–39, and is in part intended as a guide to the literature of recent criticism. Some information as to the books and articles in Dutch and the Scandinavian languages can be found in C. Lindhagen, *De tre sista decenniernas Ebed Jahveforskning*, in Svensk Teologisk Kvartalskrift, viii (1932), pp. 350–75.

BALLA, E. *Das Problem des Leides in der israelitisch-jüdischen Religion*, in ΕΥΧΑΡΙΣΤΗΡΙΟΝ (FRLANT, NF, 19). Studien zur Religion und Literatur des Alten und Neuen Testaments Hermann Gunkel . . . dargebracht, hrsgg. von Hans Schmidt, Bd. i. Göttingen, 1923.

BARNES, W. E. *Cyrus the servant of Jehovah*, in JTS, xxxii (1931), pp. 32–9.

BAUDISSIN, W. W. Graf von. *Die Entwicklung des Gebrauchs von 'ebed in religiösem Sinn*, in Beiträge zur alttestamentlichen Wissenschaft, Karl Budde gewidmet, hrsgg. von K. Marti. (BZATW, no. 34.) Giessen, 1920, pp. 1–9.

BEER, G. *Die Gedichte vom Knecht Jahwes in Jesaja 40–55 : ein textkritischer und metrischer Wiederherstellungsversuch.* (BZATW, no. 33.) Giessen, 1918, pp. 29–46.

BEGRICH, J. (1) *Das priesterliche Heilsorakel*, in ZATW (NF), xi (1934), pp. 81 ff.

BEGRICH, J. (2) *Studien zu Deuterojesaja* (BWANT, 4te Folge, 25). Stuttgart, 1936.

BLUNT, A. W. F. *The 'Servant' Passages in Deutero-Isaiah*, in The Interpreter, viii (1911–12), pp. 184–91.

BOEGNER, A. *À propos d'Ésaie LIII*, in Revue de Théologie, xxi (1912), pp. 368–72.

BROWN, S. L. *Introduction to the Study of Isaiah 40–66*, in The Interpreter, vii (1910–11), pp. 396–403.

BRUSTON, CH. *Le Serviteur de l'Éternel dans l'Avenir*, in Vom alten Testament. Festschrift Karl Marti zum 70. Geburtstage gewidmet, hrsgg. von K. Budde. BZATW, no. 41 (1925), pp. 37–44.

BUDDE, K. (1) *Jesaja 40–66*, in Kautzsch (hrsgg. v. A. Bertholet), Heilige Schriften des Alten Testaments, i, pp. 633 ff. (4te Auflage), 1922.

BUDDE, K.   (2) Review of Eissfeldt, *Der Gottesknecht*, in Theologische Literaturzeitung, 1933, no. 18, Spalten 323 ff.

BURROWS, E.   *The Gospel of the Infancy and other Biblical Essays.* Edited by Edmund F. Sutcliffe. London, 1940.

BUTTENWIESER, M.   *Where did Deutero-Isaiah live?* in JBL, xxxviii (1919), pp. 94–112.

CASPARI, W.   (1) [Abstract of a lecture at an ' Alttestamentlertagung' in a congress at Munich, 1924] in ZDMG (NF), iii (1924), p. lxxiii.

CASPARI, W.   (2) *Jesaja 34 und 35*, in ZATW (NF), viii (1931), pp. 67 ff.

CASPARI, W.   (3) *Lieder und Gottessprüche der Rückwanderer* (BZATW, no. 65). Giessen, 1934.

CONDAMIN, A.   *Les prédictions nouvelles du chapitre XLVIII d'Isaie*, in Revue Biblique, 1910, pp. 210–16.

CORNILL, C. H.   (1) *Einleitung in die kanonischen Bücher des Alten Testaments.* 7te Auflage. Freiburg i. B. und Leipzig, 1913.

CORNILL, C. H.   (2) *Der israelitische Prophetismus.* 13te Auflage. Berlin und Leipzig, 1920.

CRIPPS, R. S.   *The Prophets and the Atonement*, in The Atonement in History and in Life. London, 1929.

DALMAN, G. H.   *Jesaja 53, das Prophetenwort vom Sühneleiden des Gottesknechtes* (Schriften des Instituts für Judentum in Berlin, no. 13). Leipzig, 1914.

DELITZSCH, F.   *Die grosse Täuschung*, ii, pp. 78 ff.   Stuttgart und Berlin, 1922.

DIETZE, K.   (1) *Ussia, der Knecht Gottes, sein Leben und sein Leiden, und seine Bedeutung für den Propheten Jesaja* (Abhandlungen und Vorträge hrsgg. von der Bremer wissenschaftlichen Gesellschaft, iv, 1–2). Bremen, 1929.

DIETZE, K.   (2) *Ein Nachwort zu Ussia.* Bremen (Selbstverlag), 1930.

DIMMLER, E.   *Isaias.* M.-Gladbach, 1920.

DIX, G. H.   (1) *The influence of Babylonian ideas in Jewish Messianism*, in JTS, xxvi (1925), pp. 241–50.

DIX, G. H.   (2) *The Messiah Ben Joseph*, in JTS, xxvii (1925), pp. 130–43.

DUHM, B.   *Das Buch Jesaja.* 3te Auflage, 1914 ; 4te Auflage, 1923.

DÜRR, L.   *Ursprung und Ausbau der israelitisch-jüdischen Heilandserwartung*, pp. 125–52. Berlin, 1925.

EISSFELDT, O.   (1) *Einleitung in das Alte Testament.* Art. 40, pars. 1–5, pp. 373–83. Tübingen, 1934.

EISSFELDT, O.   (2) *Der Gottesknecht bei Deuterojesaja (Jes. 40–55) im Lichte der israelitischen Anschauung von Gemeinschaft und Individuum.* 1933.

EITAN, J.   *A Contribution to Isaiah Exegesis*, in Hebrew Union College Annual, xii–xiii, pp. 55–8.

ELLIGER, K.   *Deuterojesaja in seinem Verhältnis zu Tritojesaja* (BWANT, 4te Folge, Heft 11). Stuttgart, 1933.

ELMSLIE, W. A. L.   *Isaiah XL–LXVI* (Revised Version for Schools). Cambridge, 1914.

ERBT, W.   *Jesus der Heiland.* Stuttgart, 1926.

EULER, K. F.   *Die Verkündigung vom leidenden Gottesknecht aus Jes. 53 in der griechischen Bibel* (BWANT, 4te Folge, Heft 14). Stuttgart, 1934.

FELDMANN, F.   (1) *Das Frühere und das Neue,* in Festschrift E. Sachaus, pp. 162–9. Berlin, 1915.

FELDMANN, F.   (2) *Die Bekehrung der Heiden im Buche Isaias* (Abhandlungen aus Missionskunde und Missionsgeschichte, no. 14). Aachen, 1919.

FELDMANN, F.   (3) *Das Buch Jesajas.* 2. Halbband. Münster i. W., 1926.

FISCHER, J.   (1) *Isaias 40–55 und die Perikopen vom Gottesknecht* (Alttestamentliche Abhandlungen, vi, 4–5). Münster i. W., 1916.

FISCHER, J.   (2) *Wer ist der Ebed in den Perikopen Jes. 42, 1–7; 49, 1–6; 50, 4–9; 52, 13—53, 12? Eine exegetische Studie* (Alttestamentliche Abhandlungen, viii, 5). Münster i. W., 1922.

FISCHER, J.   (3) *In welcher Schrift lag das Buch Isaias den LXX vor?* (BZATW, no. 56). Giessen, 1930.

GALL, A. VON.   ΒΑΣΙΛΕΙΑ ΤΟΥ ΘΕΟΥ, pp. 178 ff. Heidelberg, 1926.

GLAHN, L. (hrsgg. von).   (1) *Der Prophet der Heimkehr.* Band i. *Die Einheit von Kap. 40–66 des Buches Jesaja.* Band ii. *Das Buch Jesaja 56–66 textkritisch behandelt,* von L. Köhler. København, 1934.

GLAHN, L.   (2) *Quelques remarques sur la question du Trito-Esaie et son état actuel,* in Revue d'Histoire et de Philosophie religieuses, xii (1932), pp. 34 ff.

GLAZEBROOK, M. G.   *Studies in the Book of Isaiah.* Oxford, 1910.

GRESSMANN, H.   (1) *Die literarische Analyse Deuterojesajas,* in ZATW, xxxiv (1914), pp. 256 ff.

GRESSMANN, H.   (2) Notice of F. M. Th. Böhl, *De 'Knecht des Heeren' in Jesaja* (Haarlem, 1923), in ZATW (NF), i, p. 156.

GRESSMANN, H.   (3) *Der Messias,* pp. 59, 60–3, 124, 152, 160, 185–8, 192, 205, 206, 209, 212, 213, 218, 287–323 (FRLANT [NF], no. 26). Göttingen, 1929.

GUNKEL, H.   (1) *Knecht Jahwes,* in Religion in Geschichte und Gegenwart, 1912, Spalten 1540–3.

GUNKEL, H.   (2) *Ein Vorläufer Jesu.* Zürich, 1921.

HALLER, M.   (1) *Das Judentum,* 2te Auflage, pp. 21–72 (Schriften des Alten Testaments in Auswahl). Göttingen, 1925.

HALLER, M.   (2) *Die Kyros-Lieder Deuterojesajas,* in ΕΥΧΑΡΙΣΤΗΡΙΟΝ (FRLANT [NF], no. 19), i, pp. 261–77. Göttingen, 1923.

HAUPT, P.   *Understandest thou what thou readest? Final Victory of the Maccabees,* in Festschrift Karl Marti zum 70. Geburtstage gewidmet, hrsgg. von K. Budde (BZATW, no. 41), 1925, pp. 118–27.

HEINISCH, P.   *Die Weissagung des Alten Testaments von dem kommenden Erlöser,* 2te Auflage, pp. 116 ff. Paderborn, 1925.

HEMPEL, J.   (1) *Vom irrenden Glauben*, in Zeitschrift für systematische Theologie, viii (1930), pp. 631–60.

HEMPEL, J.   (2) Notice of Volz, *Jesaja II*, in ZATW (NF), ix (1932), pp. 207 ff.

HEMPEL, J.   (3) *Politische Absicht und politische Wirkung im biblischen Schrifttum*, pp. 20, 21, 24 ff., 33 ff.   (Der alte Orient, xxxviii, Heft 1.)   Leipzig, 1938.

HEMPEL, J.   (4) *Das Ethos des Alten Testaments*, pp. 106–7, 159 ff., 201 (BZATW, no. 67).   Berlin, 1938.

HEMPEL, J.   (5) *Zu Jes. 52, 13*, in ZATW (NF), xiv (1937), p. 309.

HERTZBERG, H. W.   *Die Nachgeschichte alttestamentlicher Texte innerhalb des Alten Testaments*, in WuW, pp. 120 ff.

HÖLSCHER, G.   (1) *Die Profeten ; Untersuchungen zur Religionsgeschichte Israels*, pp. 320, 327 ff.   Leipzig, 1914.

HÖLSCHER, G.   (2) *Geschichte der israelitischen und jüdischen Religion*, pp. 123 f.   (Sammlung Töpelmann, i. 7.)   Giessen, 1922.

HÖLSCHER, G.   (3) Notice of S. Mowinckel, *Der Knecht Jahwäs*, in NTT (1923), pp. 104 ff.

HÖLSCHER, G.   (4) Notice of Gressmann, *Der Messias*, in Deutsche Literaturzeitung, 1930, Sp. 1739 ff.

HOLZHEY, K.   *Kurzgefasstes Lehrbuch der speziellen Einleitung in das Alte Testament*, pp. 150 ff.   Paderborn, 1912.

HOONACKER, A. VAN.   *Questions de critique littéraire et d'exégèse touchant les chapitres XL ss. d'Isaie*, in Revue Biblique, 1910, pp. 557–72 ; 1911, pp. 107–14, 278–85.

ITKONEN, L.   *Deuterojesaja metrisch untersucht* (Acad. scient. Fenn. Annales, Serie B, tom. xiv. 5).   Helsinki, 1916.

JAHNOW, H.   *Das hebräische Leichenlied im Rahmen der Völkerdichtung*, pp. 256 ff. (BZATW, no. 36 [1936]).   Giessen, 1936.

JEREMIAS, A.   (1) *Das Alte Testament im Lichte des alten Orients*, 2te Auflage (1906), p. 575 ; 3te Auflage (1916), p. 605 f. ; 4te Auflage (1930), p. 685 f.

JEREMIAS, A.   (2) *Die biblische Erlösererwartung*, pp. 139–45 (Quellen, Vorband ii).   Berlin, 1931.

JEREMIAS, J.   *Deutsche Theologie*, ii, p. 113.   Göttingen, 1929.

JIRKU, A.   *Altorientalischer Kommentar zum Alten Testament*, pp. 202–4.   Leipzig und Erlangen, 1923.

KAMINKA.   *Le développement des idées du prophète Isaie et l'unité de son livre*, in Revue des Études Juives, lxxx (1925), pp. 42–59, 130–69; lxxxi (1925), pp. 27–47.

KAUTZSCH, E.   *Biblische Theologie des Alten Testaments*, pp. 302 ff.   Tübingen, 1911.

KENNETT, R. H.   (1) *The Servant of the Lord*.   London, 1911.

KENNETT, R. H.   (2) *The Composition of the Book of Isaiah*.   Oxford, 1911.

KITTEL, R.   (1) *Gestalten und Gedanken in Israel*, pp. 414–31.   Leipzig, 1925.

KITTEL, R. (2) *Geschichte des Volkes Israel*, Band iii, ite Hälfte. Buch I, Kap. I, art. 3; Kap. 8; Buch II, Kap. I, arts. 37–8. Stuttgart, 1927.

KLAMROTH, E. *Die jüdischen Exulanten in Babylonien*, in BZWAT, Erste Folge, no. 10. Leipzig, 1912.

KÖHLER, L. (1) *Die Offenbarungsformel 'Fürchte dich nicht' im Alten Testament*, in Schweizerische Theologische Zeitschrift, 1919, pp. 33–9.

KÖHLER, L. (2) *Deuterojesaja stilkritisch untersucht* (BZATW, no. 37). Giessen, 1923.

KÖNIG, E. (1) *Die messianischen Weissagungen des Alten Testaments*, p. 272. 2te Auflage. Stuttgart, 1925.

KÖNIG, E. (2) *Das Buch Jesaja*. Gütersloh, 1926.

KÖNIG, E. (3) *Die Ebed-Jahwe Frage und die Hermeneutik*, in ZATW (NF), vi (1929), pp. 255–6.

LEIMBACH, K. A. *Das Buch des Propheten Isaias*, cap. 40–66 (Biblische Volksbücher, Heft 2). Fulda, 1927.

LEVY, R. *Deutero-Isaiah: A Commentary together with a Preliminary Essay on Deutero-Isaiah's influence on Jewish thought*. London, 1925.

LODS, A. *Les prophètes d'Israël*. Paris, 1935, pp. 268–80.

MARCUS, R. *The 'plain meaning' of Isaiah XLII, 1–4*, in Harvard Theological Review, xxx (1937), pp. 249–59.

MAYNARD, J. A. *The Home of Deutero-Isaiah*, in JBL, xxxviii (1919), pp. 94–112.

MEINHOLD, J. *Einführung in das Alte Testament*, 3te Auflage, pp. 28 ff. Giessen, 1932.

MITCHELL, H. G. *The Servant of Yahweh in Isaiah 40–55*, in JBL, xxxviii (1919), pp. 113–28.

MOWINCKEL, S. (1) *Der Knecht Jahwäs*, NTT (1921), bihefte nr. 2. Giessen, 1921.

MOWINCKEL, S. (2) *Psalmenstudien*, ii, pp. 49, 195 ff., 229 ff. (Videnskapselskapets Skrifter II, Hist.-Fil. Kl., 1921, no. 6). Kristiania, 1922.

MOWINCKEL, S. (3) *Die Komposition des deuterojesajanischen Buches*, in ZATW (NF), viii, pp. 87–112, 242–60.

MOWINCKEL, S. (4) *Neuere Forschungen zu Deuterojesaja, Tritojesaja und dem 'Äbäd-Jahwä Problem*, in Acta Orientalia, xvi (1937), pp. 1 ff. Leyden.

OESTERLEY, W. O. E., and ROBINSON, T. H. *An Introduction to the Books of the Old Testament*, pp. 262–76. London, 1934.

OETTLI, S. *Der Prophet Jesaja*, Kap. 40–66 (Erläuterungen zum Alten Testament IV). Calw und Stuttgart, 1913.

OLMSTEAD, A. T. *II Isaiah and Isaiah chapter 35*, in AJSLL, liii (1937), pp. 251–3.

PALACHE, J. L. *The 'Ebed-Jahveh-Enigma in Pseudo-Isaiah*. Amsterdam, 1934.

PEAKE, A. S.   *The Religion of Israel from David to the Return from Exile*, pp. 285–8, in The People and the Book. Essays . . . edited by A. S. Peake. Oxford, 1925.

PFEIFFER, R. H.   *Introduction to the Old Testament.* New York, 1941.

PRAETORIUS, F.   (1) *Bemerkungen zu den Gedichten vom Knechte Jahves*, in ZATW, xxxvi (1916), pp. 8–20.

PRAETORIUS, F.   (2) *Die Gedichte des Deuterojesajas. Metrische und textkritische Bemerkungen.* Berlin, 1922.

PRAETORIUS, F.   (3) *Nachträge und Verbesserungen zu Deuterojesaja.* Berlin, 1927.

PROCKSCH, O.   *Jesus der Gottesknecht*, in Abhandlungen der Herder-Gesellschaft und des Herder-Instituts, vi, pp. 146–65. Riga, 1938.

ROBINSON, H. W.   *The Hebrew Conception of Corporate Personality*, in WuW, pp. 57–60 (BZATW, no. 66). Giessen, 1936.

ROBINSON, T. H.   *See under* Oesterley.

RUDOLPH, W.   (1) *Der exilische Messias*, in ZATW (NF), ii (1925), pp. 90–114.

RUDOLPH, W.   (2) *Die 'Ebed-Jahwe-Lieder als geschichtliche Wirklichkeit*, in ZATW (NF), v (1928), pp. 156–66.

SCHLÖGL, N. J.   *Jesa'ja* (Die heiligen Schriften des Alten Bundes, iv. 1). Wien und Leipzig, 1915.

SCHMIDT, H.   *Gott und das Leid im Alten Testament*, pp. 30 ff., in Vorträge der theologischen Konferenz zu Giessen. Giessen, 1926.

SCOTT, P. B. Y.   *The relation of Isaiah 35 to Deutero-Isaiah*, in AJSLL, lii, pp. 178–91.

SEIDELIN, P.   *Der 'Ebed Jahwe und die Messiasgestalt im Jesajatargum*, in Zeitschrift für die neutestamentliche Wissenschaft, xxxv (1936), pp. 194–231.

SELLIN, E.   (1) *Der alttestamentliche Prophetismus*, pp. 82 ff. Leipzig, 1912.

SELLIN, E.   (2) *Einleitung in das Alte Testament.* Leipzig, 2te Auflage, 1914; 6te Auflage, 1933.

SELLIN, E.   (3) *Mose und seine Bedeutung für die israelitisch-jüdische Religionsgeschichte*, pp. 77 ff. Leipzig und Erlangen, 1922.

SELLIN, E.   (4) *Hosea und das Martyrium des Mose*, in ZATW (NF), v (1928), p. 33.

SELLIN, E.   (5) *Tritojesaja, Deuterojesaja und das Gottesknechtsproblem*, in Neue kirchliche Zeitschrift, 1930, pp. 73–93, 145–73.

SELLIN, E.   (6) *Geschichte des israelitisch-jüdischen Volkes*, ii, p. 78. Leipzig, 1932.

SELLIN, E.   (7) *Die Lösung des deuterojesajanischen Gottesknechtsrätsels* in ZATW (NF), xiv, pp. 177 ff. (1937).

SIMCOX, C. E.   *The Role of Cyrus in Deutero-Isaiah*, in Journal of the American Oriental Society, lvii, pp. 157 ff.

SKINNER, J.   *The Book of the Prophet Isaiah, cc. XL–LXVI* (The (Revised) Cambridge Bible for Schools and Colleges). Cambridge, 1917.

SMART, J. D. *A new approach to the Ebed Jahwe Problem*, in Expository Times, xlv (1933–4), pp. 168–72.

SMITH, SIR GEORGE ADAM. *The Book of Isaiah*, vol. ii (new and revised edition). London, 1927.

SNAITH, N. H. *The Exegesis of Isaiah xl, 5–6* in Expository Times, lii, no. 10, pp. 394–6.

STAERK, W. (1) *Die Ebed-jahwe-Lieder in Jes. 40 ff.: ein Beitrag zur Deuterojesaja-Kritik* (BWAT, Erste Folge, no. 14). Leipzig, 1913.

STAERK, W. (2) *Zum Ebed-Jahwe-Problem*, in ZATW (NF), iii (1926), pp. 242–60.

STAERK, W. (3) *Zur Exegese von Jesaja 53 im Diaspora-judentum*, in Zeitschrift für die neutestamentliche Wissenschaft, xxxv (1936).

STEUERNAGEL, C. *Lehrbuch der Einleitung in das Alte Testament*, pp. 516–22 (Sammlung theologischer Lehrbücher). Tübingen, 1912.

STEVENSON, W. B. *Successive Phases in the Career of the Babylonian Isaiah*, in Glasgow University Oriental Society Transactions, viii, pp. 26–8.
Same title, in WuW, pp. 89–96.

STUMMER, F. (1) *Hauptprobleme der Erforschung der Alttestamentlichen Vulgata*, in WuW, pp. 234–5.

STUMMER, F. (2) *Einige keilinschriftliche Parallelen zu Jesaja 40–66*, in JBL, 1926, pp. 171–89.

THEODORET. *Kommentar . . . zu Jesaja*, hrsgg. von A. Mohle. Göttingen, 1932.

TORREY, C. C. (1) *The Second Isaiah*. Edinburgh, 1928.

TORREY, C. C. (2) *Some important editorial operations in the Book of Isaiah*, in JBL, lvii (1938), pp. 109–39.

VISCHER, W. *Der Gottesknecht, ein Beitrag zur Auslegung von Jes. 40–55*, in Jahrbuch der theologischen Schule Bethel, 1930.

VOLZ, P. (1) *Jesaja 53*, in Beiträge zur altorientalischen Wissenschaft Karl Budde zum 70. Geburtstag gewidmet, hrsgg. von K. Marti, pp. 180 ff. (BZATW, no. 34). Giessen, 1920.

VOLZ, P. (2) *Jesaja II* (Kommentar zum Alten Testament). Leipzig, 1932.

WELLHAUSEN, J. *Israelitische und jüdische Geschichte*. 7te Auflage, p. 152. Berlin, 1914.

ZIEGLER, J. *Untersuchungen zur Septuaginta des Buchs Isaias* (Alttestamentliche Abhandlungen, xii. 3). Münster i. W., 1934.

ZIEMER, E. *Jesaja 53 in der neueren Theologie*. Kassel, 1912.

ZIMMERLI, W. *Jesaja*, in Der Grundriss, i (1939), pp. 14–19.

ZORELI, F. *Das vierte Ebed-Jahwe-Lied*, in Biblische Zeitschrift, 1916, pp. 140–6.

Page 1.

1. Paul de Lagarde, *Deutsche Schriften*, quoted by G. Bertram, *Das Problem der Umschrift und die religionsgeschichtliche Erforschung der Septuaginta*, p. 97 in WuW. Characteristically de Lagarde also said, 'Each verse of the Bible has 72 interpretations, a different one for each people of the earth'. He confused interpretation and malversation, as extreme nationalists do; but why are the peoples restricted to 72?

Page 2.

2. Euler, pp. 132–46.

3. R. Levy's commentary is useful for its account of rabbinic interpretations; Euler and Ziegler show some aspects of the interpretation by the Septuaginta. Much that is described as due to this prophet's influence on Jewish thought is in reality the effect of rabbinic thought on interpretation of the prophet.

4. Summary history of criticism in Skinner, pp. xvi ff.

5. In the first edition of his Commentary, 1892.

6. Kennett (2), pp. 23–42.

7. xl; xli, 1–7, 21–9; xliii; xliv, 9–20, 24–8; xlv, 1–13; xlvi; xlvii; xlviii, 12–15, 20, 21.

Page 3.

8. A. Bertholet, *Zu Jesaja 53: ein Erklärungsversuch* (Freiburg i. B., 1899), pp. 22 ff., found historical incidents of the Maccabaean period referred to in this chapter; a similar dating is the basis of Haupt's essay.

9. A sound criticism will be found in G. B. Gray's commentary on *Isaiah I–XXXIX* (International Critical Commentary), p. lix; see also Skinner, pp. xxxii–xxxiii. For the Aramaic in these chapters see E. Kautzsch, *Die Aramäismen im Alten Testament*, Halle, 1902, p. 100; he admits only two, סגד in xliv, 15, 17, 19, xlvi, 6, שלק, xliv, 15, and two cases in 'late additions', בחר in xlviii, 10 and הן in liv, 15. Pfeiffer, p. 467, considers the fairly frequent use of אתה an Aramaism and compares its use in Job; it cannot point, however, to the late date postulated by Kennett, nor even that given by Torrey.

10. The proposed dates of the LXX version and of the latest documents in Isaiah do not leave a sufficient margin, Skinner, p. lxxii, note 1.

11. This statement can be easily tested by a perusal of c. xli. According to Kennett, vv. 1–7 are by an author of the 6th, vv. 8–20 by an author of the 2nd century; yet there are no differences in the three respects named.

12. Thus Volz (2), p. xxxiii, says: 'The Hebrew text is on the whole well preserved in Deutero-Isaiah. But where there are corruptions and difficulties, the old versions do not help for the most part (a different position from that in Jeremiah), a sign that the damage arose at a very early date.' Yet Volz's proposed emendations and excisions are very drastic and extensive.

13. A good example is liii, 10, where the consonantal text is

ויהוה חפץ דכאו החלי אם תשים אשם נפשו

for which Begrich (2), p. 58, ingeniously and probably correctly proposes to read

וַיהוָה חָפֵץ דַּכְּאוֹ הֶחֱלִים אֶת־שָׂם אָשָׁם נַפְשׁוֹ

But yhwh was pleased at His oppressed one,
made him whole who set his life as a sacrifice.

This avoids many violent disturbances of the text, undertaken with much confidence. The Masoretic pointing is partly responsible for this corruption.

14. Itkonen.

15. Volz (2), pp. xxxi–xxxii: 'It seems that Deutero-Isaiah was not so strict in metre . . . as earlier prophets; at any rate prudence must be exercised in undertaking alterations of the text on . . . metrical grounds. Thus he changes the metre pretty freely. . . . Perhaps, however, there is not so much irregularity as poetic intention, which we can no longer recognize clearly. . . .' Mowinckel (4), p. 9, on Praetorius (2), Itkonen, and Volz, says: 'So far as metrical problems are concerned, none of the works named really introduces anything new; all of them depend on Sievers's basic theory, but it is a considerable question whether a solution of the problem can be arrived at on this basis at all. . . . It is not surprising that most scholars are satisfied with the statement that Hebrew metre prefers irregularities and "mixed metres", or that the prophetic style had no strict verse measures at all.' Caspari (3), pp. 206–7, argues that the differences of metre point to many authors; but he does not show whether this could lead to regularity, without assuming several authors of certain short units. Begrich, in OLZ, 1938, Sp. 478, in criticizing Nyberg's scepticism as to the justification of securing metrical schemes by emendation, makes considerable claims for

the metrical test; it affects something called *Stilistik*, that is, presumably, the laws governing composition. But the prophets were individuals, and it is bad criticism to apply to the writings of one man principles derived from the writings of others. Literary criticism cannot use mass methods, or reduce individual expression to set formulae.

16. On Babylonian verse see H. Zimmern, *Ueber Rhythmus im Babylonischen*, ZA, xii, 382–92. Sievers applied his system, 'Schallanalyse', *Beiträge zur babylonischen Metrik*, ZA (NF), iv, 1 ff. Such attempts are bound to be wrong; it is impossible to deduce, from a necessarily conventional transcription, rising and falling tones and degrees of stress. One feature of Babylonian verse is, however, fairly certain; the grammatical units do not exceed the double line. The failure to observe this rule, which our English verse of the 'Sing a song of sixpence' type also necessarily observes, has misled some scholars into impossible overlaps and caesuras, see ZA (NF), iii, p. 90, Kol. 2, lines 2–3; p. 91, Kol. 2, lines 16–19.

Page 4.

17. This can be seen in Akkadian verse, where the same unfortunate use of the word 'strophe' has been introduced in an inaccurate way for, e.g., the division of a short passage from the Creation Epic in ZA (NF), iv, pp. 29–33; or in the still more ingenuous division of another narrative poem into 'strophes' of four lines, two lines as 'introductions' or 'ends', five lines and three lines, ZA (NF), iii, pp. 88 ff. On these principles Milton's *Paradise Lost*, Shakespeare's longer dramatic speeches, and, surely, Browning's 'Pied Piper', should be divided up like a Greek chorus. When in ancient copies of Akkadian poems stanzas are intended, they are marked; good examples will be found in E. Ebeling, *Keilschrifttexte aus Assur religiösen Inhalts*, Heft iii, no. 96, last translated by Ebeling in H. Gressmann, *Altorientalische Texte zum Alten Testament*, 2te Auflage, 1926, pp. 284–7 and in W. von Soden's transliteration and translation of a text in ZA (NF), x, pp. 32–5.

18. If c. xlvii, which is in a regular 3 : 2 rhythm, could be divided into five stanzas of 7 lines each, as Duhm and others thought, there would still be no regular equivalence justifying the term ' strophe ', but there might be some reason for accepting the necessary excisions and emendations. But Haller (1) rejected this and divided into stanzas of 8, 7, 12, 9, Torrey (1) into 7, 4, 6, 6,

6, 5, while Volz, who considers the poem 'finely constructed', divides into six 'strophes' of 6 lines each, excising two phrases and assuming two omissions of half-lines. These schemes not only contradict one another but also show a failure to recognize that the only reason for such analysis should be the clear intention of the author. The basis of division is not really formal; the results are paragraphs according to sense.

H. Möller, *Strophenbau der Psalmen*, in ZATW (NF), ix, pp. 240 ff., attempted to define more strictly the meaning of the term 'strophe' in Hebrew poetry. He demanded the following characteristics. (1) Precise basic units must exist, out of which the strophe is constructed. (2) There must be at least one, or more, repetitions with the same construction. (3) The close of the strophe must mark an end in the idea expressed. These modest demands are nowhere fulfilled by any section in chapters xl–lv.

19. Examples: Elliger, p. 244, on xlv, 6; Caspari (3), p. 85, note 3; Volz, p. 170, notes *c, d*. See also Caspari in OLZ XXIX (1926), pp. 778–9.

20. Caspari is typical, see (2) and (3), pp. 4–8. He says of Praetorius (2) in (3), p. 207, Anm. 1, 'Praetorius often restores the text ingeniously, but does not follow the Greek sufficiently faithfully where that is possible, and so reduces the probability of his restorations'. He therefore believes that so idiomatic a matter as the use of the definite article, bound to differ in different languages, can be deduced not from the Hebrew, but from the Greek, text. This betrays a lack of feeling for the idioms of living speech; words become no more than symbols to be equated.

21. Volz (2) is typical. See especially the textual notes on the 'servant' passages, pp. 170–2.

22. See Ziegler. Torrey (1), pp. 207–15, is a fair statement.

23. G. Bertram, *op. laud.*, p. 109 in WuW.

24. Several hands, H. Gressmann, *Ueber die in Jes. c. 56–66 vorausgesetzten zeitgeschichtlichen Verhältnisse*, Göttingen, 1898; Volz (2). Mowinckel (4), pp. 27–8 still accepts several authors, but is inclined to reduce the period of time covered, and to connect all the pieces with the rebuilding of the Temple by Zerubbabel. He regards this as a necessary result of Odeberg's study. One author is assumed by K. Elliger, *Die Einheit des Tritojesaja* (BWANT, 3te Folge, nr. 9), Stuttgart, 1928; idem, *Der Prophet Tritojesaja* in ZATW (NF), viii (1931), pp. 112–41; H. Odeberg, *Trito-Isaiah* (Uppsala Universitets Årsskrift), Uppsala, 1931.

Page 5.

25. E. König (2); L. Glahn (1), Band I; Torrey (1).

26. Torrey (1), Scott, Olmstead.

27. The same applies to lvii, 14, lxii, 10. From the time regular roads were used in the Achaemenean period, the figure was bound to become popular.

28. Torrey (1), pp. 28–31, 42. On this see Mowinckel (3), p. 100, note 2.

29. Torrey (1), p. 53, repeated in (2).

30. Torrey (1), pp. 367–8, 44 ff. The natural sense of these passages is also avoided by Begrich (2), p. 67, who uses the argument from silence, 'none of them know of Cyrus', and dates lii, 11–12 before 547.

31. G. Hölscher in Kautzsch (hrsgg. von A. Bertholet), *Heilige Schriften des Alten Testaments*, 4te Auflage, Esra. Mowinckel (3), p. 244, note 1; (4), p. 27.

Page 6.

32. See *Palestine Exploration Quarterly*, Jan. 1941, pp. 5 ff., and the references quoted p. 8, note 2 and p. 9, notes 2, 3.

33. See H. Gunkel, *Die Propheten*, Göttingen, 1917, pp. 104 ff., in the introduction to Hans Schmidt, *Die Grossen Propheten*, 2te Auflage, Leipzig, 1923, pp. xxxiv ff., and in ZATW (NF), i (1924), pp. 182–3.

34. The final form may be seen in Begrich's edition of Gunkel, *Einleitung in die Psalmen*.

35. *Sitz im Leben.*

36. The 'ecstatic' has played a great part in forming some modern views of Hebrew prophecy, see G. Hölscher (1), Gunkel in Schmidt, *op. laud.*, pp. xxiii ff., and Gunkel, *Die Propheten*, pp. 111 ff.; Dr. T. H. Robinson, *Prophecy and the Prophets*, p. 50. For words of caution see N. Micklem, *Prophecy and Eschatology*, pp. 13–44.

37. Gressmann (1).

38. Gressmann's argument was directed against Staerk (1), and the view that c. xl is a unity. His points, (1) pp. 257–8, were as follows: (1) vv. 1–2 are not a 'motto', because that is a modern conception. (2) The three sections, vv. 3–5, 6–8, 9–11, considered introductory, are not properly balanced by vv. 27–31. (3) A three-fold introduction is most unusual. (4) The connexion of the three sections is fragile. Since the first section describes

God's homecoming through the desert, the second should state that Israel returns with Him to Palestine, but this is the theme of the third section. This cannot be remedied simply by the transposition of vv. 9–11 before vv. 6–8 as Marti proposed, because (5) 'it is impossible, after the prophet has just described the revelation of God in the desert, that he should say, " Hark, there is an utterance; and I said, What shall I proclaim?" How can a prophet speak so, when he is in the middle of proclaiming?' 'That something new begins after v. 5 is proved by the words, "For the mouth of Yahweh hath said so".' This argument is superficial, and does not prove the 'units' independent. The first does not even tell against Staerk's view. Mowinckel (3) p. 88, on vv. 1–2, practically repeated Staerk: '... der programmatische Spruch ... den Anfang hat bilden müssen ... die ganze deutero-jesajanische Botschaft *in nuce.*' Points 2 and 3 are observations; they do not prove anything. Point 4 imposes a sequence the author did not observe *because* Gressmann's view would demand it; that is not good exegesis, and not an argument against unity. Point 5 is purely verbal. There is no reason why a command to proclaim some further message should not be in logical sequence. The last clause of v. 5 is not a 'formula', see Lecture III, note 44a.

Page 7.

39. If xli, 1–xlii, 9 is a unit, as is possible, then the repetitions of theme in that ' speech ' are not only forceful, but the repetition is given special justification in xli, 27a. It would be interesting to study Arabic oratory, if that were possible, to see whether many features of Hebrew prophecy, such as abruptness of change in theme and person, the regular use of direct speech, not always introduced, and repetition, were not to be found there. The Qur'ān is, for instance in the rapid change of the pronouns, in some passages analogous, e.g. Sūra vii, vv. 138–41 and 142–4. The abrupt changes in Babylonian and Assyrian letters, which are, formally, direct speech, are notable.

40. The element of persuasion is frequent in these chapters; many of the rebukes for lack of courage, or reproofs for lack of faith, are also persuasive, see e.g. xlv, 9–13.

41. Gressmann (1), p. 264: 'If the utterances of Deutero-Isaiah are compared with those of Amos, Hosea, Isaiah and Jeremiah, they agree roughly in length. Exact calculations have not yet been made; it will probably prove to be the case that the " units " of Deutero-Isaiah are somewhat longer than those of his predecessors. Thus a gradual increase of bulk in the prophetic

utterances may be assumed, which is very intelligible from the point of view of literary history, whereas a poem of 333 verses would be an absolute enormity in Hebrew prophecy.' This schematic increase, obviously thought to be an argument in favour of the theory, seems *a priori* improbable, unlike any proved development, since literature, like life, is not schematic; the theory closely resembles discarded schemes of Homeric criticism.

Caspari (3), pp. 69–70: 'The extent of individual intellectual productions as written down, which was then usual, leads to the expectation that the book is a composite of several such, and gives this expectation the preference over the assumption of a coherent individuality.' This is criticism with a fixed idea.

Mowinckel (4), p. 10, on what he calls Gressmann's *Programmschrift*: 'The task here was, to use the methods of *Gattungsforschung*, based on the arguments of Gunkel, as a means both for the delimitation of the original units within the composite works which nearly all the prophetic writings in fact are, as also for the reconstruction of a livelier picture of the psychological origin. . . . '

Elliger, p. 243, considers that some of Mowinckel's 'units', e.g. xliii, 15–xliv, 5 and xliv, 6–22, are too long.

No one has yet shown why these chapters are supposed to be more closely associated, in respect of the length of the 'units', with the prophecies that preceded them than with those that followed. Volz divides cc. lvi–lxvi into the same short units as xl–lv, presumably on the same argument from analogy; there is no other obvious advantage.

42. Gressmann (1), p. 259.

Page 8.

43. Gressmann (1), pp. 259–60.

44. Gressmann (1), p. 260.

45. Gressmann (1), p. 261. The same complaint is made by Elliger, p. 135, of previous *Gattungsforscher*: ' . . . no one has yet to my knowledge refused to admit that cc. 54–55 are from beginning to end by Deutero-Isaiah. . . . The contents were not in any respect objectionable; no further attention was paid to the style. '

46. The formulae are divided according to types. (*a*) For oracles. Introductory. כה אמר יהוה, common; קול אומר or קול קורא, only once each; נאם יהוה. End formulae. אמר יהוה: כי פי יהוה דבר: נאם יהוה, once only, xl, 5. (*b*) Other prophetic formulae. Invective, הוי, only xlv, 9–10. Imperatives and interjections, 'as out of them, as can be demonstrated from

Hebrew literature, all poetry arose ', p. 263. [This curious statement is not a hasty error; it is clear from other passages that
Gressmann really believed this to be true.] (c) Lyrical introductions. Orders to the audience to be quiet and listen, xli, 1;
xlii, 18; xliv, 1; xlvi, 3, 12; xlviii, 1, 12; xlix, 1; li, 1, 4, 7, 21,
but these are not always at the beginning. (d) Introductory
formulae of the hymns. Commands to sing or rejoice, xlii, 10;
lii, 9; liv, 1, and many other ' typical introductions '.

Thus of specific formulae Gressmann only adduces those under
(a), and these must be reduced to two, כה אמר יהוה and נאם יהוה
for introductions, and two, אמר יהוה and נאם יהוה for ends. For
קול אומר and קול קורא are intentionally parallel; this prohibits
the division Gressmann posits. כי פי יהוה דבר is dependent,
and not a formula. That נאם יהוה does not always represent a
complete break in the sense is recognized by Elliger, p. 142.

Köhler believed that ' Fear not ' is an introductory formula for
' revelations of God ', Offenbarungen, see Köhler (1) and (2), p. 125.
It can be the opening clause of an oracle, as in xliv, 2, but is not
necessarily so, xli, 10; its use in other languages, e.g. Babylonian,
shows that it is proper to warlike encouragement to a nation as
well as to comfort for individuals in distress.

47. See Knudtzon, J. A., *Assyrische Gebete an den Sonnengott für
Staat und königliches Haus aus der Zeit Asarhaddons und Asurbanipals*,
Leipzig, 1893; and Klauber, *Politisch-religiöse Texte der Sargoni-
denzeit*.

Page 9.

48. c. xli will serve as an example. Gressmann found three
units, vv. 1–13, 14–20, 21–9. In the first unit he excised vv. 6–7,
which he inserted into vv. 19–20 of c. xl. This resulted in subsequent critics of the school making two units, vv. 1–5, 8–13, out
of Gressmann's one. But within vv. 8–13 the expletive ' Behold '
is an introductory formula, so that there are again two units for
one, vv. 8–10, 11–13. In the first unit, vv. 1–5, it is possible to
find sense in vv. 2–4a without v. 1, which becomes an alternative
introduction; vv. 4b–13 are then kept as a unit without excising
vv. 6–7. According to still another view, v. 5 is an editorial
' suture ', to be excised with vv. 6–7. Begrich (2), p. 1, recognizes
the complete confusion. ' The first task is, to assure the delimitation of units in Deutero-Isaiah. The necessity for this cannot be
disputed, if the different divisions of the text are compared.
Chapter 40 will serve as an example. Budde combines it with
c. 41, and sees in both an introduction to what follows. Staerk

considers 40, 1–31 a unity, and so also Torrey. Volz splits the chapter into the independent units 1–11, 12–26, 27–31, and Caspari similarly. According to Duhm the chapter contains five units, 1–11, 12–16, 17–20, 21–6, 27–31. Gressmann has the same number but divides quite differently, 1–2, 3–5, 6–8, 9–11, 12–31. That these distinctions are not without importance for the interpretation and deductions from it, can easily be inferred.' Begrich himself, without questioning the principle that causes confusion, or asking whether the 'units' do not ultimately depend on exegesis, states that the units are six in number, vv. 1–8, 9–11, 12–17, 18–20 (plus xli, 6–7 plus 25–6), 21–4, 27–31. It only remains for someone to produce 4 and 7 units; for Gressmann (3), p. 322, said, 'Science cannot allow a halt to be called, until every possibility has been explored', and this kind of literary criticism claims to be science, not an art!

48 a. Who, for instance, is to decide that xli, 13 belongs to the unit that precedes? It announces an intention that is a prerequisite for the fulfilment in verse 14, and logically need not be separated from what follows, though it continues what precedes.

49. Perhaps xl, 3–5 and xl, 6–8.

50. None against Israel. Against Babylon, indirectly expressed, xli, 11 ff., xlii, 14 ff., xlix, 26, li, 22 ff., liii, 14–15.

51. Practically every unit.

52. xlv, 9–13, xlii, 18–25 joined to 'promises'; xliii, 22–8, xlviii, 1–2, l, 1–2a.

53. lv, 6–7; joined to hymn, xliv, 21–2; joined to promise, xlviii, 18a; at end of 'servant' passage, l, 10.

54. lv, 1–3 also partly warning; xl, 27–31, li, 17–20, liv, 1–6, utterances of the prophet: xl, 1–2a, xlvi, 12–13, xlix, 15–17, li, 7–8, li, 12–13, spoken by YHWH.

55. xli, 1–13, xli, 21–9, xliii, 8–13, xliv, 6–20, xlv, 20–1, xlviii, 12–16, and a short reference in xliii, 26.

56. At end of xlv, 18–25, xlii, 17, xlv, 17, xl, 6–8, lv, 6–11.

57. li, 1–3.

58. xl, 9, lii, 7–8.

59. xlvii, 1–15, xlvi, 1–2.

60. Appear for the most part as extensions of the introduction or end. There are two longer hymns; xl, 12–26 is an introduction to xl, 27–31, xlii, 10–13 an introduction to xlii, 14–17. The smaller hymn elements are common.

61. Gressmann (1), p. 295.

Page 10.

62. Begrich (2), p. 2. A simple *credo* in the possibility of dividing all the prophetic writings into exact classes will be found in OLZ, 1938, Sp. 478.

63. xli, 8–13, 14–16, 17–20; xlii, 14–17; xliii, 1–7, 16–21; xliv, 1–5; xlv, 1–7, 14–17; xlvi, 3–4, 12–13; xlviii, 17–19; xlix, 7, 8–12 (13), 14–21, 22–3, 24–6; li, 6–8, 12–16; liv, 4–6, 7–10, 11–12 plus 13*b*, 14*a* plus 13*a*–17; lv, 8–13. As a *motif* in other connexions, xlix, 6, li, 22–3, lv, 4–5. Imitations of the oracular answer to national lament, xli, 17–20; xlii, 14–17; xliii, 16–21; li, 6–8; lv, 8–13.

64. xli, 1–5, 21–9; xliii, 8–13, 22–8; xliv, 6–8; xlviii, 1–11; l, 1–2*a*. Begrich says of this label: 'This expression, introduced by Gunkel and appropriated by other scholars, can, of course, only be accepted as a collective designation, though a very useful one. For a comprehension of the individual types which refer to legal procedure, it is insufficient.' He then distinguishes the summons of an accused party or debtor to a legal decision, the speeches of both parties in court, the judge's summing up, and the description of the procedure in court.

65. xl, 12–17, 18–20 plus 25–6, 21–4, 27–31; xliv, 24–8; xlv, 9–13, 18–25; xlvi, 5–11; xlviii, 1–11, 12–15; l, 1–3.

66. xlviii, 20–1; lii, 1–2, 11–12; liv, 1–3.

67. xliv, 21–2; lv, 6–7.

68. xl, 9–11.

69. lv, 1–5.

70. The only real hymns are xlii, 10–13, xliv, 23.

71. Lamentation, l, 4–9; li, 9–16. Thanks, xlix, 1–6.

72. xlix, 13.

73. lii, 7–10.

74. xlvii, 1–15.

75. Gressmann (1), p. 267.

Page 11.

76. Begrich (2), p. 77. In spite of Begrich's statement, there is nothing quite like this about the eschatological 'last day'; the verse is the contemporary expression of a transient, not unjustified, hatred, not of a religious belief about the future.

77. The resemblance between his 'units' and the paragraphing of exegetes was known to Gressmann; he tried to avoid the inference by pointing out, (1), p. 264, that though Budde, for

example, produced about the same number of paragraphs as his own 49 'units', Budde often divided into two what in his scheme was a 'unit', and often combined what in the scheme was divided. The argument fails, because the same fate has befallen Gressmann's own 'units' at the hands of other *Gattungsforscher*. It is by no means certain that different scholars always have the same conception of units. Elliger, p. 227, says :'When Volz treats xl, 3–5, 6–8, and 9–11 as three strophes of the same poem, the close relation of subject deceives him. The pieces are, formally, independent.' That seems to mean that any change in form prohibits logical connexion; in that case Elliger's 'units' in c. xl differ basically from Gressmann's, but they are none the less paragraphs. Elliger, p. 264, distinguishes between *gedankliche Einheiten* and *literarische selbständige Einheiten*, so that there are variable criteria.

78. There is in these chapters a use of cross-reference, much neglected. lv, 3 is unintelligible, in its immediate meaning for contemporaries, without a knowledge of lii, 6 and xlix, 6; lv, 4 will only be rightly understood by one who bears in mind xlii, 1–4, xliv, 28, xlv, 1. lv, 5 must be interpreted by xlv, 14. lv, 8–9 is the theme of xlv, 8–13. lv, 11 is meant to recall xl, 5 and xl, 8, which are intentionally parallel. These cases are not confined to c. lv; thus li, 7 could only be understood in its immediate significance if the contemporary observer bore in mind l, 4–10; the words are no mere general truth. Other examples are given in the third lecture. Pfeiffer, pp. 467–9, has argued that there are peculiarities in vocabulary, syntax and figures of speech due to direct imitation of the book of Job, but not one of his examples can be considered convincing. His best observation, the constant use of the participial clause, is due in both cases to influences not confined, as Pfeiffer seems to suggest, to Egyptian literature, but common in other early Semitic languages. G. Hoffmann argued from the similarities to Job he found in xl, 2; l, 9; li, 8, that Job was written later than Isaiah xl–lv, see *Zeitschrift für Semitistik*, ix, p. 165.

79. Köhler (2), p. 84.

Page 12.

80. Köhler (2), p. 85, 'Verlangen nach Fülle und Rundung'.

81. Köhler (2), p. 119, quoted with approval by Kittel (2), p. 208. Pfeiffer has expressed the same judgement, p. 465 : 'The poet's intense enthusiasm, fanciful Oriental imagination and burning passion lift him above the world of reality to the realm

of fantastic dreams. . . . It is in vain that one looks for logical sequence and arrangement in his poems. . . . His book is an incoherent succession of shouts, his thoughts are poured out, glowing and fluid, like a molten metal before it has hardened into a definite shape. Consequently, the dilemma posed by critics—is the work a unit, or an anthology of separate poems?—is meaningless. . . . Is. 40–55 is neither a literary unit like the Book of Job, nor an anthology like Lamentations : it is a passionate and effusively incoherent rhapsody in which the emotional moods, the dominant thoughts and the prevalent style furnish the only bond uniting detached poems into a whole, just as rocks and earth are joined ephemerally into an avalanche. . . .' The critic has fallen into the trap of the style he thinks he is describing; what this 'incoherent rhapsody' of 'a succession of shouts' really means, remains unexplained. Those interested in general literal criticism will note that the same critic says, p. 463 : 'The magnificent grandeur of Is. 40–55 and of Deuteronomy lent itself particularly well to rendition into superb Elizabethan prose. Accordingly, Is. 40–55 and Deuteronomy are more impressive literary masterpieces in the Authorised Version than in the original Hebrew'. Does this mean that Elizabethan prose is most suitable for making nonsense sound grand?

82. This poverty of vocabulary is considered by Elliger, p. 18, a characteristic of his 'Trito-Isaiah'; but in this case the repetition of a word or phrase where necessary, rather than absence of a synonym, is the basis of the charge. Such criticism of a living language by a foreigner would not deserve mention.

83. The Babylonians also measured grain etc. by 'thirds'; see Thureau-Dangin in *Revue d'Assyriologie*, xxxi (1935), pp. 49–50, who suggests that the term arose through the measuring out in heaps with a bushel-measure. In Hebrew, the measure itself received the name 'the third'.

84. פלס as opposed to מאזנים must be the only other known form of balance in common use.

85. Liquid, air, powder, solid.

Page 13.

86. So Volz (2), *ad loc.*, against the usual view, that the answer should be 'God'. The point is, that no one can estimate the extent of God's creations, rather than God's care for minute parts of His creation.

87. Perhaps because of a conception of *Gattungsforschung*. Gressmann, *Die Aufgaben der alttestamentlichen Forschung*, p. 26, in

ZATW (NF), i (1924), says, 'The history of the type has ... very little to do with aesthetics'; a criticism of style so based leads, apparently, to Köhler's results.

88. Caspari (3), pp. 239–40. Abraham Lévy, *The Song of Moses* (Deut. 32), Paris, 1930, also assumed several authors.

Page 14.

89. Caspari (3), pp. 139, 163.

90. 'Your nakedness shall be revealed, your shame shall be seen.' The allusion must be to the punishment of unfaithful wives, as in Ezekiel xvi, 35 ff., and Hosea ii, 3; the two passages are discussed by L. Köhler, *Archaeologisches*, p. 146, in ZATW, xxxiv (1914). This punishment was applied, in the 17th century B.C., under Amorite law, to wives who denied their husbands, see *Proceedings of the Society of Biblical Archaeology*, xxix, p. 180, line 14, and in the 15th century, under Hurrian law, to wives who married on the death of their husbands, see C. H. Gordon, *The Living Past*, p. 172. Most commentators excise v. 3, but it is essential: the point is lost if there is no announcement of God's vengeance and its nature. The sentiment that leads to the excision is ill judged. Babylon had been an agent of God, and had exceeded the limits imposed, xl, 2; the bitter hatred expressed is not out of place and is found in other prophets. Caspari himself admits the possibility or probability that xlvii, 4 is an interpolation, but claims that 'the feeling of the interpolator that a traditional formula suitable for a congregation or a composite of such formulae belonged here ... would be a direct testimony for a public appearance of its speaker.' There is no need to assume this; the interpolation is due to the adoption of the book for reading in the synagogues, not to the original purpose.

91. Caspari (3), p. 170.

92. For another example see Caspari (3), p. 69. The rhetorical repetition of a word, ἐπίζευξις, is thought to show that words in these 'units' were recited in chorus, 'the repetition shows that the speaker does not stand alone, so that no one needed to bother about him'.

Page 15.

93. While confining the possibilities of individual expression, Caspari multiplies the possibilities of artificial literary development. Thus in his treatment, (3), pp. 188–9, of xlii, 13–15, he assumes the existence of 'an unknown Epic' containing 'a description of a divine struggle', and concludes, 'for Deutero-

Isaiah such expressions have nothing of the warlike left in them, properly speaking'. So individual an act as borrowing from some little-known literary work, and the deliberate use of such borrowed passages to mean something other than the words say, ill fits the idea that these are marching songs, which must be immediately comprehensible.

94. Only some such explanation can account for liii, 1-6 where the 1st pers. pl. can only designate a body of people closely associated with the 'servant'; all Israel cannot be intended, for that would not fit the expressions in vv. 1-2, and the passage cannot originally have been meant for congregational use as a penitential psalm, for whether the 'we' be all Israel or only part, the 'servant' cannot in either case be the Jewish nation personified, since 'the servant' and 'we' cannot be identical. Only the need to interpret thus could be thought to make the language suitable. Perhaps the 'we' were members of an order of prophets, associated with the author of cc. xl ff., who had not taken any active part in his mission.

Page 16.

95. For criticisms of the statistical method as applied by Elliger to both cc. xl-xlv and lvi-lxvi, and also by Odeberg, *Trito-Isaiah*, to cc. lvi-lxvi, see W. Caspari, *Der Geist des Herrn ist über mir*, in *Neue kirchliche Zeitschrift*, xl, no. 11 (1929), pp. 729-47; O. Eissfeldt (1), pp. 377, 384, 386; Mowinckel (4), pp. 23-6.

96. Elliger, chapter vi.

97. Elliger, pp. 245, 255, 264-5, 268 (2).

Page 17.

98. That there was no basis for separation in style and language was recognized by Duhm. The reaction from his excisions on the basis of thought and theme, though justified, has gone too far, and the view that c. liii must be by the author of the other three 'servant' passages that refer to an individual, maintained for example by Hempel (2), p. 211, neglects the unique character of theme, thought, and formal expression in that chapter. Begrich (2), pp. 145-50, maintaining that the 'servant' is the prophet, and that c. liii is by him and refers to him, is driven to the conclusion that the chapter represents a prophecy of his own martyrdom and resurrection, a view so artificial that it cannot be correct. That the death of the 'servant' is spoken of as a past event has been shown by Cripps. Since liii is worded as the lament of a special community who had not followed the 'servant', the only

natural explanation is that it was written to express the opinion of that community, not by the 'servant', and not by the prophet whose mission cannot be distinguished from that of the 'servant'. Volz is justified in his view that liii is a separate piece; but there seems no good reason for refusing to admit the identity of the 'servant' of liii and the 'servant' of xlix, 1–6 and l, 4–10. Mowinckel (4), pp. 37–9, maintains that his theory of composition, advanced in (3), proves that the individual 'servant' passages were inserted after the original compiler's work had finished, a thesis suitably answered by Sellin (7), pp. 179–81.

99. It is this combination which gives rise to some of the major difficulties in the discussions of Gressmann, *Der Ursprung der israelitisch-jüdischen Eschatologie* (FRLANT, nr. 6), art. 30, pp. 317 ff.; Gressmann (3), pp. 308 ff.; Mowinckel (3), pp. 245–7; Elliger, pp. 66–102; Begrich, chapter vi. Only Caspari escapes the necessity of reconciling incompatibilities in xlii, 1–4 and 5–9 as compared with the other passages.

100. Peake, Budde (1), (2), König (2), Torrey (1), Eissfeldt (2), H. W. Robinson, Pfeiffer, Lods. Rudolph (2), p. 157, points out the variations in the collective interpretation König has to adopt, but puts his own case unfortunately, p. 156, when he says that 'by "servant of Yahweh" in the present text of Isaiah 40–55, the people, Israel, is to be understood in every passage' and distinguishes from the present an original text, for this seems to justify the reply of König (3). It is precisely because the present text has not been satisfactorily explained that the interpretation of the 'servant' as the collective, 'Israel', fails. Peake practically admits this. Pfeiffer, p. 478, and Lods, p. 277, avoid the difficulties by re-writing, without explaining how the simple text they produce could ever have been misunderstood. Budde's exegesis takes refuge in symbolism; Torrey's follows the late tradition, which sought, as the Septuagint shows, to bring the individual into line with the collective 'servant'. Eissfeldt and Wheeler Robinson have recently introduced an adaptation of the ideas of J. Pedersen, *Israel*, pp. 263–79; but their views are by no means simple, and would hardly be understood by an audience. Thus Wheeler Robinson says, of the prophet in xlix, 1–6, 'He *is* Israel, created to be the Servant; he is Israel, though working alone to make Israel what she ought to be; he is Israel finally become a light of nations'. This is an esoteric explanation, possible for a solitary; it could not occur to anyone first hearing the original words, and is not comparable to the admirable

treatment of the 'I' in the Psalms. Eissfeldt (1), p. 382, claims that the personification of Jerusalem and Samaria in Ezekiel xvi and xxiii exceeds in individual characteristics anything in the four 'servant' passages. This is not the point. In Ezekiel xvi and xxiii every characteristic in the personification could immediately be transferred to the known history of Jerusalem and Samaria; point by point the application of the elaborate simile is clear. But in the case of the 'servant' this is not so; therefore in the exegesis of the death of the 'servant', for instance, Wheeler Robinson says 'the prophet's spirit has become that of the nation, and . . . Yahweh has vindicated the faith of his Servant by a national resurrection from the grave of exile'. This is forced, the application of Ezekiel xvi and xxiii not so, for the true counterpart of those chapters is—c. xlvii. Mowinckel (4), pp. 29–31, argues that Eissfeldt has misunderstood Pedersen.

Once the interpretation of the 'servant' as Israel is abandoned for these passages, there is very little in favour of any of the other 'collective' explanations. The latest of these may be found in Father E. Burrows's posthumous book, who suggests that the 'servant' is the house of David, past, present, or future. Others prefer an ideal, 'prophecy'.

101. Gressmann, *Der Ursprung der israelitisch-jüdischen Eschatologie*, pp. 312–33; and Gressmann (3), pp. 287–323.

102. Mowinckel (3), p. 257. But there is no clear indication of the meaning in his later utterance (4), pp. 37–9.

103. Mowinckel (2), pp. 49, 195 ff., 230, 238 ff., 247, 251, 253, 256 ff., 273 ff., 282–6, 292 ff., 334–5, 339. His argument is that all passages referring to ancient myths or legends in which the God of Israel appears as conqueror or king, and many passages which in his opinion can be connected in some way with such themes, e.g. the road through the wilderness, are recognizably the same *Gattung* as Psalms 93–100 but later in date. For discussions of Mowinckel's basic hypothesis see C. R. North, *The Religious Aspects of Hebrew Kingship*, pp. 34–7 in ZATW (NF), ix (1932); O. Eissfeldt, *Jahwe als König*, in ZATW (NF), v (1928), pp. 81–105.

104. The Babylonian texts which have so far been adduced as parallel are (1) the Tammuz laments, (2) the New Year ritual text with explanations, E. Ebeling, *Keilschrifttexte aus Assur religiösen Inhalts*, Heft iii, nr. 143, and Heft vi, nr. 219, translated in S. Langdon, *The Epic of Creation*, pp. 34 ff. (to be used with

caution), and by Ebeling in Gressmann, *Altorientalische Texte zum Alten Testament*, pp. 320 ff.; (3) *ludlul bel nimeqi*, translated by S. Langdon, *Babylonian Wisdom*, pp. 35 ff., by Landsberger in Lehmann-Haas, *Textbuch zur Religionsgeschichte* (2te Auflage), pp. 311 ff.; by Ebeling in Gressmann, *Altorientalische Texte zum Alten Testament*, pp. 274–81; (4) an unpublished text transliterated and translated by Ebeling, *Tod und Leben nach den Vorstellungen der Babylonier*, nr. 1, pp. 1–9. Gressmann and Dix adduced the first, Dürr mentions the second and compares the third, Böhl, *De Knecht des Heeren*, introduced the fourth.

Gressmann's comparison was too general in nature to be examined in detail. The Tammuz laments as known to us in Sumerian texts contain nothing specifically comparable with Isaiah c. liii. There is no need to throw doubt on the interpretation of the ritual text, (2), as referring to the death of Marduk, as Rudolph (2), p. 164, note 1, does, to agree with his verdict, ibid., note 4, and previously (1), pp. 105–6, note 2, that Isaiah liii cannot be treated as analogous to it. The interpretation of no. (3) which led to its introduction into the discussion is almost certainly incorrect. Text no. (4) has no relation to the matter, see the translation by W. von Soden, *Die Unterweltsvision eines assyrischen Kronprinzen*, in ZA (NF), ix, pp. 1–31.

Connected with this question in the discussions, but unrelated in fact, is Staerk's view that the expressions in c. liii are not to be understood literally. In the Psalms, sufferers refer to themselves as dead, and this 'style' led to the wording in c. liii. The answer has again been clearly stated by Rudolph (2). It is clear that this chapter is not a psalm by the sufferer, and the 'style' indicated would not, according to Staerk's own theory, be applicable to a lament for the sufferer.

105. The basis of this exegesis, liii, 10–12, may originally have had a much simpler sense. 'He shall see seed' יראה זרע can be said of a man who has progeny who can perform, after his death, pious acts to commemorate him; while his children live his 'name' abides, his existence is prolonged, so that the clause יאריך ימים is justified. But the 'servant' seems to have been condemned as a felon, and such can have no 'name', their civil rights cease, children are no longer in a position to 'prolong the days'. For this reason it is said that God 'restored him to health, who set his life as a sacrifice', see note 13. The sentence, passed doubtless by the prophet's enemies, had been abrogated, his rights restored. Only when the beliefs about existence through

the 'name' were forgotten, and ideas unknown in the 6th century were current among Jews, would the idea in liii, 8,

כִּי נִגְזַר מֵאֶרֶץ חַיִּים מִפֶּשַׁע עַמִּי נֶגַע לָמוֹ

'for he was excluded from the land of the living, he was stricken because of the error of my people', become in the Septuagint ὅτι αἴρεται ἀπὸ τῆς γῆς ἡ ζωὴ αὐτοῦ, ἀπὸ τῶν ἀνομιῶν τοῦ λαοῦ μου ἤχθη εἰς θάνατον, with different implication, so that the question in Acts viii, 34 could arise. In vv. 11–12 the Hebrew imperfects denote action developing, see Kennett, *Hebrew Tenses*, pp. 10–11, and the translation by futures can mislead. In v. 12 the שלל which the 'servant' is sharing with 'the strong' is the שכר and פעלה of c. xl, 10; the armies of Cyrus have won the exiles as booty, but the 'servant' has his part, though he died in achieving his mission. In lii, 13 there is nothing necessarily referring to resurrection. But all this belongs, not to the history of 538, but to the history of the development of ideas.

106. Sellin (3) and (4).

Page 18.

107. Sellin, *Serubbabel: ein Beitrag zur Geschichte der messianischen Erwartung und der Entstehung des Judentums* (Leipzig, 1898). There have been two more recent attempts. Dietze, accepting the view that the 'servant' was a leper, identifies him with Uzziah, and thinks that the prophet is Isaiah *ben 'Amoṣ*. Palache takes xlii, 19, *Mᵉšullam*, as a personal name, and refers it to the 'servant'; he proceeds to identify him as the son of Zerubbabel, 1 Chronicles iii, 19. Professor Hooke has pointed out to me that D. S. Margoliouth, *Lines of Defence of the Biblical Revelation* (London: 1900), pp. 116 ff., also regarded *Mᵉšullam* as the name of the prophet Isaiah, and used that view to establish the unity of authorship of the whole book.

108. Kittel (2), III. i, art. 34, pp. 222–39; S. A. Cook in CAH, iii, pp. 489–98; Rudolph (1), pp. 108–11; Hempel.

109. Haller (1) and (2), Balla, Schmidt, following Mowinckel (1); Volz (2), Sellin (5) and (6), Elliger, Begrich (2).

110. For a short general statement see Gressmann, *Die Aufgaben der alttestamentlichen Forschung*, pp. 28–30 in ZATW (NF), 1 (1924).

111. Gressmann, *Der Ursprung der israelitisch-jüdischen Eschatologie* (FRLANT, nr. 6), Göttingen, 1915, and Gressmann (3).

112. See Gressmann (3), pp. *13–*15. Any feature thought legendary or mythological is apparently included. How little

'eschatology', as employed by some modern writers, has to do
with its original sense may be seen in Elliger, p. 141, on lv, 1–7:
'In the assertion that the sentences are not meant eschatolo-
gically, we must refuse to follow Volz. Why shouldn't they be?
Is such preaching, both persuasive and warning, impossible in
the eschatological situation? . . . the translation, "now, when he
is to be found", "now, when he is near", causes no difficulty.'
If it does not, it is because the author is, not an eschatologist in
the true sense, but an 'Adventist'.

113. Thus the passages about the road, xl, 3–5, xli, 14–20,
xlviii, 17–21, xlix, 8–13, lv, 12–13, and all the 'individual servant' passages come into Gressmann's treatment (3), pp. 185–8,
287–339.

114. For a criticism of this see Mowinckel (4), pp. 18–19, who
sums up thus: 'So far as Deutero-Isaiah is concerned, Volz can
employ the word "eschatologist" more correctly of him. None
of the older prophets comes so near to the conception of a final
divine new order as he; and in none is what is to come depicted
in such supernatural figures, the whole future apprehended
religiously and seen and depicted mythologically in accordance
with the apprehension. But the conscious idea of τὰ ἔσχατα is
not to be found in him, and the inevitable consequence of every
true eschatology, dualism, he did not know.' Begrich (2), p. 76,
on the other hand, says: 'By this term [i.e. eschatology] is understood a series of ideas which occur in connexion with one another
and somehow belong together, which relate to the broad sphere
of the world and have to do with the future end of present
world conditions. The employment of the conception eschatology
with reference to this cycle of ideas may perhaps be considered
incorrect. It must in fact be admitted that these ideas relate to
a horizon that limits and cuts off further vision, whether this line
is to be regarded as the practical end to what came before, or as
the absolute end. If this question be kept in mind, the term,
though not exact, may be kept for practical reasons, without
harm, for the sum total of ideas meant.' Begrich's argument in
his third chapter represents this so-called eschatology as possessing
fixed features which the prophet could recognize in events before
547; he acknowledges that the complete 'picture' is nowhere
presented, but assumes that isolated features justify a reconstruction. On such reasoning it would be possible to deduce the
existence of the Hellenistic mystery religions in Egypt and Asia
in the 7th century and earlier; but that is not historical reasoning.

The fact is, that in these chapters there is the thought of a change from 'former things' to 'new things', but not of an end, of any kind. It is, possibly, true that 'it was the Second Isaiah who made of the hope in a fantastically glorious future an essential half of Judaism before A.D. 100. He may therefore be called the father of the apocalypse', Pfeiffer, p. 470. But that hope arose from later interpretation; the prophet's intention concerned an immediate, not a distant, future.

A special development of this view introduces Persian comparisons. Thus Kittel (2), III. i, art. 34 (9), p. 234, speaks of 'the strongly eschatological orientation. . . . Everything sounds much as in Zarathustra, who so often speaks of the judgement near at hand and the great god—without it being necessary to think of any direct derivation.' Yet the instances of 'God's judgement' and the isolated phrases he quotes have nothing to do with a final judgement on the last day, but refer to judgements on the claims of heathen gods, or to the prophet's certainty that God will justify him in the immediate present. Previously von Gall, pp. 41, 175–6, 178–89, 214, 219, stressing the idea of the righteous age when God is king, claimed that this is borrowed from Zarathustra. Kittel (2), p. 211, note 4, rightly replies that the idea of God as King is earlier in the prophetic literature than the assumption of von Gall would allow. The real truth is that the words in lii, 7 must not be taken out of their context, and that in their context they bear no eschatological significance at all, but simply announce the restoration of rule by a chosen deputy of the only God, even though that deputy is not of the house of David. Simcox pursues the attempt to find Zarathustrian analogies, mainly by using the *Zamyad Yašt*, a document much too late for the purpose. If there were really intentional reference to an eschatological kingdom of God, it should have been possible for L. Dietrich, *Die endzeitliche Wiederherstellung bei den Propheten*, (BZATW, no. 40), who gives a list of terms used in eschatological passages, pp. 63 ff., to cite more convincing examples in these chapters than הָאַחֲרוֹן‎, נחם‎, יסד‎.

Gressmann saw Persian influence in what he calls the 'mythical cosmography', depending mainly on his particular interpretation of the road through the desert, see *Eschatologie*, p. 224, and (3), p. 186; but he insisted that this influence was due to the prophet's residence in Babylonia: 'As Deutero-Isaiah lived in Babylonia, at a time when it was conquered by Medes, there is no difficulty in assuming the influence of Persian ideas'. This is a baffling statement, from the historical point of view; there is no

reason whatever for believing that any one would become closely
acquainted with Persian ideas without direct contact with Persians,
and the prophet's residence in Babylonia before 539 (even if it is
to be accepted as a fact) has nothing to do with the question.
The 'Medes' must be due to some error. But there is no
'mythical cosmography' in these chapters, only references to
contemporary facts. Begrich, partly owing to his chronology, is
opposed to the idea of any Persian influence at all, (2) p. 68, but
this is equally extreme. See Lecture III, note 33.

115. The theory of two different stages in the prophet's career
arose apparently with Staerk (1), who argued that cc. xl–xlviii
were written in Babylonia, cc. xlix–lv in Palestine; this was a
side-issue of the controversy about the place of authorship, see
Lecture III, note 64. A different explanation was suggested by
Haller (2), who thought that the same or similar descriptions
were applied both to Cyrus and the 'servant' because the prophet
transferred his expectation from Cyrus to the mission he himself
had undertaken. Volz (1) and (2) agreed with this view, taking
the 'servant' of the first three passages only to be the prophet.
Hempel (1), believing that the 'servant' is not the prophet of
cc. xl–lv, but an unknown contemporary, also considered that
the prophet recognized his 'error' in basing his hopes on Cyrus,
and that the 'servant' passages were later 'corrections'. Mowinckel's latest point of view, (4), pp. 37–9, seems favourable
to this standpoint, with the radical difference that the 'servant'
passages are said to be by another prophet, not the author of the
Cyrus passages, and everything in cc. xl–lv was, it is asserted,
written in Palestine.

The factual argument relied upon is put by Volz, pp. xxxiii–
xxxiv: 'The names of Babylon and Cyrus, repeatedly mentioned
in cc. xl–xlviii are completely absent in cc. xlix–lv, and that is
the more striking because in cc. xlix–lv the release and return
still appear throughout as future events. . . . Between the songs
of the first part and those of the last chapters there lies some lapse
of time, and . . . in this interval Babylon fell, but the edict for
the release had not yet been published. The indisputable differences are most easily explained if Babylon had been taken mean-
while, but remained unharmed, and the prophet was unwilling
to announce Cyrus any longer as the instrument of Yahweh in
the decisive fight for monotheism owing to his friendly behaviour
towards the hereditary enemy, Babylon, and the god Marduk.'
This view is only correct if there are no allusions to Cyrus in

xlix–lv, and this has become a dogma. There is no reason why liv, 16 should not be a reference to Cyrus as the one appointed by God to destroy any future attack on Jerusalem. In any case, the argument from absence is a bad one till it is established that the present order in the text is not partly due to subject.

Page 19.

116. This view is based on xli, 25, יִקְרָא בִשְׁמִי, on which, see Lecture III, note 11.

117. Thus Mowinckel, for example, (4), p. 36, says: 'Then Cyrus went off and became a worshipper of Marduk instead of a worshipper of' YHWH. This is based on the Cyrus cylinder, on which see Lecture II, note 150.

118. Hempel (1).

119. See Mowinckel (3), pp. 250–1, note, for a just criticism.

120. See Lecture II, note 96.

121. See Baudissin, pp. 2–4; Caspari (3), pp. 190–203, would whittle down the evidence, see especially p. 191.

122. This statement still applies, even if these utterances were for public delivery only before a restricted or secret assembly. They are often treated as if they were enigmatic intentionally, like Delphic oracles addressed to foreign potentates in terms not likely to prove wrong in any event. But veiled allusions must be distinguished from ambiguity. It is to these two passages in particular that the remark of Gressmann, *Eschatologie*, p. 319, applies: 'The author could only be content to leave the "servant" unnamed if he was commonly known and occurred naturally to everybody, as every one had to know who was meant.' The first person pronoun prevented there being any riddle; the prophet must have been well known.

Page 20.

123. Begrich (2), Kapitel VI, 11–13, pp. 145–51.

124. J. B. Koppe, the translator of Lowth's Isaiah, advanced the thesis that the individual 'servant' was Cyrus. The suggestion was renewed by T. H. Weir, *A New Theory of 'The Servant of Jehovah' in Isaiah 40–55*, in *The Westminster Review* (1908), pp. 309–14. Haller (2), following a hint by Mowinckel (1), argued that xlii, 5–9 referred to Cyrus. This was accepted by Mowinckel (3), pp. 93–4, who considers that there is a difference between the 'servant' of vv. 1–4 and the one of vv. 5–9: 'The servant in verses 1–4 is a servant gentle in word, who quietly and without

exciting attention spreads the teaching for which the isles and coast-lands wait; the one addressed in verses 5 ff. is a man of energy in action, which presumes the employment of force, who is to lead the prisoners out of the dungeon, an expression which ought not to be spiritualised, but presumes a task that is not to be fulfilled by *tōrā*.' This is doubtful exegesis, for the distinction has been shown unnecessary in the essay of Professor Barnes. Elliger, pp. 64–5, after admitting the possibility that xlii, 5–9 refers to Cyrus, decided that it is in fact an 'Israellied'; this shows that the terms employed describe an activity and are not peculiar to a personality. The decisive point ought to be the logical connexion of vv. 1–4 and 5–9; the distinction between 'units' has misled the adherents of the 'type' theory.

Torrey (1), p. 33, says that the view that the 'servant' of xlii, 1–4 or 5–9 is Cyrus 'inevitably makes the author of the passage ridiculous'. Yet he regards the argument of all these chapters, rightly, as an appeal to history. Is it ridiculous to see the action of God in contemporary history? Is not Torrey under the influence of Duhm's purely verbal dialectic on xli, 21–4? and of his own conviction that the exile had no historic importance?

The cause of the argument about the identity of the servant of xlii, 1–4 and 5–9 is that certain terms are applied in these chapters to Israel, Cyrus and another, as was noted by Gressmann, *Eschatologie*, p. 302: 'His words all move, to a certain extent, on the same level, whether he speaks of Yahweh, or the 'Ebed, of Israel or of Cyrus. That makes it extremely difficult to decide who is meant.' It is the more remarkable that Gressmann sought, for the passages concerning an individual 'servant', a single explanation, for in *Eschatologie*, p. 317, he seems to recognize the danger of error in combining what does not belong together.

125. A few scholars maintain that the whole section, cc. xl–lv, was written after the fall of Babylon. E. Meyer, *Entstehung des Judentums*, p. 234, seems to have taken this view, as did G. Hölscher (2), art. 54, note 2; Mowinckel (3), p. 244, note 1, adheres. Buttenwieser, pp. 102–3, rebutted the view as stated by Torrey and H. P. Smith. Begrich (2) dates everything 553–546.

126. Gressmann (1), p. 255, says: 'If he (Deutero-Isaiah) lived among the exiles in Babylonia, public activity was perhaps limited for political reasons in many respects, as the Babylonians would certainly not have allowed any public proclamation by a Hebrew prophet before the fall of Babylon; but like Ezekiel, Deutero-Isaiah will not have been satisfied in every case with the written

distribution of a word of God; a prophet who only writes is a self-contradiction.' Gressmann did not pursue this question and explain his views on publication. There is no reason to see any argument as to the place of authorship in this matter; if the prophet had lived in Palestine, he would not have been allowed to preach publicly about the impending fall of Babylon. If his message was, as it seems to be, to Jews of all classes, then distribution of a written document would not in itself suffice, for comparatively few could read.

127. So Volz (2), pp. xvi–xvii: 'Even if it is impossible to speak of a regular synagogue and a developed service at the time of the exile, yet the beginnings date back to the exile ... (Ezekiel viii, 1). . . . Deutero-Isaiah was in any case the man who gave these Sabbath gatherings an important content, and raised the word of God above every ceremony. Certainly he contributed beyond all others to giving such services an abiding form, and we can with some justification call him the founder of the synagogues.' It is not easy to see the justification. Hempel (2), p. 210, criticized: 'I pass over the fact that the characterisation of the prophet's activity as that of a Sabbath preacher seems to me insufficiently based, because in his work the Sabbath is not mentioned at all and every allusion to a cult outside Jerusalem is carefully avoided, so that the view that Deutero-Isaiah lived in Babylonia, where he thinks of the exiles as living in "holes", and certainly the view that he founded the synagogues, become uncertain.'

128. Duhm; Begrich (2), pp. 136–7.

129. Caspari (3), pp. 129–40. The reasoning is exceptionally difficult to follow, even in this consistently difficult writer.

130. Caspari (3), pp. 211–16, who says: 'The justification in research into types for the expression "book-speech", *Buchrede*, is easily comprehended, at any rate within Old Testament writings. One component of the compound expression removes so much precision from the other that one is no longer aware of any "type" in the subject of discussion. . . . The formula "book-speech" is intended to overcome the correct recognition that a book cannot be a speech, a speech cannot be a book.' This sounds pointed but is inept. Good speeches have at all times since the invention of writing been composed and delivered from a written original or notes or memory. There is no need to suppose that the 6th century differed from any other in this respect.

131. So H. Ewald and K. Budde, followed by Sellin (6), ii, pp. 66, 67, 69, 73, and Volz (2), p. xxvi.

132. Caspari (3), p. 216: 'Characteristic, for a fly-sheet, would be, beyond everything, reproduction in great quantities, which would not be possible with the means of writing then in use.'

Page 21.

133. Anxiety to prove that the section cc. xl–lv is not a book has not quite stifled this opinion. Duhm considered that the contemplated speeches were never delivered but only written. Volz (2), pp. xxxiv–xxxv, though he insists that these 'songs' were delivered publicly, is still of the opinion that the prophet wrote them down and published the collection himself. Begrich (2), p. 93, writes: 'To judge from the circumstances in which the exiles in Babylonia lived, it can hardly be imagined that Deutero-Isaiah was ever able to work otherwise than by the written word. But there is no trace of this in his method of expressing himself. All his utterances are conceived as spoken words. He always sees himself in the presence of others, addresses them directly or thinks of them as a silent audience. . . .' Hempel (2), p. 210, says: 'In form, psychology and content we are on different ground in Deutero-Isaiah from that in the older prophets. That is a point to be considered in the question of determining whether his "songs" were intended for delivery by word of mouth or through the productions of an author. . . .' All these remarks betray the difficulty in accounting for the retention of the form of spoken words in a conscious and deliberate style of writing. Lods seems to deny that the prophecies were ever spoken at all, for he says of another critic that he 'part de l'idée que les oracles du Second Esaïe ont été lancés au grand jour dans le public; ce n'est nullement évident', p. 269. Again, 'Rien dans son œuvre ne suggère qu'il ait, comme les prophètes antérieurs, essayé d'agir *par la parole* sur un cercle déterminé d'auditeurs. . . . If faut sans doute se le représenter rédigeant des feuilles volantes, dont les copies, colportées dan les juiveries disséminées dans l'empire, circulaient sous le manteau, sans nom d'auteur', p. 271. This view completely neglects the actual form of the prophecies.

134. Thus xliii, 14 is quite isolated, without relation to what precedes or follows. If the explanation given in Lecture III is correct, that is intelligible; it is an urgent message conveying good news of a decisive success, which needed only to be brief.

135. Thus xli, 1–xlii, 9 can be understood as a logical unity; but there are no close links in the paragraphs, and the style is not

ruled by what Volz (2), p. xxxvi, calls 'germanischer Ordnungs-sinn'.

136. xliv, 26. Most editors emend.

137. Caspari (3), p. 220.

138. That the Epic of Creation was recited at the New Year Festival in Babylon is now well known; but it is not perhaps generally recognized that all Babylonian verse compositions were similarly declaimed, and that our written copies owe their existence to this fact, just as, say, early copies of Homer did. On this subject see E. Ebeling, *Bruchstücke eines politischen Propagandagedichtes aus einer assyrischen Kanzlei*, p. 1, and the evidence there quoted for the existence of reciters.

139. Caspari (3), pp. 216–17, note 5. The supreme example of this type is the text published by Thureau-Dangin, *Une relation de la huitième campagne de Sargon*. See A. Ungnad, *Der Gottesbrief als Form assyrischer Kriegsberichterstattung*, in OLZ, xxi, 72–5. Another example was edited by Weidner in AfO, ix, (1935–6), pp. 101–4. For this style in Sumerian see A. Falkenstein, *Ein sumerischer Gottesbrief* in ZA (NF), x (1937), pp. 1–25. The end of the verse account is quite sufficient to prove that it does not belong to this class.

140. Mowinckel (3) seeks to show that the individual 'units' are arranged in their present order either because catchwords, *Stichwörter*, led to their association by the compiler, or because of an accidental resemblance in theme. As an illustration his treatment of xl, 9–11 will serve. The catchword is קולך, which reminded the compiler of קול in vv. 3 and 6. The subject, good news for Jerusalem, connected this 'unit' accidentally with verse 1. The formal resemblance, in that an undefined person, מבשרת ציון is to give the message, connects the 'unit' with vv. 2 and 3, where there are unnamed persons implied, or with the prophet himself in verse 6. It is extremely difficult to believe that any compiler can have wasted such ingenuity. To these reasons Mowinckel adds: 'Whether the purely external assonance, *der rein äusserliche Gleichklang*, between הבשר in verse 6 and מבשרת in verse 9 contributed, may be doubtful.' Indeed it may, for there is no assonance between *habbāsār* and *mᵉḇasseret* in any normal sense. Even 'introductory formulae' can serve as catchwords, p. 105, on xlix, 7–13. For a full and conclusive criticism of Mowinckel's theory see Elliger, Kapitel VI. This has obviously not convinced Mowinckel and is not mentioned by him, (4), pp. 11–12, in a restatement of his views. The chief importance of this strange

theory is that Mowinckel seeks to prove that the four 'servant' passages have been inserted into the text because they are connected, by catchwords or other superficial resemblances, in each case, not with the passage that precedes, but with that which follows. On this see Sellin (7), pp. 179–81, where 'catchwords' on Mowinckel's principle are found to connect the passages with what precedes. This theory of 'catchwords' was earlier than Mowinckel's essay, see König, *Neue kirchliche Zeitschrift*, 1898, p. 933; Sellin, *Studien*, i, p. 40. It is even accepted by Mowinckel's critics, see Caspari (3), p. 71: 'The addition of c. xl, 9–11 is conditioned by the catchword, cf. vv. 3 f., 6.' Eissfeldt (1), p. 376, calls this principle 'sehr äusserlich'; might it be termed superficial?

141. Haller (2) argued that there was a chronological sequence because there was no other perceptible basis for the arrangement; the 'Cyrus songs', as he calls them, were written down in a journal, an idea first proposed by Gunkel. The view that cc. xl–lv are to be divided into two parts, cc. xl–xlviii and xlix–lv, on the basis of the supposed absence of any mention of Cyrus in cc. xlix–lv and the different place of authorship (see note 115), necessitates the view that a sort of chronological sequence exists. Volz accepts this idea but divides at c. li, 9.

Though it would be wrong to assume that the present arrangement is based on chronological sequence, it is probable that in fact c. xli is the earliest utterance and that cc. lii–liii are the latest; there may then be some correspondence between historical events and the arrangement, but it should not be relied on for deductions.

142. Volz, p. xxxv: 'I do not believe that a chronological or thematic development can be demonstrated in the individual poems, beyond what has been said'—(xl, 1–11 introduction, lv, 12 ff. composed as end)—'. . . In any case the view must be maintained that the individual poems or collections of poems arose each independently, at first existed independently and must be expounded, *ausgelegt*, independently.' This is the fruitful result of *Gattungsforschung*. Observation of the rule is rare, for Old Testament studies are pursuing inquiries into cross-sections of all the books, and the 'units' of cc. xl–lv often illustrate matters with which they have little, if any, relation. For examples see Gressmann (3), pp. 124, 152, 185.

143. This conception of cc. xl–lv as a book which once had a separate existence led to complicated theories, and to the excisions of Duhm, based on the assumption of a long interval,

between 500 and 200 B.C., during which the book suffered at the hands of scribes and editors. Kittel (2), p. 203, still said: 'We call him thus (the second Isaiah) because his book appears as an addition to the book of Isaiah.' Though the earliest parts of the book of Isaiah date from the 8th, and the latest perhaps from the 4th, century, it is not possible to produce any evidence for or against diverse possibilities as to publication of sections; internal coherence of a series of chapters, e.g. xl–lv, is no argument for separate issue as a written book.

144. G. B. Gray, *Critical and Exegetical Commentary on the Book of Isaiah, i–xxxix*, p. xlviii, held to the theory of such a roll, partly owing to his interpretation, p. xxxviii, of 2 Chron. xxxvi, 21. But the name Jeremiah there may be one of the simple errors, constantly committed at all times, a fault of memory or an accidental mistake in writing, see Sellin (2), p. 82; Volz (1), p. xxxvi, note 1.

Page 22.

145. Eissfeldt (1), p. 388: 'To the question, how the inclusion of cc. xl–lxvi in the book of Isaiah, that is the ascription of these parts to the prophet of the 8th century, is to be explained, we cannot give a decisive answer, but must leave two possibilities open. One of these is based on a mechanical accident, the other brings into consideration the thematic relation between cc. i–xxxv (xxxix) and xl–lxvi. It is conceivable that cc. xl–lv and lvi–lxvi came to stand after Isaiah i–xxxix in the same roll as anonymous prophecies, and that then gradually these anonymous parts were attributed to the prophet last named, Isaiah.... There is greater likelihood, however, in the other possibility, the assumption that cc. xl–lv were united with i–xxxv (xxxix) and lvi–lxvi with xl–lv or i–lv because stylistic and thematic resemblances suggested the derivation from the same author. That there exist close connexions between cc. lvi–lxvi and xl–lv has been repeatedly emphasized. But the relation between cc. i–xxxix and xl–lv is no less important. . . .' This is the clearest statement in any textbook. It must be remembered that certain parts of cc. i–xxxix may be later than anything in cc. xl–lv.

146. Hertzberg, p. 120. See also Kittel (2), p. 203: 'The prophet could be called by that name (the second Isaiah) with the more justification because the spirit of the old Isaiah in fact celebrates its resurrection in him. That is not to say that his book is a repetition of the book of Isaiah. But his passionate and sarcastic manner seems in several sections to have gone for its model back

beyond Ezekiel and Jeremiah, who were more nearly contemporary, to the great Isaiah. . . .'

Page 23.

147. This must be stressed. As, or if, knowledge of the history of the period develops, the more clear contemporary allusions may be expected to become; the contribution made by the new information as to the exploit of Nabonidus in Arabia is only small, there is still much that is inexplicable.

ADDENDUM

Page 21, four lines from bottom.

The hypothesis that there were two rolls depends on the average measurement of a papyrus roll, and the average 'page' of Greek or Aramaic script on such a roll. See Sir Frederic Kenyon, *The Bible and Archaeology*, p. 342.

LECTURE II

BIBLIOGRAPHY

In these notes, apart from the abbreviations, references to the names of authors refer to the following books, or articles.

BAUER. *See* LANDSBERGER.

CAMERON, G. G. *History of Early Iran.* Chicago, 1936.

CHRISTENSEN, A. *Die Iranier* in *Kulturgeschichte des alten Orients*, IIIter Abschnitt, 1te Lieferung (Handbuch der Altertumswissenschaft, IIIte Abteilung, 1ter Teil, IIIter Band; hrsgg. von W. Otto). München, 1933.

DOUGHERTY, R. P. *Nabonidus and Belshazzar* (Yale Oriental Series, vol. xv). New Haven, 1929.

DUSSAUD, R. *Sur le chemin de Suse et de Babylone*, in *Mélanges Franz Cumont*, pp. 143–50 (Annuaire de l'Institut de Philologie et d'Histoire Orientales et Slaves, Université libre de Bruxelles, tome IV). Bruxelles, 1936.

GALLING, K. *Syrien in der Politik der Achaemeniden bis 448 v. Chr.* (Der alte Orient, Band 36, Heft 3/4). Leipzig, 1937.

HERZFELD, E. *Archaeological History of Iran* (Schweich Lectures, 1934). London, 1935.

KÖNIG, F. W. (1). *Naboned und Kuraš*, in AfO, vii (1931–2), pp. 178–82.

KÖNIG, F. W. (2). *Älteste Geschichte der Meder und Perser* (Der alte Orient, Band 33, Heft 3/4). Leipzig, 1934.

LANDSBERGER, B., and BAUER, THEO. *Strophengedicht von den Freveltaten Nabonids und der Befreiung durch Kyrus*, in ZA(NF), iii (1926), pp. 88–98.

LAWRENCE, A. W. *Herodotus, Rawlinson's translation revised and annotated.* London, 1935.

LEUZE, O. *Die Satrapieneinteilung in Syrien und im Zweistromlande von 520–320* (Schriften der Königsberger gelehrten Gesellschaft, geisteswissenschaftliche Klasse. II. Jahr. Heft 4). Halle (Saale), 1935.

LUCKENBILL, D. D. *Ancient Records of Assyria and Babylonia*, vols. i and ii. Chicago, 1926–7.

NABONIDUS. Inscriptions quoted by the numbering in S. Langdon, *Die neubabylonischen Königsinschriften* (Vorderasiatische Bibliothek, Stück 4). Leipzig, 1912 (pp. 218–97).

WEISSBACH, F. H. *Die Keilinschriften der Achämeniden* (Vorderasiatische Bibliothek, Stück 3). Leipzig, 1911.

WEISSBACH, F. H., art. *Kyros* in Pauly–Wissowa, *Realencyclopädie der klassischen Altertumswissenschaft*, Supplementband IV, Spalten 1130–65.

The Nabonidus Chronicle, and the Persian verse account of Nabonidus published in BHT, are called the chronicle and the verse account. The inscription of Cyrus in Babylonian on a clay cylinder edited by Weissbach is called the cylinder.

Page 24.

1. Josephus, *Contra Apionem*, i, 21, based on Berossus. Eusebius gave a garbled version. Schnabel, *Berossos*, p. 274, arts. 53, 54.

2. This depends on whether Nabonidus no. 9 refers to the father or mother. For possible, and some impossible, arguments in favour of the mother see Dougherty, pp. 18–27. His points 1, 2, 4, 5 are not cogent. The strongest argument, apart from the probability (not a certainty) that the parent commemorated died in the 9th year, is that the father is nowhere else called a priest of Sin. The argument against identification as the mother depends on the place of the mother's death, near Sippar, which does not account for the wording of the inscription, col. ii, 24–9, and Herodotus. H. de Genouillac, in RA, xxii (1925), p. 74, places too much faith in Dhorme's interpretation of doubtful signs as a feminine name.

3. Nabonedochus (Abydenus apud Eusebium, derived from Megasthenes); Nabonnedus (Berossus apud Josephum); Nabodenus (Alexander Polyhistor in the Armenian version of Eusebius); Nabonadius (Claudius Ptolemy, Syncellus); Naboandelus (Josephus) equated with Baltasar.

4. i, 74, 77, 188. There is no sound reason against identifying Labynetus in each case with Nabonidus, and the most natural view is that Labynetus the son is meant in cc. 74 and 77. Dougherty's identification of Labynetus I as Nabonidus, and of Bel-shar-uṣur as Labynetus II, has nothing in its favour, since c. 188 would then state that Cyrus marched against Bel-shar-uṣur; the statement, p. 34, note 128, that in BHT, p. 43, Labynetus I is said to be Nebuchadrezzar in one paragraph and Nabonidus in another is incorrect.

5. Lawrence, p. 42, note 3 on i, 74.

6. On this fact has been based a theory that Nebuchadrezzar married an Egyptian princess, and that the daughter of the marriage, given the Egyptian name *Nt.iqr.t*, was Nabonidus's queen, Dougherty, pp. 42–66. This is not history.

7. Dougherty, p. 43, note 147, argues from Berossus's mention of the furbishing of the quay walls on the river, τὰ περὶ τὸν ποταμὸν τείχη, in Josephus, *Contra Apionem*, i, 20, by Nabonidus, and from Herodotus's statement i, 186, about the emptying of the river-bed

of the Euphrates by Nitocris for the purpose of lining the banks
with brick and building quays. Nabonidus did in fact do some
work on the river-bed, which narrowed it, see Lawrence, p. 120,
and the references there. This hardly seems a sufficient basis for
the identification of Nitocris as the wife of Nabonidus, in view of
Nebuchadrezzar, no. 13, col. i, line 61—col. ii, 18, in Langdon's
collection of texts.

8. At Dur-karashu above Sippar on the Euphrates, Chronicle,
ii, 13. Presumably a military camp, *karašu*, with a fortified wall,
duru.

9. The Crown Prince and the troops mourned for three days
in Nisan. In Siman, two months after, an official mourning took
place in Akkad. The delay was obviously due to the absence of
Nabonidus at Taima, Dougherty, p. 26.

10. The odd view has been expressed that 'Nabonidus would
certainly have drawn attention to this in his inscriptions. For not
alone would pride in this great connexion have induced him to
do so, but the fact that he owed his elevation to the throne to it
would have made it imperative for him to record it', JTS, xxxii
(1931), pp. 24–5. No Babylonian king was likely to state in so
many words that he was not in the line of succession, or to
mention the deeds of a concubine, even a favourite. Nabonidus
was known to be a usurper.

11. τούτου δὲ ἀποθανόντος βιαίῳ μόρῳ Ναβοννήδοχον ἀποδεικνῦσι
βασιλέα προσήκοντά οἱ οὐδέν. Dougherty, p. 75, reads ἀποδείκνυσι,
3rd per. singular and takes Neriglissar as the subject, an impossible
view, see H. H. Rowley in JTS, xxxii (1931), p. 26. The verb is
3rd plur. indefinite. But why ought Megasthenes to have stated
that, though not related to Labashi-Marduk, Nabonidus 'had
stood in close connexion with Nebuchadrezzar'? The sources do
not, by their nature, permit such arguments.

Page 25.

12. Landsberger and Bauer, p. 96: 'Aber ebendieses Ara-
mäertum N.'s lässt uns vielleicht das Rätselhafte dieser Gestalt
begreifen.' B. Meissner, *Könige Babyloniens und Assyriens*, p. 276.

13. Landsberger and Bauer, pp. 96–7: '. . . so dass es schliess-
lich dem Aramäerfürsten N. gelang, seiner Stammesgruppe zum
Königtum zu verhelfen.'

14. B. Meissner, *Babylonien und Assyrien*, ii, p. 60.

15. CAH, iii, p. 407.

16. CAH, iii, p. 218.

Page 26.

17. See the verse account and the discussion of the evidence in BHT, pp. 44–68. The further argument there, pp. 68–76, based on the verse account, ii, 2–3, that Nabonidus was accused of controverting the accepted Babylonian beliefs, has been denied by Albright, in JRAS, 1925, pp. 293 ff., and 1926, pp. 285 ff., and by Landsberger and Bauer, pp. 90 and 95. The basic argument, that the clause in line 2 is dependent, can only be correct if the clause in line 3 is also dependent, for the two lines form a single metrical unit, with obvious *parallelismus membrorum*; and it is contrary to the usage of Babylonian verse to make a double-line dependent. The details of the argument fall with the basic assumption. There is not room for Landsberger's restoration *pitiqtu* at the end of line 2. If a relative is to be understood in line 2, it must be understood also in line 3, and there can be no distinction between *ul* and *la* on Landsberger's lines. Both are, of course, regularly used, with different emphasis, in principal clauses. *ibnu* in line 2 requires an object, which can only be *Mummu*, the name of a primeval being, a participial form also applied to Ea. Albright argued that in col. v, 16, *Mummu* must be understood as the adjective applied to Ea for grammatical reasons; he misunderstood the construction of verbs meaning 'to fashion' with the double accusative, see Thureau-Dangin, *Huitième Campagne de Sargon*, p. 62, line 401. The meaning of v, 16 must depend on ii, 2. In line 3 Landsberger produced a new transliteration based on the idea of 'artificial writing'. The signs *UD-ma (il)A-nim* he combines to read *um-ma-(il)a-nim, ummanim*, comparing, as the only parallel, *i-(il)nanna, inanna*, from the poem *ludlul bel nimeqi*. Now there are other examples of such tricks of writing; they all, like *ludlul bel nimeqi*, go back to the orthography of the early Kassite period, when the obscure use of signs with rare values was scribal art as practised in the southern cities, see Gadd and Thompson in *Iraq*, iii, pp. 87 ff. Before such orthography can be considered probable in a New Babylonian text, a parallel must be produced from contemporary tablets. Further it should be noted that in these writings all the signs are generally necessary. In *i-(il)nanna* the sign *(il)* is essential for the reading. But in *um-ma-(il)a-nim*, the *(il)* is otiose, and not a true parallel to its use in *i-(il)nanna*. If *UD-ma* may in fact be read *um-ma* in a New Babylonian text, then it is better joined with what pre-

cedes, and the archaic *šutma*, a stumbling block in my former transliteration, presents no further difficulty.

> *ul idi zikiršumma (il)Anim Adapa*
> Adapa did not know the name of him, of Anu.

The plain interpretation may therefore be retained on grounds of sense, of grammar, and of rhythm; for the assumptions that these lines are dependent clauses and that the writing is 'artificial' do not seem to give a readily explicable meaning, or at any rate one that has yet been explained.

18. The chronology of the reign was settled by Weissbach in ZDMG, lv, p. 211; an old error in the use of the Canon of Ptolemy was repeated, inexcusably, in BHT, pp. 107–10, and all the years there given are one too late. The erroneous dating is still to be found in Volz, p. xv, Dussaud, p. 146, and elsewhere.

19. For valuable evidence about the Babylonian administration at Tyre, see Unger, *Nebukadnezar II und sein Šandabakku in Tyrus*, in ZATW (NF), iii (1926), pp. 314–17.

Page 27.

20. Herodotus i, 74.

21. In Nabonidus no. 9 a parent of Nabonidus is said to have served Sin at Harran continuously through the reigns of Ashurbanipal, Ashur-eṭil-ilani, Nabopolassar, Nebuchadrezzar, Neriglissar, Nabonidus. The only known domination for any time by the *Umman-manda* therefore fell immediately before Nabonidus's accession in 556, though the destruction of the temple took place 54 years before 556, that is in 610, see Nabonidus no. 1. If the priesthood of this parent had been interrupted at any other time, there is no reason why he or she should have returned to office.

22. Unpublished fragment of a chronicle.

23. This ingenious conjecture of E. Herzfeld, pp. 26–7, that the tribe derived its name from *Parṣuaš*, and that the name *Parsumaš* derives from the tribal name, has much in its favour, since it would serve to explain the etymological connexion.

Page 28.

24. *Parṣuaš* (or *Parsuaš*, Sargon, 8th campaign, line 38) was visited by Shalmaneser III in his 26th, 30th, and 31st years, by Shamshi-Adad V, Adad-nirari III, Tiglath-pileser III, Sargon in his 6th and 8th years. All these connect the land with the Medes, Messi and Mannai, and the position of the Mannaean territory

immediately south of Lake Urmia is certain. Sennacherib says that in his 8th year the king of Elam gathered a confederation which included men of *Parṣuaš*, *Anzan*, *Ellıpi*, and all the Chaldaeans and Aramaeans. This may show either a southward extension of *Parṣuaš*, or perhaps (less probably) favour an identification of *Parṣuaš* and *Parsumaš* at this date. According to the inscription at Karagundiz described by Lehmann-Haupt, *Armenien Einst und Jetzt*, II, i, p. 37, *Corpus Inscriptionum Chaldicarum*, no. 15, Ispuinis and Menuas, kings of Urarṭu, conquered *Parṣuaš* about 810–800 B.C.; the capital city is there called *Mešta*. According to Forrer, *Provinzeinteilung des assyrischen Reiches*, pp. 89–90, the capital of the Assyrian province *Parṣua* was Nikur.

In the Assyrian letters, Waterman, *Royal Correspondence of the Assyrian Empire*, nos. 61, 165, 311, there is mention of the city, no. 61, or the land *Parsua*—*s*, not *ṣ*—which must be identical with *Parṣuaš*; these letters all probably date to the time of Esarhaddon, and show that the rendering of the foreign sibilant by different scribes differed. *Parsua* was a centre of the traffic in horses called *Kusaya*, no. 61; lay north of the Upper Zab, no. 311; the *Mannai* could intercept the horse traffic between *Parsua* and the city of Ashur, no. 165. Probably the move of the *Parsa* southward took place in Esarhaddon's time.

25. On the location see M. Streck, *Das Gebiet der heutigen Landschaften Armenien, Kurdistan und Westpersien nach den babylonisch-assyrischen Keilinschriften*, in ZA, xv, pp. 311 ff.; his remarks on the geography and the possibility of etymological connexion between *Parṣuaš* and *Parsa* are still sound. The possible conclusions are, that the Mannai inhabited the land round Ushnu and to the south, and that they were able to cut the road from the east before it reached Rayat. *Parṣuaš* lay east of them, in the valleys of the rivers flowing into Lake Urmia from the south-east. The horse traffic started further north-east, see Sargon's 8th campaign, lines 170 ff. By Sennacherib's time *Parṣuaš*, become independent, may have reached to the road between Baghdad and Hamadan; that would explain its part at the battle of Halulie. Cameron, p. 142, puts *Parṣuaš* west of Lake Urmia, the Mannai east, not in accordance with the evidence. F. W. König (2), pp. 8–9, is not clear. Herzfeld, pp. 9–10, reconciling Sennacherib's mention with the earlier occurrences, locates in Ardalan and Garrus.

26. An inscription of Shamshi-Adad V published by Schroeder in *Keilschrifttexte aus Assur historischen Inhalts*, Heft 2, nr. 142, edited by Weidner in AfO, ix (1933–4), pp. 101–4, has been

thought to mention a land [*Par*]*samaš*, which must be identical with *Parsumaš*. Cameron, pp. 146, 179, concludes that the migration took place before 815 B.C. The conclusion is so contrary to probability that the restoration must be erroneous.

The submission of Cyrus I of *Parsumaš* is recorded in Ashurbanipal's inscriptions published by E. F. Weidner, *Die älteste Nachricht über das persische Königshaus: Kyros I, ein Zeitgenosse Assurbanaplis*, in AfO, vii (1931–2), pp. 1–7; Campbell Thompson in LAAA, xx (1933), pp. 86, line 115; 95; 98–9.

In the Assyrian letters, Waterman, *op. laud.*, nos. 1309, 1311, *Parsumaš* is closely connected with the affairs of Shamash-shum-ukin and the city *Hidalum*; these references, therefore, date from just before 650.

27. Both Cambyses I and Cyrus II are called *šar Aššan*, in Gadd and Legrain, *Ur Excavations, Texts, I, Royal Inscriptions*, no. 194, as is noted by Herzfeld, p. 24. The chronicle, ii, 1, calls Cyrus II king of *Anšan*, and king of *Parsu*, ii, 15. Weissbach, art. *Kyros*, Sp. 1142, held that this showed that Cyrus was king of *Anšan* originally and conquered *Parsu* after he had defeated Astyages. This has influenced F. König (2), p. 9, who regards *Anšan* as the smaller territory falling within the greater *Parsu*. Cameron, pp. 31–2, also distinguishes between *Anšan* and *Parsumaš* as neighbouring territories. On the early evidence examined by König, art. *Anšan* in *Reallexikon der Assyriologie*, *Anšan* must at times have been the eastern neighbour of the ancient Babylonian city Der, modern Badrah; but periodically the principality disappears and is not mentioned in wars where, if it always reached so far west, it should play a part. It is therefore necessary to assume that the westward extension was temporary. Herzfeld seems to be right in assuming absolute identity of the kernel of *Anšan* and *Parsumaš*; variations of political borders at different times make any assumption of complete identity impossible. The chronicle entries are not good evidence that the two terms must differ, for the chronicles were compiled from different documents which might use alternative geographical terms.

28. Pasargadae was built, or partly built, by Cyrus II, see Herzfeld's reports on the site in AMI, i, pp. 4–38. Whether the site was previously inhabited there is at present nothing to show. K. Galling, p. 27, note 3, has announced an essay to be entitled 'Pasargadae—the ancestral memorial of the second dynasty of the Achaemenids'; he means by the 'second dynasty' the succession started by Darius I.

R

29. The son's name, (m)A-ru-uk-ku, is considered by F. W. König in AfO, vii (1931–2), p. 6, note 23, not to be 'Aryan'. He rightly compares Daiukku (by some thought to be the same name, but not the same person as Deioces), Paaukku and Maš-daukku. In (2), p. 30, he calls the name 'Subaraean'. Herzfeld, p. 25, note 2, regards the -ukku as a hypocoristic ending, which seems very probable.

30. So Herzfeld, AMI, i, p. 113 and ii, p. 123. Weidner in AfO, vii (1931–2), p. 5, regards Achaemenes as the father and immediate predecessor of Teispes; similarly Cameron, p. 179 and Table V, dates Achaemenes about 700–675. Weissbach, art. *Kyros*, thought that Cyrus II either deposed Arsames or succeeded him, so that Hystaspes never reigned. Herzfeld, AMI, i, pp. 106–12, argues that Hystaspes was called 'king' because he was satrap of *Parthava* and a member of the Achaemenid house.

31. Cameron, p. 212, holds that Teispes at his death was master of *Parsumaš* and *Anšan*, and of a recent conquest, *Parsa*. Aria-ramnes, the younger son, was made 'great king, king of kings, king of the land *Parsa*'; Cyrus I, the older, was subordinate, king of *Parsumaš*. Further, p. 214, he suggests that Cyaxares probably brought the rule of Ariaramnes to an end and prevented Arsames and Hystaspes from assuming the title 'king'. This cannot be correct. Cyrus I could not accept the overlordship of Ashur-banipal even symbolically if he was subject to Ariaramnes. There is in existence an inscription of Arsames on gold from Ecbatana, in which he is called 'king over *Parsa*'. F. W. König, *Relief und Inschrift des Königs Dareios I am Felsen von Bagistan*, Leiden, 1938, p. 60, says that *dwitaparnam*, 'in two-fold succession', means that the Achaemenids ruled over a *monarchia bipartita*, and compares King and Maharajah in Nepal. This would require a differentia-tion of titles between the senior and junior lines which either did not exist or cannot be proved to have existed.

32. The gold tablet of Ariaramnes published by Herzfeld in AMI, ii (1930), pp. 113–27, has been confidently dismissed as an ancient forgery of late Achaemenean date by H. H. Schaeder in *Sitzungsberichte der preussischen Akademie der Wissenschaften, phil.-hist. Klasse*, 1931, pp. 635–45: W. Brandenstein in *Wiener Zeitschrift für die Kunde des Morgenlandes*, xxxix (1932), pp. 14–19, also argued that it was a forgery, written about 360 B.C. I have heard from other scholars the opinion that it is a modern forgery. Herzfeld replied in AMI, iv (1932), pp. 132–9; viii, pp. 17–46. E. Ben-veniste in Meillet, *Grammaire du vieux Perse* (2nd ed., Paris, 1931),

pp. 1 ff., accepts the inscription as genuine and of the early 6th century. This gold tablet is more than an inscription; it is an antiquity. To forge it in modern times, a man must have thorough knowledge of the Old Persian language in its later stages, and of comparative phonetics, must be practised in the use of the cuneiform syllabary, able to copy the ancient technique in writing on metal, and be sufficiently cognizant of local conditions in Hamadan to plant a forgery successfully just when genuine inscriptions were turning up. It is difficult to believe in this paragon. Schaeder's view must stand or fall by its inherent probability. The motive for such an ancient forgery must be stronger than Schaeder has suggested. It would be difficult to find historically sound reasons for forgery about 360 B.C.

33. This supposition is only possible owing to our complete ignorance of events in Media between 585 and 558. There may have been refusal to admit the overlordship of Astyages on his accession, soon after his marriage with the daughter of Croesus.

34. Inscription of Darius at Bisutun, arts. 35 and 36; see Weissbach, p. 43.

Page 29.

35. On the probable length of reign see Weissbach, art. *Kyros* Sp. 1131; Herodotus gives 29 years, Ctesias and Justin 30; the difference may be due to the months of the Babylonian accession year, 'beginning of kingship'. This date of Cyrus's accession is in no way dependent on the 'third year' in Nabonidus no. 1, which is not connected with the regnal years of Cyrus in Anshan.

36. But not a lampoon, for there is no attempt at irony, and the charges brought are not accompanied by violent invective. In *Deutsche Literaturzeitung*, 1926, Spalte 752, this document is inappropriately labelled a *Schmähschrift*, with the comment, 'also ein literarisches Erzeugnis, das in einem gewissen Grade mit dem Trostbuche des Deuterojesaja verglichen werden kann'. If the reference is to Isaiah c. xlvii, the comparison is bad. Landsberger and Bauer, p. 97, used the same term, *Schmähschrift* and, note 2, *Schmähgedicht*.

No other Assyrian or Babylonian document as yet found really falls into this class of polemic. E. Ebeling, *Bruchstücke eines politischen Propagandagedichtes aus einer assyrischen Kanzlei* (*Mitteilungen der altorientalischen Gesellschaft*, Band xii, Heft 2), pp. 1–2, classes a heroic poem dealing with a war of an Assyrian king, Tukulti-Enurta I, against the Kassite rulers of Babylonia, with the verse account of Nabonidus; it is actually similar to the poem dealing with Sargon of Agade, *šar tamhari*. Modern propaganda about races seems to have influenced the views of von Soden, *Der Aufstieg des Assyrerreichs* (*Der alte Orient*, Band 37, Heft 1/2), Leipzig, 1937, pp. 25–8, on this poem.

The Biblical critics have not as yet used the verse account much. Caspari (3), pp. 80–1, sought to support his interpretation of Isaiah xl, 8, as due to an actual drought, by citing Landsberger and Bauer's translation of the verse account, i, 4; unfortunately the translation is wrong, for *kuruppu* does not mean *Wasserzufuhrgerät*, but 'garden', 'cultivated land', see BHT, pp. 91–2. Caspari (3), p. 140, note 4, also assumed, owing to that translation, that there is mention of the literary type *Arbeitlied*, but *alala* cannot be so interpreted. Galling, too, used the Landsberger–Bauer translation, see notes 64 and 98. There is no reconsideration of the historical interpretation of cc. xl–lv in the light of the historical facts established by the verse account in the commentaries and essays published between 1924 and 1939, though such might have been expected in Stevenson's essay, and more especially from Begrich (2), p. 66, to justify his statement: 'Finally it may be noted that there are no indubitable references in individual texts to contemporary events which would argue for the date rejected here.' The true position is that Begrich's dating is in itself so improbable that general references to contemporary events tell against his argument; they need not be precise. The historical background ought not to have been neglected in recent 'Introductions' to the Old Testament.

37. Landsberger and Bauer impugn the accuracy of only one passage, p. 97, note 2: 'the fact that Nabonidus is charged with the suppression of the Arab population by the author of the lampoon on this occasion (the expedition to Tema') is not to be taken seriously.' No reason for this is given, nor why, if this statement is unreliable, others can be accepted; the criticism is due to the fact that the words cannot be reconciled with an untenable theory of Nabonidus's purpose.

38. The relief, illustrated in A. Upham Pope and Phyllis Ackerman, *A Survey of Persian Art*, vol. iv, plate 78, was once said to represent Cyrus, see, e.g., Williams Jackson, *Persia Past and Present*, pp. 278–93. Herzfeld, in Sarre-Herzfeld, *Iranische Felsreliefs*, pp. 159–60, rightly controverted this; but his own description, 'Genius', accepted by Weissbach, art. *Kyros*, is not satisfactory, because liable to misunderstanding. Though the figure resembles

the winged human figures performing ritual acts which are a regular subject of Assyrian art, it is not derived solely from them and may not be, as they are, apotropaic, since the Assyrian figures generally form part of a scene, or are represented smearing the bull colossi; the relief at Pasargadae has no connexion with a building and no immediate apotropaic significance, since the figure stands alone. The degraded form of the Egyptian crown must, in spite of Herzfeld's contrary view, go back to Phoenician art, and ultimately to forms found in Syria in the 18th century B.C. There is no certainty that the figure is not a god, then; for always in Syria, from the end of the XIIth Dynasty (examples quoted in *Alalakh and Chronology*, pp. 13–14) to the Hellenistic period this crown is reserved for gods. But even if the figure is a god, it is not a Persian god; the dress is, as Dieulafoy noted, much like the Elamite, it may even be compared with some representations of Syrian dress, but it is certainly not Persian. The significance of this sculpture has been missed; it points to the employment of sculptors trained in a school where motives and methods were derived from many sources; the religious ideas involved are syncretic and beyond our knowledge. It may be that the relief testifies to conceptions current in the 6th century, not among the Persians but among the subjects of the western provinces of Cyrus's empire. It should be noted that though reproductions seem to show that the figure carries an object in the right hand, this is said by Herzfeld to be an illusion due to the inner edge of the wing. The frontispiece shows how strong the illusion is. See note 119.

39. 2 Chronicles xxxvi, 22–3, Ezra i, 1–11.

40. Ezra vi, 3–5.

41. Daniel x, 1. There is some still unexplained mystery in the choice of Cyrus's 3rd year (as king of Babylon, presumably, rather than as king of *Anšan*) and of the Hiddeqel, the Tigris. In Daniel viii, 1 the 'third year of Belshazzar' should mean the 3rd year of Bel-shar-uṣur's rule as deputy of the king, i.e. 550–549, the year of Cyrus's final victory over Astyages. There may be some special appropriateness in the year 536–535 as the setting of Daniel c. x, as viii, 4 explains the setting of c. viii in 550–549.

Page 30.

42. Most conveniently by Weissbach, art. *Kyros*.

43. Meyer, *Geschichte des Altertums* (1te Auflage), III. i, art. 5, p. 9; Christ-Schmid, *Geschichte der griechischen Literatur* (6te Auflage), 1ter Teil, p. 517.

44. The sober judgement of Christ-Schmid, 'Mit den über-
lieferten Tatsachen wird sehr frei umgesprungen', true because
of the nature of Xenophon's source, becomes in Leuze, p. 162 [6],
'Manche Züge sind historisch, anderes aber ist, den Absichten des
Werkes entsprechend, sehr frei umgestaltet oder ganz erfunden',
or, p. 165 [9], 'Wie er aber auch sonst sich nicht scheute, von
Herodot abzuweichen, so hat er *in majorem gloriam Cyri*, die Sache
in Kyros' Zeit verlegt und die Gelegenheit, bei der die freiwillige
Waffenhilfe erfolgt sein soll, frei erfunden, wobei es ihm begegnete,
dass ihm seine Phantasie an der späteren Stelle (viii, 6, 8) etwas
anderes eingab als an der früheren (vii, 4. 2).' This amounts
to a charge of falsifying history without the wit to achieve consistency, an aspersion on the character and sense of Xenophon.

In addition to the legendary material, the nobles must have
preserved records of the officers of Cyrus who were members of
their family. Such records might not be comprehensive and must
not be treated as complete, but Leuze's question, p. 162 (6), 'Is
it conceivable or probable that Xenophon, who was in Asia about
400, could still have authentic information as to the way in which
Cyrus arranged the satrapies one and a half centuries before, and
about the names of the men to whom he first entrusted the
government of the satrapies?' can be answered with some certainty.
It is not only conceivable, but extremely probable that Xenophon
constantly met men who could give an account of the satrapies and
name their governors, because these matters were part of family
history, information not likely to be false because others would
be quick to correct errors in matters affecting honour and pre-
cedence, by reference to the written records that unquestionably
existed. Language difficulties have introduced mistakes and ob-
scurities. The question indicates little understanding of Oriental
tenacity in traditions concerning genealogies and offices.

45. Herodotus, i, 95 ὡς ὧν Περσέων μετεξέτεροι λέγουσι οἱ μὴ
βουλόμενοι σεμνοῦν τὰ περὶ Κῦρον, ἀλλὰ τὸν ἐόντα λέγειν λόγον, κατὰ
ταῦτα γράψω, ἐπιστάμενος περὶ Κύρου καὶ τριφασίας ἄλλας λόγων ὁδοὺς
φῆναι. How then can E. Meyer know what Xenophon derives from
Herodotus, and not one of the other three? i. 214 τὰ μὲν δὴ κατὰ τὴν
Κύρου τελευτὴν τοῦ βίου πολλῶν λόγων λεγομένων ὅδε μοι ὁ πιθανώ-
τατος εἴρηται. Xenophon, *Cyropaedia*, 1. 2. i ὁ Κῦρος λέγεται καὶ
ᾄδεται ἔτι καὶ νῦν ὑπὸ τῶν βαρβάρων. Ctesias drew on such songs.
I have not been able to consult G. Hüsing, *Beiträge zur Kyros-Sage*,
Berlin, 1906, and Lessmann, *Die Kyros-Sage in Europa* (Schulpro-
gramm), Charlottenburg, 1906.

Page 31.

46. C. J. Gadd, *Early Dynasties of Sumer and Akkad*, pp. 26–8.

Page 32.

47. What is said of Assyria in CAH, iii, pp. 94–5, applies to Babylon in the 6th century. T. H. Robinson, *Palestine in General History* (Schweich Lectures, 1926), London 1929, p. 42, states the common, but erroneous, view, with a reservation. On instances of dream-oracles from various sources dealing with state affairs at this period see Weissbach, art. *Kyros*, Spalte 1144.

48. It is very difficult to believe that the use of omens from dreams for oracular purposes, according to the system used in Western Asia from early times till the Hellenistic period, arose independently in different lands at different times. The technique required and the usages involved are much too complicated to have developed on the same lines in different lands. The earliest known case of incubation is Gudea's dream, see Gadd, *Sumerian Reading Book*, pp. 90 ff., in the 22nd century B.C. The earliest 'dream-book' is the Egyptian text, Papyrus no. III A, in *Hieratic Papyri in the British Museum, Third Series*, vol. i, pp. 9–23, by Dr. A. H. Gardiner. The centre of dissemination cannot, therefore, be discerned on the present evidence; but the fact of dissemination ought not to be doubted.

49. The procedure adopted can be deduced from that used in the case of liver omens, as revealed by Nabonidus no. 8, col. xi; no. 7, col. ii; no. 3, col. ii, 41–7.

50. Nabonidus, no. 1, col. i, 26–30. On the *Umman-manda* as a confederation see J. Lewy, *Forschungen zur alten Geschichte* (MVAG, 1924, Heft 2, 1925), p. 13; Landsberger and Bauer, pp. 81–3, 87–8 (where the derivation proposed is impossible, since, apart from the inherent improbability, the etymology depends on forms which did not exist in the 17th century, the time to which the earliest mention refers). The view advocated by Thureau-Dangin, *La Fin de l'empire assyrien*, in RA, xxii (1925), pp. 27–9, that the *Umman-manda* who, with Nabopolassar, besieged and took Nineveh in 612 and occupied Harran in 610 were Medes only, disregards much evidence about the Scythians; for a summary account with references see L. Piotrowicz, *L'Invasion des Scythes en Asie antérieure*, in *Eos*, xxxii (Leopoli, 1929). E. Herzfeld, *Sakastan*, pp. 12–13, in AMI, iv, maintains that the *Ašguzai* Scyths settled in Azerbaijan, in a former Assyrian province, the land of the Mannai, and yet took no part in the capture of Nineveh and Harran; if his

geographical assumption is right, his conclusion is improbable. That there is some difference between Medes and *Umman-manda* in the Nabopolassar Chronicle is, in spite of assertions to the contrary, the only reasonable explanation of the wording, see C. J. Gadd, *The Nabopolassar Chronicle*, pp. 90–1, in *The Expositor* (Ninth Series), iii (1925), and JRAS, 1927, pp. 570–1.

51. Hence 'king of kings' as a title. The title 'king' for the tribal and provincial rulers was probably abolished by Cyrus; it was certainly abolished before the reign of Darius. But the great Persian families maintained semi-dynastic state, and retained certain offices in succession, so that personal names of governors recur in different periods, a feature of Sassanian times too. For that reason Leuze's arguments about Artakamas, p. 165 [9], note 2, are not convincing.

Page 33.

52. Thus Weissbach considers that Nabonidus was informed for the first time by the oracle of events that he did not know, and argues that the third year is Cyrus's third year, as king of *Anšan* (see art. *Carrhae* in PRE, Band x, Sp. 2013 f.), and that Cyrus's victory over Astyages fell in 556–555. It is probable on other grounds, see note 35, that Cyrus began to reign in 558; but Weissbach's hypothesis is impossible, because the Chronicle does not in fact admit the doubt he assumes, but makes it quite certain that Ecbatana fell in 550–549. There is as little difficulty in an Akkadian *imperfectum propheticum* as in a Hebrew *perfectum propheticum*.

Another cause of misunderstanding 'in the third year when it arrives' would only arise if the translation 'two years afterwards', given in ZA (NF), iii, p. 91, line 17, for the same phrase restored in the verse account, were adopted for Nabonidus no. 1, col. i, line 28. Fortunately that is impossible, for the 'afterwards', *darauf*, is inserted in translation, and there is nothing in no. 1 to which it can refer. But this translation is inaccurate in the verse account, see note 64; the numbering must be understood to refer to the reign of a king.

In CAH, iii, p. 220, the rising of Cyrus is correctly dated to 553–552, but the note states that 'the Chronicle says his sixth year'; this is incorrect, it is Cyrus's final victory the chronicle dates, while the cylinder dates the rising.

53. Presumably the inscription Nabonidus no. 1 was meant to be deposited simultaneously in the three temples to which it refers. The temple of Harran was not complete till 553, and it

is improbable that either the Shamash temple at Sippar or the Anunitum temple in the same city was complete before then. H. de Genouillac, *Nabonide*, in RA, xxii (1925), p. 75, assumes that Nabonidus's oath in the verse account, ii, 10–11, means that the king proclaimed national mourning till the temple at Harran was consecrated, and the wording points to that, though not certainly. The New Year Festival was in fact omitted during Nabonidus's stay at Tema', and the period of *tazimtu* and *nissatu*, ii, 16, must therefore have been extended. Landsberger and Bauer ingeniously transliterate ii, 16 *nismat*, proceed to assume an otherwise unknown *tazimtu = nizimtu*, and translate 'Wunsch'. But *tazimtu*, I.AN.UD, means 'disaster, mourning', and is not rare; it is unwise to solve difficulties by positing unknown meanings.

54. The reference to the *Umman-manda* as still in Harran dates the oracle to 556. In 554 Nabonidus was already in Syria; according to the verse account combined with the chronicle Nabonidus set out for Syria at the end of 555 or in the first two months of 554.

55. The two best examples are the expedition to Muṣaṣir, in Sargon's eighth campaign, Luckenbill, ii, arts. 169–72, and Esarhaddon's invasion of Egypt, Luckenbill, ii, arts. 554–9, 561–4, and Delitzsch, *Die Babylonische Chronik (Abhandlungen der phil.-hist. Klasse der königl. sächs. Gesellschaft der Wissenschaften*, Band xxv, nr. 1), pp. 15, 23, col. iv, lines 13–18; CAH, iii, pp. 52–3, 85.

56. The best example is Merodachbaladan, CAH, iii, pp. 62–6.

57. The word actually occurs in Darius's inscriptions, see Herzfeld, pp. 41–2, and also *Altpersische Inschriften*, Berlin, 1938, p. 81.

58. Chronicle, i, 7, *ana hume*, where *humu* may be a variant form of *hamu, hammu*, 'rebel', from the root *hamu*, a cognate of Hebrew עוה, Arabic غوى, or a Pu'al formation, 'one led into error'. It must not be deduced from this word that there had been revolts in the provinces after Nabonidus's accession, see note 68.

59. Nabonidus no. 1, col. i, ll. 38–46 *ušatbamma ummania rapšati ultu (mat)Hazzati paṭ (mat)Miṣir tamtim eliti abarti (nar)Puratti adi tamtim šapliti šarrani(pl.) rube(pl.) šakkannake(pl.) u ummania rapšati ša (il)Sin (il)Šamaš (ilat)Ištar bele(pl.)ea iqipuni ana epišu E.HUL.HUL bit (il)Sin*. Langdon, p. 221, followed by Galling, p. 9, mistranslated *rube* as if it were the adjective GAL.MES, *rabuti*, and *ša* 'because', though it is the relative, 'the wide-flung troops which the gods Sin, Shamash, and Ishtar entrusted to me'. This leads to *ana epišu E.HUL.HUL* being taken with *iqipuni*, which ends the subordinate

clause in the normal way, instead of with *ušatbamma*. Galling's comment, 'that the king gambled with the safety of *Ebir nari* as a part of the Babylonian Empire, to proceed more quickly with his temple building' was followed by the statement in Begrich (2), p. 71, 'Nabuna'id on his own admission actually ordered the Babylonian garrisons as far as the Egyptian border to Harran'. This is a misunderstanding of a very simple institution, the levy. Translate: 'I ordered my wide-flung troops to arise, from Gaza on the border of Egypt, the Upper Sea beyond the Euphrates (Mediterranean), as far as the Lower Sea (Persian Gulf), [that is] kings, princes, governors, and wide-flung troops that my lords Sin, Shamash, and Ishtar entrusted to me, for to make the temple of Sin.' These troops are conscripts, not garrisons.

Page 34.

60. Chronicle, i, 7.

61. Perhaps long aiter, for a levy in the west would explain the chronicle, i. 14, *šarru ummanšu* [*idki*]; this would date the western levy to 553.

62. *ušatbamma . . . ana epišu E.HUL.HUL*, see note 59.

63. E. F. Weidner, in JSOR, vi (1922), pp. 117–20, has proved that Sp. ii. 407, published by Father Strassmaier in *Hebraica*, ix, p. 5, is a text of Nabonidus containing information about his 2nd and 3rd years, 554 and 553. It is badly broken but mentions, under 554, in line 2, a mountain way, in 3, death, a weapon, in 4, the people of the *Hatti*-land. This might point to fighting in northern Syria, but no safe inference can be drawn. In Iyyar of 553 someone 'took the head of his army in Babylon'; this presumably refers not, as Weidner thought, to Nabonidus, who seems to have stayed in Syria, but to his son, Bel-shar-uṣur, as also does the levying of troops in the next line. Then came a description of the capture of the town Ammananu and the slaughter and impaling of its inhabitants, which is certainly to be connected with the mention of the mountain Ammananu where, according to the chronicle, i, 11, something happened in the month Ab, as Weidner says. It seems more probable that this town, in a mountain mentioned also by Tiglathpileser III and Sennacherib for its stone quarries, is in the Jabal Druz, east of Jordan, than in Anti-lebanon, as Winckler and Weidner proposed, since its capture would be preparatory to Nabonidus's march south along the route used by caravans. The inference drawn from this text by Olmstead in AJA, xxxiv, p. 275, that the campaign against Tema' cannot

have commenced in the 3rd year, is not warranted, as can be
seen from a comparison of other entries with actual campaigns.

64. Verse account, ii, 17. Landsberger and Bauer, p. 91, pro-.
pose a much better reading than mine for the broken signs, so
that the whole line runs

ibnu ikkibi šipri la mesu   šalulti šatti ina kašadi

Landsberger and Bauer, however, split the line; the first half they
take as dependent on *ištu* in line 16, the second half with *karaš
ipteqid* in line 18. This is not permissible, because in Babylonian
verse the rhythm is not broken by such caesuras. Moreover, the
translation 'zwei Jahre darauf' is misleading; there is no reference to any event mentioned in the text. F. W. König in AfO,
vii (1931–2), p. 179, has been misled, 'Das ist also zwei Jahre
nach Fertigstellung von E.HUL.HUL . . .'; and also Galling,
p. 10, 'Nach zwei Jahren war der König fertig . . .'; *šalultu šattu*
should refer, as in Nabonidus no. 1, col. i, line 28, to the 3rd year
of reign. The phrase *šalulti šatti ina kašadi*, 'when the third year
arrives', is tantamount to 'at the commencement of the third
year'; *ibnu*, the imperfect, a state, not a tense, is best translated
as pluperfect. Landsberger translates *šipri la mesu* 'das unheilige
Werk', but *mesu* is a substantive, not as he translates, an adjective.
I take it to mean *sacrum*, 'holy thing', used both of ritual and of
concrete object, and as a cognate of Phoenician מס, מאש (on which
see A. M. Honeyman in JEA, xxvi (1941), pp. 58–9), used of
votive objects, statues, &c. Landsberger's view that *mesu, parṣu*
and similar words refer to ritual is correct in certain cases, not
always, see JRAS, 1928, p. 624; in the present instance *šipru* and
la mesu both clearly mean the temple, nothing else, as *ibnu*, which
does not mean 'vollbracht', shows. The line should be literally
translated

He had built the abomination, the work (that was a) no-sanctuary
   when the third year was coming in.

65. Galling, p. 10, note 1, writes 'Belsazar d.h. Bel-schar-usur
bzw. Nabu-Bel-dan-usur (vgl. Sidney Smith S. 119)'. There is
some misunderstanding here. I read the name of an official in
the chronicle, i, 15, not previously deciphered, *Nabu-Bel-dan-uṣur*.
Tallqvist had previously suggested, on the basis of a copy,
Nabu-tad-dan-uṣur, and Baumgartner in ZATW (NF), iii, p. 46,
repeated that, after seeing the new copy. As an emendation there
is much in favour of this reading, for *taddan* is a known element
in such names whereas *Nabu-Bel-dan-uṣur* cannot be paralleled.
But it is not a possible reading of the signs. The late form of *tad*

can be seen in BHT, plate xviii, line 16; it does not resemble
(*il*)*EN*, a ligature. Baumgartner's objection that the ligature is
differently formed in other places in the chronicle depends on the
fact that the head of a horizontal falls behind instead of in front
of the perpendicular; no one accustomed to reading tablets would
urge such a point, for such slips are not uncommon.   The unique
Nabu-Bel-dan-uṣur, if not an error of the scribe, can only be a
ritual name, and was probably given to the man when adult
because he had taken part in a ritual; he may have been a slave
or a foreigner. If the name is correctly written, it is possible
that it is the original form of בלטשאצר, because such corruptions
are not due to scribal errors, as Baumgartner seems to demand
('ein graphisch so wenig naheliegender Schreibfehler'), but to
analogy. Now in Daniel iv, 19, 'Daniel whose name was Belteshazzar', this name is introduced without further use by the
author, possibly because the name appeared as the original in
a form of the story he was adapting. If the name were a pure
invention, there must have been some further use or purpose in
its introduction. That some features of that story appear in the
verse account Baumgartner denies with some emphasis, apparently
because that view would make Hölscher's thesis, that the author of
the book of Daniel was using unwritten stories, untenable; but
a reasonable interpretation of facts must not be rejected to preserve a theory. In reply to this, von Soden, *Eine babylonische
Volksüberlieferung von Nabonid in den Danielerzählungen* in ZATW
(NF), xii (1935), pp. 81–9, has claimed that the Nebuchadrezzar
of Daniel cc. i–ii is Nabonidus in every respect. That is an
exaggeration. But there is a reasonable case for believing that
the writer of the book of Daniel used a story which is itself
derived from Persian propaganda against Nabonidus, and may
have used corrupt forms of names in the cuneiform document.
(Thus though Baumgartner, p. 43, note 3, rejects my rendering of
i, 17, *ittekiršu šedu*, 'a demon altered him', and renders 'benahm
sich feindlich gegen ihn', a correction I accept, the essential point
remains; for the enmity of a *šedu* entails disordered behaviour
such as is attributed to Nebuchadrezzar. Landsberger and Bauer,
p. 89, render 'es verliess seinen Platz der Schutzgott', but they
have not justified the ellipsis of *manzazu* or some similar word
that they assume, the omission of *-šu* in translation, or the statement that *šedu* must have the adjective *limnu* to mean 'demon'.
Both *ilu* and *šedu* could in the Babylonian conception be good
and bad at once, since the interference of divinities in human
affairs might benefit some, while injuring others; indeed the

Babylonians continually aimed at securing goodness and kindness from the great gods, so can hardly have conceived them good, or minor deities bad, by nature. Landsberger's translation is not even acceptable as a free rendering of the sense.) But even if *Nabu-Bel-dan-uṣur* be the original, the corruption Belteshazzar is not Belshazzar; Josephus, *Antiq. Jud.* x, 11, 2, confounded them and equated both with Naboandelos, Nabonidus, but that does not justify a modern scholar in doing so, as Galling has done.

66. The verse account, ii, 20 *iptaṭar qatasu*. Landsberger and Bauer translate this 'Er legte (die Herrschaftsembleme) aus der Hand', but give no explanation why they assume this meaning and no ground for the important ellipsis. *paṭaru* in Akkadian generally means 'to release, free', but also, in accordance with the root meaning in other languages, 'to strike, split, break through'. In ritual texts, where meals prepared for the gods are called *riksu*, 'things bound on', the phrase *rikse paṭaru* would mean 'to remove the dishes', because in the ritual some attachment of the offering table to the figure of the god made it proper to call the food offered *riksu*, see H. Zimmern, *Beiträge zur Kenntnis der babylonischen Religion* (Assyriologische Bibliothek, xii), p. 94. Hence *ipaṭar agu* might *possibly* mean (if it occurred) 'he removes the royal hat' from someone's head, though this is not certain; *ipaṭar qatasu* might possibly mean 'he frees his hands' from bonds, though the additional words are required and are not a natural ellipsis. But this does not justify Landsberger's translation. Only if *irkus qatasu* could mean 'he took (the sceptre) into his hands', and the ellipsis of the primary object was possible, would *ipṭur* (not *iptaṭar*) *qatasu* mean 'he put (the sceptre) down out of his hands'. Landsberger is forced to translate verse account v, 26 *ipaṭṭaru qaqqadsunu izakkaru mamit*, where the action of striking the head is the ordinary gesture of respectful obedience, *sie entblössten ihr Haupt*. Baring the head has at all times been shameful in the Near East, and cannot be the gesture appropriate to taking an oath. The well-known illustration of the ceremony of installing an officer, *Assyrian Sculptures in the British Museum from Shalmaneser III to Sennacherib*, plate xxv, shows that the striking of hands by the king, or by one man empowering another to act for him, was normal; from that ceremony the use of *qatu, qatatu* 'hands' for a deputy arose. The decisive argument against Landsberger's translation is, that it implies that Nabonidus abdicated, an implication enhanced by the translation of verse account ii, 20 *iptaqidsu šarrutam* 'übergab jenem das Königtum'. There is no evidence in the words in favour

of this assumption, and it is quite certain that Nabonidus did not abdicate; Bel-shar-uṣur was simply his deputy. *šarrutu* never means 'kingdom', but only 'kingship', and *paqadu* does not mean 'to hand over' a possession once for all, but 'to entrust' it for safe-keeping temporarily. Finally, it is very doubtful whether the 'sceptre of righteousness' mentioned in descriptions of rituals, see BHT, p. 148, would be voluntarily relinquished by any king between one New Year Festival and the next; certainly only the god could bestow it on another. It should also be noted that the *t* form of the verb is only explicable of mutual action, 'he struck his hand (in return, while his own was struck)'. This manner of deputing and accepting power must be compared with the custom instituted by 'Omar when taking the oath of allegiance to Abu Bakr as Caliph, see J. G. L. Kosegarten, *Taberistanensis . . . et*

Taberi Annales, I, p. 8: فقال عُمَرُ آبْسُطْ يَدَكَ لِأُبَايِعَكَ فقال ابو

بكر بَلْ أَنْتَ يَا عُمَرُ فَأَنْتَ أَقْوَى لَهَا مِنِّى وكان عمر أَشَدَّ الرجلين وكان

كُلُّ واحد منهما يفتح يده يضرب عليها ففتح عمر يد ابى بكر وقال إنَّ

لَكَ قُوَّتِى مَعَ قُوَّتَكَ ''Omar said, "Unclose your hand, so that

I may take the oath to you". Abu Bakr replied, "No, you do it, 'Omar, for you are stronger to do so than I". 'Omar was, in fact, the more vigorous of the two. Then each opens his hand, strikes thereon (i.e. on the hand of the other). And 'Omar opened the hand of Abu Bakr, and said, "Behold, my strength joined to your strength is yours".' This primitive symbolism is exactly that indicated in the verse account, in the Akkadian term for 'deputy', and the relief, though it does not seem to have been generally understood yet.

67. The verse account, ii, 19 *ummane matitan uta'ir ittišu*. Dougherty, pp. 107–8, is certainly right, in referring -*šu* to Bel-shar-uṣur; I previously translated it, clumsily, as reflexive. But Dougherty is wrong in translating *ummane matitan* 'the troops of the land', for *matitan* is certainly an adverb. Landsberger and Bauer translate 'die Truppen von allüberall unterstellte er dessen Befehl', construing the adverb with a noun, an impossible construction, even if *matitan* means 'allüberall'.

68. This not uncommon illusion, a projection backwards of events still to come, appears in the general histories, e.g. CAH, iii, p. 219: 'Babylon was rapidly nearing her end. With con-

tinual internal dissensions barely kept in check, it is a matter for
wonder that Nabonidus should have been able to retain his throne
as long as seventeen years. . . . With the accession of the new king
came one of the usual revolts in the provinces. . . . Yet in spite
of this flourish of trumpets, Babylon was falling from her high
estate. . . . Persia was almost at the very gates of Babylon and
the writing on the wall was unmistakable: "thus saith Yahweh
to his anointed Cyrus, whose right hand I have holden to subdue
nations before him".' There is no evidence for the revolts in the
provinces, no sign of disturbances except at Erech, in 546 and
540, where the trouble was due to intervention of some kind from
Elam, perhaps ordered by Cyrus, perhaps not.

Page 35.

69. *Excerpta historica jussu Constantini Porphyrii confecta*, iii (edited
by de Boor), pp. 23–33, c. 26.

70. F. W. König. AfO, vii (1931–2), p. 179.

71. Chronicle, ii, 16, *i-rab*, for *i-bir*, a metathesis that proves
that the document was copied from dictation; the error could
not arise from copying the signs.

72. Calah was in ruins; so was Nineveh, see Thompson and
Hutchinson, *A Century of Excavation at Nineveh*, pp. 137–8. Andrae,
Das wiedererstandene Assur, pp. 164 ff., dates some shrines and
dwelling-houses in the city of Ashur to this period; may they not
be late Achaemenean or Seleucid?

Page 36.

73. Lehmann-Haupt in *Klio*, xvii, 114. This conjecture is maintained by A. Götze, *Kleinasien*, p. 194, note 1.

74. By F. W. König, in AfO, vii (1931–2), p. 180, note 10.
He says that in the copies the horizontals are 'somewhat slanting'.
This is incorrect, and an example of reading copies against the
copyist's decipherment. The sign cannot be *su* as König reads it.
It is most like *iš*, and at the time of republication it seemed to me
possible that *iš-par-da*, a variant form for *sa-par-da*, Sardis, might
be correct. But *lu* is not impossible. Apart from the epigraphical
argument, there is a verbal difficulty in reading (*mat*)*Subartu*.
When Cyrus crossed the Tigris he was already marching to Subartu; in Iyyar he must have passed through the greater part of
the land, and could hardly have been said to be marching to it.

75. Herodotus, i, 46, 71–3, 75.

76. Lehmann-Haupt in *Wiener Studien*, xlvii, 123 ff., maintains
that Croesus attempted suicide.

Page 37.

77. Verse account, ii, 21–3. In the next line Landsberger and Bauer rightly corrected my former reading *harranu* to *ṭudu*; the line should read

   iṣṣabat ṭudu nisutu   urhu ultu ulla la ina kaša(di)

Landsberger also read *ullanu* for *ulla la*, and translated, 'Nun schlägt er den Weg ein, die weite Reise; sofort nach seiner Ankunft | den Fürsten von Tema tötet er mit der Waffe'. *nisutu* is therefore taken with *urhu*; this is opposed to universal Akkadian practice, which demands that an adjective follow the noun unless exceptional. The rhythm of the line is completely broken by the caesura at the half-line; it is against the Akkadian verse practice to split a line, and take the second half with what follows. *ultu ullanu* does not mean 'immediately'. The best translation is still

   he took the long road,   the way not within reach from of old.

78. Arguments are set forth at length in Dougherty, pp. 138–40, and in *A Babylonian City in Arabia*, in *American Journal of Archaeology*, xxxiv (1930), pp. 296–312. The only serious opposition has been raised by the distinguished Czech traveller, Alois Musil. Though he admitted that the city of Tema' whose inhabitants are mentioned by Tiglathpileser III was the oasis of Taima, in *Northern Heǧaz*, p. 288, and also that the Adumu conquered by Sennacherib was the oasis of Jawf, Dumat Jandal, al in *Arabia Deserta*, p. 493, he argued against the identification of Tema' in the verse account with Taima, and therefore also against the identification of . . . *dummu* in the chronicle with Jawf, *Northern Neǧd*, pp. 225 ff. The arguments against the identification of Tema' will not hold. There is no reason why the term Amurru should be considered adverse to the identification; it is a vague term and is similarly used of the desert south of Palestine in the cylinder inscription of Cyrus. There is no land *Aruba*, to which Musil thinks it should be said to belong. The fact that the verse account mentions no difficulties in the long journey is not so surprising, for it passes over the siege of a town recorded in the chronicle. Musil's own proposal, to locate Tema' in northern Edom, at *al Twanah*, lacks all probability, for that cannot have been far outside the borders of the Babylonian province. His argument, p. 226, about the donkey and the king's food, is a misunderstanding of the text, which mentions a camel; Dougherty corrected the error, p. 115, note 379. It is true that it is 'more than improbable that Taima could be a centre of Assyrian or

Babylonian administration'; that is why Nabonidus appointed a deputy while remaining king. But Musil puts clearly one point of great value: 'Residing in *al Twanah* in northern Edom, king Nabonidus would have been in a far better position to control all trade routes converging on Egypt and Syria from south-western and eastern Arabia . . . than from the oasis of' Taima. 'The natural location of' Taima, 'far from the main trade routes, precludes it from exercising any influence over the oases and tribes of north-western Arabia'. Musil provides part of the answer himself. 'Only caravans marching to Egypt . . . from the Persian Gulf had to cross the oasis of' Taima, 'and for these alone' Taima 'was an important station'. The other part of the answer is, that the route up the eastern coast of the Red Sea had to be cut, because Egypt could monopolize the trade there. And Taima was a convenient point, outside the Egyptian sphere of influence, from which to conduct operations. Musil wrote purely from the geographical point of view, and took no account of political conditions.

79. Chronicle, i, 17, . . . *-du-um-mu it-ta-du-u*. For *nadu*, I, 1, 'to pitch camp', and so 'to besiege' with *ina eli*, see C. J. Gadd, *The Fall of Nineveh*, plate II, line 20; *nadu*, I, 2 with *ina eli*, ibid., plate III, line 26, but with *ina libbi* ibid., plate II, line 16. Restore perhaps [*ina eli (al)A*]*dummu ittadu*. The mystification about *ina eli* in ZA (NF), iii, pp. 85–6, is superfluous: it should be translated 'at', with Mr. Gadd, or 'over against'.

80. Esarhaddon, Prism, I R., 45, col. ii, 55; Luckenbill, ii, art. 536, *Adumu al dannuti mat Aribi*. It is incorrect to read (*mat*)*Aribi* as Landsberger and Bauer do, p. 95. *Aribi* is always the gentilic adjective, in the genitive, never simply a geographical name. That there *is* a gentilic in -*u*, besides one in -*aiu*, is proved by such forms as *Aramu, Habiru, Ari*(? or *a*?)*bu*; נבטו, שלמו in Nabataean inscriptions. This is tacitly recognized by Theo. Bauer, *Das Inschriftenwerk Assurbanipals*, Teil II, p. 109, sub *Mat-Aribi*. The inscription refers to the campaign of Sennacherib recorded in *Vorderasiatische Schriftdenkmäler*, Heft I, plate 77, lines 22 ff., Luckenbill, ii, art. 358. There is also a reference to Sennacherib's campaign and later events in Ashurbanipal's inscriptions, Winckler, *Keilinschriftliches Textbuch zum Alten Testament*, pp. 48–9, Luckenbill, ii, arts. 940, 943 (not altogether reliable). In these inscriptions it appears that Haza'il, king of the Aribi, and Te'elhunu the queen fled before Sennacherib's troops to the fortress Adumu, also called Adummatu, and that Te'elhunu fell into the hands of the As-

syrians. On Esarhaddon's succession, Haza'il asked for the return of the gods of the Aribi and the queen; the Assyrian ordered that the gods be restored, and sent back with the girl Tabua, born in his palace, perhaps Te'elhunu's daughter. Ashurbanipal's own activity is unknown owing to breaks in the text.

Sennacherib's inscription calls *Adumu* by the feminine form, *Adummatu*, and says that it lay 'in the *madbar*'. To judge from other passages, *madbaru* does not mean, at any rate necessarily, the sandy desert, see M. Streck, *Assurbanipal*, ii, p. 70, lines 87–90, for the description there is of the terrain east of Jordan; p. 72, line 108. It thus resembles the Hebrew *mid̠bār*, and is, in Akkadian, certainly a loan-word.

81. Landsberger and Bauer rightly corrected my previous reading of the verse account, ii, 26, *ašib ali[šu] matsu kullišunu uṭṭab[bihu]* to *ašib ali [u] mati sugullišunu uṭṭab[bihu]*. The purpose of killing off the flocks was partly to secure food till supplies arrived, partly to drive out the local inhabitants to make room for the soldiery. This statement, with others, is a strong argument against Landsberger and Bauer's strange view, pp. 97–8, that Tema' was an Aramaean centre which Nabonidus expected to rally against Persia; they accordingly have to deny that it is to be taken seriously, p. 97, note 2, against the rules for the use of historical evidence. Landsberger's views depend on his as yet unproved doctrine that the names of Aribi recorded are all exclusively Aramaic, and on the erroneous assumption that the people of Tema' were Aribi.

82. Dougherty, p. 96.

83. Dougherty, pp. 114–15.

84. Or at any rate not mentioned by them. The omission is probably due to the fact that the Persians were one of the peoples who have no written history, only legends and tales. One of the strangest features of their civilization is the almost total disappearance from popular memory of the Achaemenid kings; such vague allusions as there are have been discussed, with widely different interpretations, by Herzfeld, *Zarathustra*, in AMI, i and ii (1929–30), and A. Christensen, *Les Kayanides* (Det Kgl. Danske Videnskabernes Selskab., Hist.-fil. Middelelser, xix. 2, 1931).

85. Here used of the kingdom in its greatest extent, the Roman Idumaea. The difficult question as to the dominant power in the region between Wadi Sirḥan and the Gulf of 'Aqaba in 550 B.C. cannot be definitely answered. Albright, in *Bulletin of the American Schools of Oriental Research*, no. 82, p. 14, argued that

in the time of Nabonidus all the territory to Ezion-Geber was part of the kingdom of Edom. It is, however, possible that Nabataean tribes had conquered this whole territory before Nabonidus attacked.

86. If Adummu was in Edom, then the distance from watered land to Taima was about 280 miles; Musil's estimate that the march across would last about 20 days, *Northern Neǧd*, p. 225, may be excessive. But even if all the army were mounted, which is unlikely, the need for supplies of food and water for men and horses would prohibit any delay or diversion on the way from Syria to Taima after watered land was left. Now if Adummu was Jawf, there was, in addition to the march there, the march thence to Taima across the great Nafūd. That is why Musil convinced me in 1923, during conversations, that (*A*)*dummu* in the chronicle could not be Jawf, and must lie in Edom; but his own view, that *Adummu* in the chronicle is distinct from *Adumu, Adummatu*, is extremely improbable. In JRAS, 1926, p. 285, note 2, Albright stated that 'the strategic difficulties supposed to exist are imaginary'. Difficulties in watering men and horses such as the Nafūd causes need no particular military training to be comprehended, and miles of such desert are not imaginary. No doubt Jawf did fall into Nabonidus's hands, as he would need the oasis for his line of communications with Babylon. It could easily be taken after Nabonidus had established himself at Tema'. But a campaign entailing a march from Syria to Jawf, a siege, and then a march to Taima, is incredible.

There is one instance of an Assyrian army being mounted on camels, that of Esarhaddon's expedition against Egypt, Luckenbill, ii, art. 558. The Arab kings, of course, supplied the camels, because the enemy attacked was Egypt. It is not likely that they supplied camels to Sennacherib or Nabonidus for use against themselves.

Page 38.

87. The translation of the account of this campaign in Luckenbill, ii, arts. 817–31. For the geography see Musil, *Arabia Deserta*, pp. 487–9; on the location of Qedar, p. 490, on the Nabaite, p. 492. This discussion has settled the main lines of the tribal areas, which cannot be altered much. Landsberger and Bauer, p. 95, say that the reasons for the statement that Jawf lay in the territory of the Nabaite are unknown, yet there was a not inconsiderable literature on the point when they wrote. The only argument they adduce against placing Adummu in Edom depends

upon a confusion as to 'Edom', which was meant to refer to the later kingdom, not the Edom of the seventh century. In a list of kings who acknowledged Esarhaddon as overlord, Luckenbill, ii, art. 690, the king of Edom appears, with the kings of Tyre, Judah, Moab, Gaza, Askelon, Ekron, &c., under the heading 'kings of *Hatti*-land'. The term *Hatti*-land here is given an unusual extension to southern Palestine and is obviously loosely used. The Edom meant is a political creation within very narrow borders, lying within what was subsequently central and south-western Edom. This evidence does not 'cause the untenability of' the location in north-eastern Edom, that is the Kingdom of Idumaea, 'to spring to the eye'. The original reason for equating Adumu-Adummatu with Jawf was assonance, and a misunderstanding of the ninth campaign of Ashurbanipal by Glaser and Winckler.

88. Job vi, 19.

89. See note 129.

90. The text is in Strassmaier, *Inschriften von Nabuchodonosor*, p. 194, no. 329, lines 13 ff.; for a translation see CAH, iii, p. 304. Winckler, *Altorientalische Forschungen*, Reihe i, pp. 511–15, introduced the speculation, without real evidence, about Greek mercenaries and Pittakus of Mytilene, which has had an undeserved influence on the interpretation of this document. For some imaginative views about *Puṭu-Yaman* see F. W. König (1), pp. 47–8, 50. Lawrence, pp. 290–1, has revived the doubtful suggestion of Pinches that *Puṭu* is Egyptian *Pwn.t*, but wrongly rejected the possibility of Dougherty's view that *Yaman* can be the Red Sea coast, as well as the Babylonian transliteration of the Greek form of 'Ionia'. Weissbach, in ZA (NF), ix, p. 281, characterizes this location as 'more than doubtful', but the identification as Ionia in this case is inexplicable. In Dougherty, *Records from Erech. Time of Nabonidus*, no. 168, rev. lines 3, 5, large amounts of iron from *Yamana* and the Lebanon are mentioned, besides copper from *Yamana* in obv. line 1; this iron more probably came from Tall al Khalaifah than from a Greek colony. The proof that in the 14th century at Ras Shamra *Ṣapuna* means 'the northern' indicates that *Yaman* here simply means 'south'. There is no other possible theatre for this war than the district at the head of the Red Sea and round the Gulf of 'Aqaba. The 'distant district in the midst of the sea', which is not identical with *Puṭu-Yaman*, might be the Sinai peninsula. For trade between Tema' and Babylon early in Nebuchadrezzar's reign see Dougherty, p. 117.

91. This is fully discussed with comprehensive references by W. W. Tarn, *Ptolemy II and Arabia*, in JEA, xv (1929), pp. 9–25.

92. Woolley, *Excavations at Ur 1929–1930*, in *The Antiquaries Journal*, x (1930), pp. 316 ff., 'The Work on the City Wall'. Sir Leonard Woolley believed that the Euphrates still flowed past the west side of the city at this time; but that is impossible in view of the evidence from Erech, which shows that the main river was then flowing, in the general line, along a bed farther east. What lay along the western wall of Ur was probably a stream canalized farther north along an old bed.

93. This is clear from Sennacherib's campaigns, see Luckenbill, ii, arts. 261, 241–2, 246.

Page 39.

94. Weidner in AfO, vii (1931–2), p. 3, line 14; R. Campbell Thompson in LAAA, xx, p. 86; Leroy Waterman, *Royal Correspondence of the Assyrian Empire*, ii, no. 521; Schawe in AfO, viii, p. 52.

95. So Herzfeld, pp. 25–6.

96. Periodically theories or geographical identifications are advanced that necessitate the assumption that there were such campaigns. Thus Dr. Campbell Thompson, in JRAS, 1933, p. 890, identified the land Bazu with the Biblical Buz, and located both in eastern Arabia. But Jeremiah, xxv, 23–4, is good evidence that Buz lay on the Dedan–Tema'–Jerusalem trade route, most probably in the Wadi Sirhan, see Musil, *Northern Neğd*, pp. 224–5, and the land Bazu cannot lie there, in spite of Musil's argument in *Arabia Deserta*, pp. 482–5, because Adad-nirari II cannot possibly have invaded a district in Edom or Arabia Petraea, see Luckenbill, i, art. 382. Dr. Campbell Thompson's identification of Bazu and Buz therefore fails. The personal names of the kings of districts in Bazu, said to be Arabic by Dr. Campbell Thompson and by Meissner, *Könige Babyloniens und Assyriens*, 1926, p. 296, who places Bazu in the 'Syrian desert', though it is not mentioned by Ashurbanipal, are misinterpreted; thus *Agbaru* cannot be the Arabic elative, *'akbar*, which would not in any case be a possible personal name till after Muḥammad, but is a variant form of Ugbaru, a Gutian name.

97. Landsberger and Bauer, p. 98, say: 'It is also hardly probable that Nabonidus controlled the traffic through Arabia from Tema', in order to obtain a revenue for himself by that means; any one of his officials would have sufficed for that, and

the king could have devoted himself to his threatened empire.'
This is a misunderstanding or a misstatement of the explanation
tentatively proposed in BHT, pp. 81–2.

98. The verse account, iii, 3–7, *idduk niše* . . . . *sinništu*
ṣahri . . . . . . *igdamar bušašunu* . . . . *šeim ša ina libbi* . .
. . . . *ummanšu anhu* . . . . Landsberger and Bauer read
in the last line *anhu u da[l-pu]*, which they translate 'müde und
schlaflos'. Galling, p. 10, has based a reading of history on this:
'For the march (against Taima) he took the troops of Akkad
with him (had they put themselves under suspicion on the eastern
border against Persia?). After the bloodthirsty victory over the
king of Taima he could have a city and a palace built there as
splendid as Babylon. In 545 there was a revolt of the troops.
The date is deduced by us from the chronicle, ii, 32, where there
is talk of an advance of an Elamite against Erech. It is possible
that Cyrus wished to provoke the rebellion by the advance
against Erech.' Nothing in verse account or chronicle justifies this.

Page 40.

99. Verse account, ii, 29.

100. Miss Caton-Thompson in *Nature* (1939), pp. 139 ff., *The
Geographical Journal* (1939), pp. 18 ff., *Asia* (New York, 1939), pp.
294–9. The dating was given by the Rev. Professor G. Ryckmans
at the Congress of Orientalists in Brussels, 1938.

Landsberger and Bauer do not accept my suggested restoration
of *(il)Sin* in the verse account, ii, 27, and I very willingly abandon
a mere conjecture, though it would fit traces and space; that
means there is no record of a temple of Sin at Tema', yet there
must have been one. Dougherty's conjecture, p. 110, is impossible
because there is not enough space.

For the persistence of the worship of Sin in the Haḍhramawt,
see the coins published by Dr. John Walker, *A new type of South
Arabian Coinage* in *Numismatic Chronicle*, Fifth Series, vol. xvii,
pp. 260–79. The interpretation of crescent and disk on South
Arabian objects as crescent and full moon favoured by Dr. Walker,
p. 20, shows the association with Babylonian and Assyrian symbolism which might be expected, for crescent and disk were the
symbol of Sin, as against the rayed disk of Shamash, see, e.g.,
the round-topped stele of Shamshi-Adad V, *Assyrian Sculptures in
the British Museum, From Shalmaneser III to Sennacherib*, plate II.

101. D. Nielsen, *Handbuch der altarabischen Altertumskunde*,
pp. 213–24.

102. EN.ZU is written in the personal names of the Cappa-docian tablets ZU.EN, and this must conceal the earliest form of the name *Sin*.

103. *Corpus Inscriptionum Semiticarum*, tome i, pp. 107–15, dated the monument to the first half of the sixth century. H. de Genouillac, in RA, xxii (1925), p. 79, says: 'Les aramisants ne pensent plus qu'elle remonte au delà de 450.' His reason for this was R. Dussaud's statement in *Syria*, v, p. 258. But Dussaud, p. 147, note 1, has obviously altered his opinion: 'Ce texte étant daté de l'an 22 ne peut être du règne de Nabonide, 555–538, comme on l'a suggéré. Il faut plutôt le rapporter au temps de Darius Ier, 521–485.' The epigraphical argument is thus aban-doned; it can never have been a strong one, in view of the forms of, e.g., the *zayin* and the *yod*. Nor is the argument from the 22nd year good; why must a Babylonian regnal year be intended? It seems far more likely that the inscription referred to the 22nd year after some grant had been made, or some ritual event took place. The difficulty about dating this stele later than the 6th century is the relief, which in no way resembles 5th-century work. The choice between 550 and 500 is one of historical probability.

104. One of the bases of Begrich's thesis, (2) Kapitel II, is that the first predictions of the return of the exiles and the coming restoration of Jerusalem were based upon eschatological notions, because in the war between Astyages and Cyrus the prophet saw the confusion of nations, 'der eschatologische Völ-kerkampf', which was to be the beginning of the end. This misconception of the historical position is similar to that remarked on in note 68. It seems to be an equally common error, for Volz wrote, p. xv, 'The decisive battle on the Halys had already been fought; thereby Cyrus took over world-leadership in place of Babylon, and it was almost an historical necessity that Babylon would fall to him sooner or later. In all the market-places and in every alley people spoke of Cyrus, and the Persians, their stature, their weapons, their victories, and again and again of their legendary heroes.' This is imaginative, but not historical. There is no comparison between the position after 547, and that after 522 when Haggai saw in the reorganization of Darius a general destruction of heathen kingdoms.

105. Herodotus, i, 79.

Page 41.

106. Hill, *History of Cyprus*, i, p. 111, note 2: 'While Herodotus, iii, 19, is not explicit as to the date of their going over to the

Persian side (he might even be taken to mean that this did not happen until Cambyses was preparing to attack Egypt in 525), Xenophon, if he is to be trusted at all in such matters, leaves no doubt that the Cypriotes had assisted Cyrus in his campaign against the Carians, *Cyropaedia*, VII, iv, i, and willingly joined the expedition against Babylon, *Cyropaedia*, VIII, vi, 8.' The Cypriotes also appear in the list of peoples ruled by Cyrus, *Cyropaedia*, I, i, 4, with the Egyptians, who were first conquered by Cambyses. Leuze, p. 164 (8), says: ' So far as Cyprus is concerned, Xenophon's assertion that the Cypriotes voluntarily served in Cyrus's army against Babylonia conflicts with Herodotus iii, 19 . . . . The sentence can only be understood to mean that in Herodotus's opinion the Cypriotes joined the Persians voluntarily for the first time under Cambyses in his attack on Egypt.' Herodotus does not *necessarily* mean this; Leuze has created a contradiction. Later he says: ' It must not be overlooked that the Cypriote help is said to have been rendered in a campaign against Caria according to VII, iv, 2, in a campaign against Babylon according to VIII, vi, 8. This self-contradiction is characteristic.' But Leuze assumes the self-contradiction; there is no reason why both statements should not be correct. This is an example of bad method in the use of historical evidence which admittedly needs criticism.

107. Landsberger and Bauer, p. 97: ' He (Nabonidus) . . . sought probably to unite the inhabitants of Arabia for the purpose of creating a counterpoise with these pugnacious peoples against the onslaught of the Indo-Germans.'

108. E. Meyer, *Die Entstehung des Judentums*, pp. 19–21; Beloch, *Griechische Geschichte*, I, ii, p. 41, II, ii, p. 154; Olmstead, in AJSLL, xlix, Jan. 1933, p. 156; M. N. Tod, *Greek Historical Inscriptions*, p. 12; Lawrence, p. 296.

109. τὰ κάτω τῆς Ἀσίας μέρη. This nomenclature resembles that found in Akkadian inscriptions concerning lands north of the Taurus boundary in Mesopotamia, ' the upper ' parts, and a district in Asia Minor, south of the Halys, the 'lower land ', see A. Götze, *Kleinasien*, pp. 61–2 and 68. But there can be no identity in the territories referred to, though the terminology may be derived from continuous use of these vague terms.

110. Dittenberger restored πᾶσαν ἀτρέκειαν, ' all truth ', which must in any case be something like the sense.

Page 42.

111. Excavations at Neirab have produced a few tablets of the New Babylonian period, see E. Dhorme, *Les tablettes babyloniennes de Neirab* in RA, xxv (1928), pp. 53 ff. Dates on these documents are: year 1 of Nebuchadrezzar, unknown year of Neriglissar, accession, 3rd, 4th, 5th, 7th, 9th, 10th, 11th, 12th, 13th, 16th years of Nabonidus, and the 1st and 3rd years of Cambyses. Galling, p. 19, who believes that Syria first actually fell to Cambyses, asks, concerning the gap between the 16th year of Nabonidus, 540, and the 1st year of Cambyses, 528, 'Sollte die Kluft ... reiner Zufall sein?' and proceeds to argue that the interval is no accident. To do this, he has to explain away the date 'ist year, Cambyses'. The document was dated from *Itum*, which he identifies with *Id*, Hit; it was, he says, sent to Neirab as a sort of messenger to prepare the way, 'er ist ein "Vorbote" des Königs'. But other documents are dated from townships round Neirab, and they simply prove that though drawn up in these small towns, they were recorded at Neirab, which must therefore have been the provincial capital. If Neirab was the provincial capital in 528, Syria must have been in Persian hands before that date, and Galling's whole construction falls. The tablets are not in any case sufficiently numerous to permit of any argument from absence. In 528 Gubaru was governor of the two provinces, *Babili* and *Ebir nari*. According to Galling, he was only ruling Syria nominally, not in fact. A document of that year from Hit on the Euphrates would in that case have been sent not to Neirab but to Babylon.

The important point for history is not this wrong deduction, but the fact that Babylonian rule was still acknowledged at Neirab in 540. That must mean that the towns along the middle Euphrates, as far as Carchemish perhaps, were still loyal. By the winter of 540 a great army under Cyrus had drawn a cordon round northern Babylonia. There must be special, that is probably local, circumstances to explain the position at Neirab.

Neirab was once a township in the Aramaean kingdom Bit Agusi, of which the capital, Arpad, paid tribute to Ashurnasirpal in 876, a formal compliment to a passing conqueror. Arpad resisted Adad-nirari III in 805–804 and Ashur-dan III in 754, unsuccessfully. The little kingdom recovered under Mati-il, who concluded a treaty with Ashur-nirari V soon after 754, and later became an ally, perhaps also a tributary client, of Sarduris of Urarṭu. Tiglathpileser III attacked and besieged Arpad in 743, defeated Sarduris's attempt to relieve the city so severely as to drive the Urartian finally out of Syria, and maintained the siege till Arpad fell in 740 B.C.; then it became a subject province, the final stage of Assyrian vassaldom, CAH, iii, pp. 93–4. Arpad rose once again to join Ilu-iau-bi'di of Hamath against Sargon of Assyria in 720, but that was the end. For a hundred years the district was an orderly province in the Assyrian empire.

Neirab lay on the periphery of the Aramaean kingdom, near Aleppo, where the resistance to Assyrian arms was never so desperate as farther north; the town is mentioned in Tiglath-pileser's inscriptions. Aleppo does not seem to have been important in the Assyrian and Babylonian periods; Neirab as a provincial capital would flourish on the trade from the Euphrates to the Orontes. Prosperity does not lead to a desire for change. It was not essential for the Persians to take Neirab and other cities which held out before attacking Babylon, and they clearly did not do so. But this evidence from Neirab must not be thought to invalidate the other evidence which shows that the provinces of the Babylonian Empire, in general terms, fell to Cyrus before 540; it merely proves that Syria was not an entity, and that local history and conditions differed and must be appreciated.

112. Josephus, *Contra Apionem*, i, 20; Schnabel, p. 274.

113. Herodotus, i, 178. The 'Assyrians' here correspond to Xenophon's 'Assyrian king'. Lehmann-Haupt, *Wiener Studien*, l, p. 152, as in previous articles there quoted, maintained that this is due to the inclusion of Assyria in the satrapy of Babylonia by Darius I. Even were this inclusion established, it would not justify this nomenclature, though it might justify calling Assyria by the name of the satrapy. The truth is that these geographical names are carelessly used very often, and that Greek authors are to be judged, not by the standards of present-day scholarship, but by the easier habits of the 16th and 17th centuries.

114. *Cyropaedia*, VII, iv, 16.

115. *Anabasis*, I, v, 1. Musil is probably right in identifying the Araxes as the Khabur, see *Middle Euphrates*, p. 221.

116. See note 111.

Page 43.

117. Darius, Persepolis, e, art. 2, and Naqš-i-Rustam a, art. 3, in Weissbach, pp. 82, 88; Weissbach, art. *Kyros*, Spalte 1153; Leuze, pp. 249–55. Herzfeld's view, AMI, i. p. 81, note 1, though he rightly accepts Marquart's identification of 'Arbaia' and Syria, introduces an unlikely etymology, 'Arbaia' metathesis from עבריא, derived from עבר נהרא. Lawrence, p. 290, note 1, on

iii, 88, identifies *Arabaia* as northern Arabia, which is unlikely, for that could not constitute a satrapy, and Syria, Phoenicia, and Palestine would remain unmentioned in these lists. There is an attempt to estimate the relation of the Persian lists and Herodotus, iii, 89–96, in Herzfeld, AMI, i, pp. 91–5.

118. *Cyropaedia*, VIII, vi, 7. Leuze, pp. 162–3 (6–7), takes it for granted that only desert Arabia can be meant, and he accordingly indulges in an argument based on a misunderstanding, finding an opposition between Xenophon and Herodotus where none exists, see note 106.

119. The evidence of tablets from Erech shows that Gubaru was governor of Babylonia and Syria from the 4th year of Cyrus to the accession year of Cambyses, see Schwenzner, *Gobryas*, in *Klio*, xviii (1923), p. 239. Two documents mention him without title in the first year of Cambyses, one, PSBA, xxxviii (1916), p. 29, calls him satrap of Babylonia only, in the 4th year of Cambyses. The omission of Syria in this last is no more than an omission; it does not prove that Syria was no longer governed by Gubaru. Leuze, pp. 181–8 (25–32), supposes that Gubaru was made governor of Syria before Cyrus had reduced that land; the reason for the union of Syria and Babylonia under one governor was the desire to keep the old Babylonian empire under a single administration. This argument not only intentionally neglects the evidence that Syria was conquered before 539, but fails to take account of the separate names for the two provinces. If there were any desire to retain the Babylonian Empire as a unity, it would not have been given two names. The union of the two provinces under one governor shows the importance of Gubaru, nothing else; Leuze's use of the evidence is not sound, more especially because he summarily rejects E. Meyer's correct inference, *Geschichte des Altertums*, iii, art. 29, p. 50, that the union of the two provinces under Gubaru implies the separate existence of *Ebir nari* prior to that date. *Ebir nari* was in fact the satrapy *Arabaia* to which Cyrus first appointed Megabyzus. One reason for uniting the two satrapies must have been the necessity for Aramaic as an official language: subsequently it became *the* administrative language. The relief at Pasargadae is positive evidence that Cyrus ruled Syria.

Galling, pp. 17 ff., accepts Leuze's views and develops them, by refusing to admit that the edict of Cyrus which was the basis of the memorandum in Ezra vi, 3–5 contemplated or led to a return of any Jews; he accordingly denies that Syria was conquered

till the reign of Cambyses. His arguments, like Leuze's, are confused by impossible deductions from the title 'king of Babylon'
held by Cambyses in 538. See note 148.

120. Weissbach, pp. 6–7: *naphar šarrani* (*MEŠ* omitted) *ašib
parakke(pl) ša kališ kibrata ištu tamtim elitim adi tamtim šaplitim ašib
. . . . . . šarrani(pl) mat Amurri ašib kultari . . .*, 'all of the kings
who abide in holy chambers, who are in all parts of the (four)
quarters, from the Mediterranean to the Persian Gulf, those
dwelling in . . ., the kings of the land of Amurru who dwell in
tents, all of them brought their heavy tribute and kissed my feet
in Babylon'. Leuze, p. 185 (29), note, arguing against Meyer's
view that all the western provinces submitted to Cyrus immediately Babylon fell, says that this passage only says 'the kings
dwelling in throne-rooms and those dwelling in tents brought
heavy tribute . . .'. This is inaccurate. The kings 'from the
Mediterranean to the Persian Gulf' submitted, all the client princes
in all the western provinces, Syria, Phoenicia, and Palestine,
some of whom perhaps acknowledged Cyrus as overlord before 539
while some had not. The kings of Amurru are distinguished
from these as desert-dwellers. All the sources, without exception,
must be rejected by those who accept Leuze's view.

121. The old view was that the 'kings dwelling in tents' were
from Palmyrene. These were doubtless included; but now that
the term Amurru is known to include places so far south as Tema',
at this period, the evidence in note 123 is conclusive in favour of
a wider interpretation.

122. Herodotus, iii, 97: Ἀράβιοι δὲ χίλια τάλαντα ἀγίνεον λι-
βανωτοῦ ἀνὰ πᾶν ἔτος. There can be no doubt about the Arabs
meant; they must be the tribes controlling the frankincense route
at the point of maximum traffic, between the Gulf of 'Aqaba and
the Haḍramawt. These are not the Arabs meant in Herodotus,
iii, 91 ἀπὸ δὲ Ποσιδηίου πόλιος . . . μέχρι Αἰγύπτου πλὴν μοίρης
τῆς Ἀραβίων (ταῦτα γὰρ ἦν ἀτελέα) . . ., presumably the tribes
lying between the brook of Egypt and the Egyptian border.
Leuze, p. 163 (7), uses this latter passage as the basis of his
assertion that 'Under Darius the Arabs were still left out of the
division into satrapies', again a wrong use of the sources, which
fails to distinguish between different uses of a general term.

123. Herodotus, iii, 88: καί οἱ ἦσαν ἐν τῇ Ἀσίῃ πάντες κατήκοοι
πλὴν Ἀραβίων, Κύρου τε καταστρεψαμένου καὶ ὕστερον αὖτις Καμβύσεω.
Ἀράβιοι δὲ οὐδαμὰ κατήκουσαν ἐπὶ δουλοσύνῃ Πέρσῃσι ἀλλὰ ξεῖνοι

ἐγένοντο παρέντες Καμβύσεα ἐπ' Αἴγυπτον. ἀεκόντων γὰρ 'Αραβίων
οὐκ ἂν ἐσβαλοῖεν Πέρσαι ἐς Αἴγυπτον. This passage has been pressed
into meaning what it does not say. Lehmann-Haupt, PRE, Bd. ii,
Sp. 82–188, art. *Satrap*, referring καταστρεψαμένου to 'Αραβίων,
speaks of efforts being made to subdue them and impose a regular
administration. This, as Leuze, p. 163 (7), rightly says, is not
the construction, for the genitive absolute must refer to the πάντες
or κατήκοοι, though this introduces a difficulty. As Lawrence,
p. 291, note 2, on c. 88 says, 'it sounds as though Herodotus
meant that a general revolt against Cambyses had occurred, which
is in agreement with what Xenophon says, *Cyropaedia*, viii, viii,
2'; yet there is no hint in the accounts of Cambyses's reign elsewhere of such a rising. Leuze attributes to Herodotus's words
a meaning they will not bear : ' The Arabs were not subjected by
either Cyrus or Cambyses; they never obeyed the Persians as
subjects at all, but became ξεῖνοι of the Persian kings at the time
of Cambyses, whom they enabled to cross to Egypt.' Galling,
p. 23, note, similarly paraphrases : 'Darius, the son of Hystaspes,
became king, and those who were in Asia were all subject—with
the exception of the Arabs—and the reason was that Cyrus
and later Cambyses again subdued them. But the Arabs (to
explain the exception) were never subject to the Persians as
slaves', and remarks, 'a subjection of the Arabs by Cyrus has
been wrongly inferred'. Herodotus does not mean the Arabs
were not subject, but that they were not subject in the same
sense, κατήκοοι ἐπὶ Δουλοσύνῃ, that all the others were; he
knew that there were grades of subjection, and he specifies one
grade, peculiar in that part of the world to the Arabs, but not
elsewhere. Moreover, the term ξεῖνοι does not imply complete
independence; the Arabs were clients.

M. Boissier published a ritual text from Erech, in RA, xxiii
(1926), p. 15, dated in the 8th year of Cyrus, 531/0, in which
a certain *Ša-Nabu-ṭabi* is mentioned, the (*amel*)*qipu* of (*al*)*Šalamu*.
Professor Langdon, in JRAS, 1927, pp. 529–30, argued that since
the Nabataean inscriptions from *al-Ḥijr*, 40 miles south of Taima,
mention a tribe שלמו, the city *Šalamu* must be in that territory,
because of the known connexions between Erech and Taima in
the reign of Nabonidus. This is not a sound argument. The
title (*amel*)*qipu* is, it is true, sometimes used for governors of border
districts, but even that does not seem to be universally true. It
is much more probable that (*al*)*Šalamu* was in the marshes than
in Arabia. This evidence is not at present relevant to any discussion of Persian dominance in Arabia, but may prove so.

Page 44.

124. This is quite clear from the clause, 'for had the Arabs been unwilling, the Persians would never have entered Egypt'. The tribes were under some obligation to assist the Persians.

125. Chronicle, iii, 14-15.

126. Chronicle, iii, 16. Christian in ZA (NF), ii, p. 314, and Landsberger and Bauer, ZA (NF), iii, p. 85, read LAL in this and certain other passages in the Nabopolassar Chronicle and emend, in the latter, Mr. Gadd's *ihhiš* to *ihhisu*, inferring that LAL = *nihesu* and translate 'zurückziehen'. But *nihesu* means 'to retire', 'zurückweichen', and that is precisely what Nabonidus did not do when he returned to Babylon; moreover, there is good epigraphical reason for reading ME, not LAL. But the reading makes no difference to the sense.

127. Berossus in Josephus, *Contra Apionem*, i, 21 Αἰσθόμενος Δὲ Ναβόννηδος τὴν ἔφοδον αὐτοῦ, ἀπαντήσας μετὰ τῆς Δυνάμεως καὶ παραταξάμενος ἡσσηθεὶς τῇ μάχῃ καὶ φυγὼν ὀλιγοστὸς συνεκλείσθη εἰς τὴν Βορσιππηνῶν πόλιν. Κῦρος Δὲ Βαβυλῶνα καταλαβόμενος . . . ἀνέζευ-ξεν ἐπὶ Βορσίππων ἐκπολιορκήσων τὸν Ναβόννηδον. Τοῦ Δὲ Ναβοννήδου οὐχ ὑπομείναντος τὴν πολιορκίαν ἀλλ᾽ ἐγχειρίσαντος αὑτὸν πρότερον. . . . It may well have been to Borsippa that Nabonidus fled from Sippar, and it is possible that he surrendered there, for the chronicle, iii, 16, might be consonant with that, *ki šibsa*, 'while he was returning', whereas *ki ihhisa* could only mean 'when he had retired'.

128. Professor Rowley, in JTS, xxxii, p. 19, appears to think it doubtful whether the words quoted do not mean that 'on the fall of Babylon, Nabonidus was captured through his delay', and says: 'He (Nabonidus) must thus have acted somewhat strangely in returning to Babylon after it had fallen into the hands of his enemies; it should be noted that the Cyrus cylinder (line 17) associates the capture of Nabonidus with the fall of Babylon.' This forces into the cylinder a meaning not in the words; and there is nothing about delay by Nabonidus in the chronicle.

Page 45.

129. R. Dussaud, pp. 143-50. If the dating adopted by Marti is correct, then there is no doubt about the correctness of the general argument. Even so, M. Dussaud has misconceived the situation at least in part, for he says, p. 147: 'On conçoit que pour se plaire dans l'oasis, le roi dut trouver un accueil empressé

auprès des Arabes de la région.' This is contrary to the historical fact of resistance to be inferred from the verse account. But Marti's dating does not suit the situation better than 648, the time of Ashurbanipal's expedition against Adummu, for then the Arabs were allies of Babylon, which would account for Isaiah xxi, 7, 9, where, according to M. Dussaud, sorrow is expressed at the fall of the city, whereas in 539 they were allied with Cyrus against Babylon. Even the time of Sennacherib's campaign must be considered, more especially since it fell within the lifetime of Isaiah *ben 'Amos*. M. Dussaud's interpretation is not, therefore, certain, but it is a great advance on previous commentators, and Galling's statement, p. 12 : ' An attack on Taima by Cyrus must not be assumed in any case', is not more than dogmatic.

130. The verse account v, 6–7, *ina (aban)narua(pl)-šu ištatar ana šepeia . . . . . . matatišu qataia taktašad bušašu altequ ana . . .*, 'he wrote on his stelae, "To my feet (I made him bow). My hands conquered his lands, I took his booty to (my own land)"', on which the preceding comment is, v, 3, *ša la ikšudu ina eli iltatar*, ' what he had not conquered he wrote thereon'. The use of the forms *ištatar* and *iltatar* side by side is worth noting ; living speech tolerates such variations, the absence of them smells of the lamp—or of criticism when the language is dead.

131. Herodotus, i, 189–91.

132. There is no means of deciding which is meant. Rawlinson proposed the Diyalah, and is generally followed, on the not very sound ground that it is the most important tributary. Col. W. H. Lane, *Babylonian Problems*, pp. 6–10, argued, not unreasonably, in favour of the 'Adhaim, because the lower course of that river presents a reasonable explanation of Herodotus's anecdote.

Page 46.

133. *Cyropaedia*, VII, iv, 12. Weissbach, art. *Kyros*, col. 1150, says, 'Cyrus came from the north-east, probably from Ecbatana'. What is the *a priori* probability which is allowed to override the sources? Why not from Pasargadae? Why not, as Xenophon says, from Sardis?

134. *Cyropaedia*, VII, v.

135. Chronicle, iii, 1–4. But no attack there matured, for the dating by Nabonidus at Erech continued till 539.

136. Chronicle, iii, 9–12. The fact that the gods of Kuthah, Borsippa, and Sippar were not brought in to Babylon seems to prove that this measure was not due to any policy affecting

religious observances; but the Cyrus cylinder, lines 9–10, 33–4, and the verse account, vi, 12–13, seem to represent it as an act of impiety.

137. The typical instance is i, 194, the account of the boats on the Euphrates, see Lawrence, pp. 127–8, on that chapter.

138. Chronicle, iii, 12–14.

139. On Tall 'Umar as the site of Opis and of Seleucia, and the change in the bed of the Tigris, see L. Waterman, *Preliminary Report upon the Excavations at Tell 'Umar, Iraq* (Ann Arbor, 1931), pp. 1–6 and chapters 4–5. An inscription which mentions *Akšak*, the alternative name of Opis, belonging to the time of the First Dynasty of Babylon, was found at Khafaje, but it does not, apparently, prove that Opis lay there.

140. Into the present bed, for instance. There have been continual changes in the bed; some may have been caused artificially, but most are due to neglect.

141. Chronicle, iii, 13–14. *niše(pl) mat Akkadi(KI) BAL KI MU.MU*, i.e., *iqqur itti napihti*, see BHT, p. 149, note on line 29.

142. Weissbach, art. *Kyros*, col. 1150: ' In the whole adventure of the Gyndes there is perhaps only this truth, that Cyrus had to cross the river', and col. 1151: 'There can be no question of a rather lengthy siege of Babylon, a romance which Greek authors have tacked on to both Darius and Cyrus.' H. H. Rowley, *The Historicity of the Fifth Chapter of Daniel*, in JTS, xxxii, p. 29: 'This whole fiction of the siege of Babylon must therefore be set aside as completely unhistorical.' Historical sources are rarely absolutely without error; but sweeping condemnations of this kind, often much favoured in 'literary criticism', are rarely justified by research, as is shown by the development of modern studies in early Greek history, because the inventive powers of ancient authors and the credulity of their readers have been, ingenuously, overrated. In the present case the Cyrus cylinder, though it purposely does not mention a siege, makes a statement which cannot well be explained otherwise. Lines 10–11 read: . . . . *ina naphar dadmi ša innadu šubatsun u niše(pl) mat Sumeri u Akkadi(KI) ša imu šalamtaš . . .* , '(Marduk took pity on) all abiding places whose dwellings had fallen, and on the people of Sumer and Akkad, who resembled skeletons (*or*, had become skeletons)'. Since the cylinder is an official, contemporary, document, the statement that in certain parts houses had been knocked down cannot be an invention, and from our knowledge of the conditions

in Babylonia down to 540, in the contracts, this position cannot be supposed to have arisen gradually. Similarly, the statement that the people resembled, or had become, skeletons, implies a famine in 540–539; and famine during war results from siege conditions. Once again the cuneiform sources agree with elements in the Greek account, which some modern criticism is most positive in rejecting.

Page 47.

143. Chronicle, iii, 14–16 ; Cyrus cylinder, 17 ; the verse account, vi, 2.

144. There has been some mystification on this subject. In the name Ugbaru, which seems to occur in the chronicle in iii, 15 and 22, the first sign is in both cases doubtful. In line 22 it probably was meant for Brünnow, *Classified List*, no. 3860, but is in any case badly formed. In line 15, if a slip of the stylus caused an unnecessary wedge, the sign is Deimel, *Šumerisches Lexikon*, 381, (11), *UD = ug*. If any better suggestion can be made, the ingenious reconciliation by Pinches of the two forms must be abandoned. But as Pinches said, the sign can in neither case be *gu*, see TSBA, 1882, p. 174 ; and there was never any sound reason for identifying the (*amel*)*pahat* (*mat*)*Gutium*, a rebel native governor of Gutium who joined Cyrus, with the (*amel*)*pahatušu*, an officer of the Persian king who bore the Persian name Gubaru, *Gaubaruwa*. The identification was, however, favoured owing to an accident. Pinches, a very able decipherer, was deceived by the close script into a wrong combination of wedges in iii, 22, and then into a wrong restoration ; in his printed characters he was not able to show clearly what was on the tablet and what was original. For ⟶ ► ⟪ he read, in iii, 22, the signs ► ⟨⟶ and completed the last sign to ⟨⟶⟩ in print, a misreading perpetuated by Hagen, who followed the printed signs rather than the tablet, see BHT, p. 99. Hagen then connected the words *ina eli* with the beginning of the next line, though there is no proof that the sentence continued so far. Now in line 23 the first sign is badly broken, and only the perpendicular with one or possibly two obliques attached is visible, with a single perpendicular at the end. Pinches read *u*, ⟨⟩, Hagen *u*, ⟨ (impossible because it neglects the perpendicular) and *mar* ⟩ (impossible because it neglects the clear perpendicular at the end). For many years the translation Hagen gave passed from book to book. I corrected this reading in 1924. Professor Dougherty, one of the few scholars who have seen the

tablet, while not committing himself to the reading DAM ⟨cuneiform⟩ for the doubtful sign, had no doubt, p. 172, note 561, that there is no *TUR*, *mar*, just as he agreed with the certain reading *BAD*, *imut* in line 22. Professor Rowley, p. 27, says, 'the consensus of expert opinion is against Dougherty'; no 'expert' since 1924 has defended Hagen's assumptions, readings, or conjectural translation, though Lehmann-Haupt, in *Wiener Studien*, l, p. 159 expressed an unfulfilled (?) intention of proving that Gobryas did not die in 539, but is identical with *Gubaru*.

The erroneous identification of Ugbaru and Gubaru led first Lehmann-Haupt and then Schwenzner to elaborate biographical reconstructions. For criticism of these see Leuze, pp. 182 (26) ff.

145. For eulogies see the cylinder inscription, lines 20–35; the verse account, vi, 1–28. There is an interesting statement in the chronicle, iii, 17–18, *BE-la ša manma ina E . SAG . GIL u ekur-rati(pl) ul iššakin u simanu ul etiq*. The late Professor Langdon rightly pointed out, in JRAS, 1925, p. 168, that, owing to similar passages in contract tablets, the first word cannot be *bela*, 'weapon', as it had always previously been translated. He assumed the existence of a word *belu* meaning 'cessation', but this is unnecessary. The true reading is *baṭla*, from the root *baṭalu*, regularly used of absconding or ceasing to work; the passage must be translated 'There was no cessation by any one (performing duties) in ESAGIL or the temples, and no appointed ceremony was omitted'. This emphasizes the rapidity and peaceful nature of the entry of Gobryas and his troops.

146. Chronicle, iii, 20 (m)*Gubaru (amel)pahatušu (amel)pahati(pl) ina Babili(KI) ipteqid*. Much discussion has centred round this passage. Schwenzner, *Gobryas*, in *Klio*, xviii, p. 236, translated, ' He (Cyrus) delivered to Gubaru, his governor, the governorships in Babylon'. This is simply a mistranslation; (*amel*)*pahati(pl)* cannot be treated as the plural abstract, the determinative shows that 'governors' are meant, and there is no reason to assume a double accusative. The words mean, 'Gubaru, Cyrus's satrap, entrusted (i.e. appointed) district governors in Babylonia', not ' in Babylon'; Leuze, however, considers the matter still doubtful, p. 186 (30). Lehmann-Haupt, *Geschichte des alten Orients*, 3te Auflage, 1925, p. 190, assumes that this entry refers to Gubaru being made satrap not only of Babylonia but also of *Ebir nari*, Syria. Now it cannot be assumed that the chronicle is a full historical record, and the argument from absence ought not to

be used so freely as it is by some scholars; but the wording is not in favour of this assumption, and until some document naming Gubaru governor of Babylonia and Syria earlier than Cyrus's 4th year turns up, it is unnecessary.

Page 48.

147. Chronicle, iii, 24–8, leaves no doubt that Cambyses in person carried out the ceremonies of the New Year Festival in 538. On his youth at the time see Prašek, *Cambyses* (*Der Alte Orient*, xiv, no. 2), p. 4.

148. Thus Lehmann-Haupt, art. *Kambyses*, in PRE, x, Sp. 1813, argued that it was originally Cyrus's intention that Cambyses should rule the Babylonian kingdom as Nabonidus's successor, as 'king' under the 'king of kings', but that he was found unsuitable by his father and dismissed before the end of the year. Leuze, p. 188 (32), rightly points out that there is not the slightest ground for this assumption, since Cambyses succeeded his father and there is no sign of any estrangement in the accounts of Cyrus's dispositions. He himself argues that Cambyses remained 'king of Babylon', but is not called so in the documents because he no longer resided in Babylonia. This assumption runs contrary to all that is known of the Babylonian kingship, even under foreign kings. A king remained a king, wherever he resided. Once the compliment to Marduk had been paid by Cambyses's participation in the ritual, Cyrus could adopt the title. Kings could be represented at the festival by objects such as a cloak, and very probably, when the special occasion had passed, Cyrus was so represented. An example of this practice can be found in Waterman, *Royal Correspondence of the Assyrian Empire*, i, no. 496, which seems to mean that the king is asked to send officers with a cloak for use on the statue of Bel at the New Year Festival held in Elul in an unknown city, because there is no (royal) cloak proper to the occasion available, *ittia ia'nu ana akit lubušti*.

Recently a quite different view of the 1st year of Cambyses has been propounded. W. H. Dubberstein, *The Chronology of Cyrus and Cambyses*, in AJSLL, lv, pp. 417–19, after adducing and classifying all the evidence, argues that this year was not 538, but 531. Cambyses was made king of Babylon in Cyrus's last year; on the death of Cyrus, the year became 'the accession year of Cambyses, king of Babylon, king of the lands', but at Babylon the dating by the original formula, 'Cambyses, king of Babylon', was retained for the whole year. The main reason adduced for this view is the Greek tradition that Cyrus appointed Cambyses his successor before his last campaign; but that tradition does not assert that Cambyses was made king, or that he was given the satrapy of Babylon. Dubberstein places some emphasis on a dating 'year one, accession year of Cambyses, king of Babylon and the lands', but this single occurrence may be due to a scribal error, for the scribe should have given the day, not 'year one', or, as is equally possible, the name of Cyrus has been omitted after 'year one'. The chief argument against Dubberstein's view is that 'Cambyses, king of Babylon' is clearly dated to the 1st year of 'Cyrus king of the lands' by Strassmaier, Cyrus no. 16, and there is no reason, in view of the chronicle, to suspect scribal error. There is not, at present, sufficient ground for rejecting the old view in favour of Dubberstein's.

149. The discussions that have gone on so long as to whether Cyrus was a Zoroastrian seem likely soon to end. It is true that Kittel, *Die Religion der Achämeniden*, in *Sellin-Festschrift*, hrsgg. von A. Jirku, 1927, pp. 87–99, argued that he was, and Volz (2), p. xviii, note 2, seems still to hold that opinion. Yet the evidence is quite clear, and scholars who have studied the early history of the Zoroastrian religion in recent years, though they differ on the important points of Zoroaster's date and whether any Achaemenid kings were followers of the Iranian prophet, are agreed that Cyrus and Cambyses were not. Thus E. Herzfeld, pp. 37–43, summing up the results of several essays, maintains that Darius, Xerxes, and Artaxerxes were adherents, and has defended his view in *Iran in the Ancient East*, pp. 216–20. H. S. Nyberg, in JA, ccxix, no. 1, juillet–septembre 1931, pp. 5–19, and *Die Religionen des alten Iran*, pp. 343–74, is equally convinced that there is no trace of the true religion in the inscriptions of these three. A. Christensen, *Les Kayanides*, p. 34, agrees with this view. E. Benveniste, *The Persian Religion according to the chief Greek Texts*, pp. 22–49, argues that the religion described by Herodotus, i, 131–2, is 'Mazda-ism', not Zoroastrianism. Kittel and others reply that Herodotus describes the popular religion which Zoroaster opposed. Amid all these doubts there is a further general agreement that certain theological and cosmic beliefs put into mythical form, such as the cycle concerning Zurvan, existed before the official acceptance of the Zoroastrian faith, and were known to Cyrus.

150. There is therefore no justification for the assumption that Cyrus was generally considered to have become a worshipper of Marduk, and the elaborate theory that his behaviour after the

fall of Babylon disappointed the prophet of Isaiah xl–lv has no historical basis.

151. CAH, iii, p. 224: 'The old king Nabonidus was given Carmania to rule, or much more probably as a place of abode in a new land'. This is based on Abydenus apud Eusebium, see Schnabel, p. 274, art. 53: τὸν Δὲ Κῦρος, ἑλὼν Βαβυλῶνα, Καρμανίης ἡγεμονίη Δωρέεται; and Josephus, *Contra Apionem*, i. 21, see Schnabel, p. 275, no. 54: Τοῦ Δὲ Ναβοννήδου . . . χρησάμενος Κῦρος φιλανθρώπως καὶ Δοὺς οἰκητήριον αὐτῷ Καρμανίαν ἐξέπεμψεν ἐκ τῆς Βαβυλωνίας. Ναβόννηδος μὲν οὖν τὸ λοιπὸν τοῦ χρόνου Διαγενόμενος ἐν ἐκείνῃ τῇ χώρᾳ κατέστρεψε τὸν βίον. Since Eusebius differs from Josephus throughout, while deriving from a common source, there is a problem in criticism here, see BHT, p. 35. If there were Cyrus legends, then this is a legendary feature, with an intelligible purpose.

152. *Cyropaedia*, VII, v, 30.

ADDENDA

Page 116, note 19.

For chronological tables of this period see now R. A. Parker and W. H. Dubberstein, *Babylonian Chronology, 626 B.C.–A.D. 45* (Studies in Ancient Oriental Civilization, no. 24), Chicago, 1942.

Page 120, note 25.

E. M. Wright, *The Eighth Campaign of Sargon II of Assyria*, in *Journal of Near Eastern Studies*, ii, p. 178, note 26 locates *Parṣuaš* in the Solduz tract. The *Mannai* he places, following others, round Saqiz, and on his map he seems to identify *Messi* with *Mešta*, Tash Tepe. It is not easy to reconcile this view with the inscription at Karagundiz, and it is not proved correct by the rock inscription of Tash Tepe, *Corpus Inscriptionum Chaldicarum*, no. 15, quoted p. 179, note 31. The latter may only show that the land of the *Mannai* bordered on *Parsua* near *Mešta*. I have not been able to consult H. A. Rigg, *Sargon's Eighth Military Campaign*, in *Journal of the American Oriental Society*, lxii (1942), pp. 130–8.

Page 140, note 90.

For the occurrence of Babylonian *Puṭu*, Old Persian *Putaya*, in lists of lands subject to Darius and Xerxes, see now R. G. Kent's summary table in *Journal of Near Eastern Studies*, ii, p. 306.

(*continued on p.* 204)

LECTURE III

NOTES

Page 49.

1. There is no general agreement, however, as to all the passages. Oesterley and Robinson, p. 263, give xli, 2, 25; xliii, 3; xlv, 9–13. W. B. Stevenson, in WuW, gives xli, 1–5; xlii, 10–17; xlv, 13. Haller (2) calls xli, 1–15; xli, 21–8; xlv, 9–13; xlviii, 12–16 'indirect Cyrus-songs'. He would include 'in the widest sense' xlvi, 1–13; xlii, 5–9; xliii, 1–7. Caspari claims xli, 2–4a; xli, 25–9; xlii, 1–4; xlii, 5–9; xlv, 9–13; xlvi, 8–11; xlviii, 12–15. Volz seems to assign xli, 1–5; xli, 21–9; xliii, 14–15; xlvi, 11; xlviii, 14 to this class. Begrich allows the following to the period after the Lydian war, xli, 1–5; xli, 25–9; [xliv, 24–8; xlv, 1–7]; xlv, 9–13; xlvi, 5–11; xlviii, 12–15; probably liv, 14–17. Not all the passages thus adduced have been considered in the lecture, as their historical application has long been recognized; the object has rather been to deal only with those passages which require a new setting in their historical context.

2. This is comment by the prophet, not part of the speech of YHWH, which is continued in verse 2. This simple metaphor is not necessarily a repetition of xl, 31. If it is, it must be intentional, not a clumsy insertion by a redactor. The western provinces must take on a new strength, by revolt, before proceeding to dismiss their idols. Dittography could not produce such excellent sense; repetition could only be objectionable if the passages were originally combined.

3. In xlv, 8 'the right', צדק, is compared to rain that fructifies, 'righteousness', צדקה, to the crop that springs up. It will never be possible to distinguish more clearly. Caspari (3), pp. 159 ff., is too ambitious. The nuance of difference in any language between 'the right' and 'righteousness' is impalpable. Haller's suggestion, that 'victory' might be the correct translation, misses the point, the combination with משפט. Hempel (4), pp. 158 ff., tries to define and illustrate the development of meaning.

4. The point of this comparison is not easy to see. Figures in these chapters are often violent and depend on a single point in the similitude. The comparison between the sword and dust may be that dust forces men to close their eyes, the sword of Cyrus blinds his enemies. From stubble there fly small pieces as arrows fly from the bow. This is only a suggestion. Volz takes חרבו as subject and has to emend. The translation 'His sword

maketh (them) as dust, his bow as driven chaff' (Levy) assumes an impossible ellipsis. Emendation can produce so simple a text that the cause of corruption becomes inexplicable. The historical fact, to which the text alludes, is that there was no pitched battle during the march from the Halys to Sardis; the emendations חרבם or יתנם miss the allusion.

5. Gressmann, *Ursprung der israelitisch-jüdischen Eschatologie*, pp. 305–6, 'Mythisch ist es, wenn Cyrus mit seinen Füssen den Pfad nicht betritt'. A wrong deduction from a mistranslation. The verb is used in the military sense. The Persians were mounted, hence the rapidity of the march.

6. Here taken as the answer to the question.

7. A theme constantly repeated, xliv, 6; xlviii, 12; xliii, 10. Volz aptly compares Gatha 31, 8: 'I recognized, O Mazda, that you are the first and the last.' The idea must be older than Zoroaster. No argument can safely be based on the omission of the article, which is only used sporadically, not according to any perceptible system, in these chapters, see Köhler (2), p. 57, § 3.

8. These verses 6–7 are usually deleted and introduced into xl, 19–20, as referring to the manufacture of figures of gods. W. E. Barnes, *Isaiah XL–LXVI* (Churchman's Bible), 1903, p. 11, rightly saw that לדבק טוב must be translated, 'saying of the armour-joint: it is good'; he comments, p. 12: 'The founder casts small plates of metal to be joined together into pieces of defensive armour. The smith receives the plates from the founder, pronounces them good, and proceeds to rivet them firmly, so that no stroke should stir them, on a leathern jerkin to form a suit of armour.' This explanation is unquestionably right, as against the view that these words have to do with idol-making, which leads to excision or transference and violent alteration, as by Volz. There is no reason to distinguish between the use of דבק here and in 1 Kings xxii, 34 (2 Chronicles xviii, 33) where a man drew a bow at a venture

וַיַּכֶּה אֶת־מֶלֶךְ יִשְׂרָאֵל בֵּין הַדְּבָקִים וּבֵין הַשִּׁרְיָן

Though the reference to 'splint armour' is certain, the distinction between דבקים and שרין is not clear. Oriental armour of this kind had a long history, recently illuminated by Bengt Thordeman, *The Asiatic Splint Armour in Europe*, in *Acta Archaeologica*, iv, pp. 117–50 (København, 1933). Little can be inferred from the illustrations on Assyrian reliefs, and the recent discovery of some scales at Ugarit (Ras Shamra), see Schaeffer, *Ugaritica I*, pp. 25–7, at Boğazköy, see K. Bittel in *Mitteilungen der orientalischen Gesellschaft*, no. 76, p. 20, fig. 8, *e*, *f*, and at Alalakh ('Atshanah), has not thrown any new light on the matter beyond proving the existence of this kind of armour in Syria in the 15th century B.C. But at Nuzu (Yalghan Tepe) considerable numbers of plates, and coherent sections of suits have been found; there is useful information in the tablets, see R. S. Starr, *Nuzi*, i, pp. 476–80, for an instructive discussion, and pp. 540–1, for E. R. Lacheman's summary of the evidence from the tablets. The whole suit appears to be called *zariam*, which became in Assyrian *siriamu*; this must be connected with Hebrew סִרְיֹן, which is not more than a variant form of שִׁרְיוֹן; the variant spellings in both languages point to the word being foreign. Perhaps in 1 Kings xxii, 34 שִׁרְיָן means only the inner layer of plates, not the whole suit, while the דבקים form the outer layer. Mr. Starr seems to have proved that there were two different systems of lacing, and the number of plates specified in the tablets for a suit show that the lacing of double rows of plates was common. For a representation of the other system, single rows on leather, see W. Wolf, *Bewaffnung des altägyptischen Heeres*, p. 98, Abb. 70. Perhaps the smith's remark means that the plate will fit another, back to back. The mention of nails is disturbing, for none have been found yet with this armour, but use of pins would be intelligible.

The words לא ימוט are specially applicable to scales, see Job xli, 15. If it is true, as some commentators hold, that the words are intrusive in either xl, 20 or in xli, 7, then they are likely to be original in this place; the contrary assumption is due to wrong interpretation. But the assumption of dittography is unnecessary when the words give perfect sense, see note 50. As Caspari (3), p. 114, saw, there is a reference to usages of war in verse 6, 'Leise Fühlung mit Kriegsbräuchen verrät xli, 6, vgl. II Samuel, x, 12; I Samuel, xxiii, 16; Jos. i, 6–7, 9, 18', and the reference in verse 7 is clear. Duhm's objection to the translation of פעם 'anvil' is due to misunderstanding and disappears when the passage is rightly understood. Critics generally treat verse 7 as prose. Kittel prints as verse. The difference may only prove that it is difficult to distinguish the two; no argument against authenticity should be based on the assumed prose form.

Page 50.

9. Begrich (2), p. 67.

Page 51.

10. There has been some strained interpretation of 'from the north . . . from the east'. Barnes, *Isaiah, XL–LXVI*, p. 19, speaks 'of the empire on the north and east'. Skinner, p. 26, says: 'The terms are poetic; the north is the region of mystery and the east the region of light. In point of fact Cyrus came from the north-east'—a mis-statement of fact. Volz refuses to see anything strange in the expressions. The real point may be the indication of a point in time, when Cyrus was at Sardis. Torrey, referring the words to Abraham's journeys, speaks of 'Israel called in the person of Abraham', a desperate expedient to avoid a plain allusion.

11. Torrey takes this as circumstantial, 'he came . . . calling on my name', which is not likely, for the wording points to consecutive action. Most commentators take יקרא בשמי to mean 'he will call upon My name', see Lecture I, note 116. Thus Skinner, 'The clause can hardly mean less than that Cyrus shall acknowledge Jehovah as God. . . . There is no difficulty in the idea that Cyrus, who was at first the unconscious instrument of Jehovah's purpose, shall at length recognize that Jehovah was the true author of his success.' Volz says: 'Dtjes. religiöse Kühnheit tritt hell zutage in der Behauptung, dass Cyrus den Namen Jahwes anrufe. Man darf aber aus diesem Satze schwerlich folgern, Cyrus habe seine Siege bewusst auf Jahwe zurückgeführt, oder Cyrus sei tatsächlich Jahwebekenner und Monotheist gewesen. Vielmehr sind solche Ausdrücke mit Mal. i, 1, oder dem Gedankengange von Jes. x, 12–15 zusammenzustellen und so zu erklären: für Dtjes. ist Cyrus nicht bloss objektiv und passiv religiös, nämlich als Werkzeug Jahwes, sondern er ist auch subjektiv und aktiv eine religiöse Persönlichkeit; weil es aber für Dtjes. nur die eine Gottheit gibt, verknüpft sich ihm alle auch fremde Religiosität mit Jahwe. Dtjes. würde z. B. auch die Frömmigkeit jenes Nebo-wortes an Asarhaddon: *ich, ich rede das Künftige wie das Vergangene*, anerkennen, er würde nur an Nebos Stelle Jahwe setzen.' Such an explanation should show there is something wrong with the interpretation. Duhm avoided the dilemma by textual emendation, אקרא בשמו. But קרא ב in these chapters does not mean 'call upon'. In xl, 26, of the stars, לכלם בשם יקרא, 'He calls them all by name', that is, uses a name for each; the ancient belief that name and existence are one is implicit. Similarly xlv, 4, ואקרא לך בשמך clearly does not mean 'I call upon your name to you', but 'I call you by your name', use your

name in calling you. Therefore xli, 25 means 'he will call or summon in My name', will use My name in calling some person or persons understood. All ambiguity disappears if יקרא · · · ויבא are taken together; it is then obvious that the persons understood are the governors, and the first clause must be mentally completed לסגנים.

12. Practically all commentators, following a hint in the Targum, emend to וְיָבָס or וַיְבֹס to avoid the grammatical difficulty, since בוא 'to attack' demands על. But the present usage might conceivably arise from such phraseology as 1 Samuel, xviii, 13, 16, where וַיֵּצֵא וַיָּבֹא לִפְנֵי הָעָם implies marching and fighting at the head of the levy. It is surely beyond our knowledge to say that any phrase like this is impossible in a living language. The emendation is objectionable because it anticipates ירמס טיט in the figure, and thus weakens the force of the simile, which has in fact suggested the emendation.

13. The figure of the potter is much used by this writer. Thus he turns to the potter's craft to enforce the same lesson as that for which the older Isaiah chose the metaphor of weapons, x, 15; xlv, 9, 'Woe to the clay that striveth with its modeller, the potsherd with those that trim the earthenware (חַרְשֵׂי אֲדָמָה: see Robertson in *Journal of Near Eastern Studies*, ii, 38). Shall the clay say to its modeller, "What are you doing, that your work has no handles?"' ופעלך אין־ידים לו. The reference is due to the sporadic use of handles in Near Eastern lands at all times, see *Alalakh and Chronology*, p. 8, note 24. Similarly the claim that YHWH has moulded the 'servant' or Israel 'from the mother's womb' is based on the figure of the potter, and it occurs in the address to Cyrus. This is language understood in every ancient pagan country of the Near East, but most familiar to us from representations of the Egyptian god Khnum in the reliefs of Hatshepsut. But in xli, 25 Cyrus is himself the potter, remodelling the western lands to what they should be, as an agent of God; this is an example of the change in application of a phrase, or figure, see note 34 a.

Page 53.

14. xli, 4.

15. xliv, 7–9.

16. xlv, 2–6.

17. The formula is *amat šarri ana NN*, cf. E. Ebeling, *Neubabylonische Briefe aus Uruk*, p. 2, nos. 2 ff.

18. See note 7. Sellin (5), p. 149, proposed אָמְרִי for רִאשׁוֹן; this is accepted by Elliger, and by Caspari (3), p. 213, note 2: 'Schon v. 26 ist jedoch am Ende unverständlich wenn man nicht *imri* oder *amarai* liest'; the reasoning is not easy to follow, for 'your words' in verse 26 forms no contrast to verse 27. Some scholars think that the question מִי הִגִּיד in verse 26 demands the restoration רִאשׁוֹן לְצִיּוֹן הִגַּדְתִּי but the negative clauses of verse 26 are a sufficient answer. Mowinckel (3), p. 94, followed Gressmann, *Ursprung der israelitisch-jüdischen Eschatologie*, p. 310, by comparing the Akkadian *mahru*, in the Creation Epic, Tablet VII, lines 126–7.

> *liṣṣabtuma mahru likallim*
> *enqu mudu mithariš limtalku*

where he considers *mahru* means 'prophet'. But *mahru* is not *mahhu*, and in conjunction with line 138

> *taklimti mahru idbubu panuššu*

mahru in line 126 must mean 'first among the wise and initiated', either in time or rank, as Langdon, *Epic of Creation*, notes. There is no parallel between this passage and xli, 27 owing to the absence of anything to correspond to *enqu* and *mudu*; רִאשׁוֹן is indispensable, but it may be desirable to insert אמר before it.

19. הִנֵּה הֵם. It is difficult to see the point of הִנֵּה: it must not be treated as the first member of a rhetorical repetition such as is frequent in these chapters, for there would be no reason to omit the suffix in that case. The proposed emendation, הִנֵּהוּ for הִנֵּה is only acceptable because the suffix might easily be neglected when the true reference of xlii, 1–4 was no longer understood, and a new interpretation was accepted before the second century B.C.

Page 54.

20. For *amur* used thus see E. Ebeling, *op. laud.*, no. 15, line 9; no. 17, lines 3, 17, 19, 23; no. 31, line 16; no. 36, lines 8, 20; no. 39, lines 5, 12; no. 40, line 15; no. 41, line 12. This use of *amur* goes back to the 15th century, see the Amarna letters in Knudtzon's edition, no. 8, line 41 (to be taken with what follows); no. 105, lines 7, 17, *et freq.* It is similarly used in the Hittite treaties, see E. F. Weidner, *Politische Dokumente aus Kleinasien*, p. 114, lines 11, 18, 19.

21. תמך is to be distinguished from חזק in xlv, 1. Sellin (7), p. 187, rightly claims that the meaning is settled by xli, 10, where

YHWH says to Israel, 'I will support thee by My righteous right hand'. Elliger, p. 92, supposed that this phrase, in xlii, 1, meant that the 'servant' was in need of some help, as Israel in xli, 10, is. Begrich (2), p. 161, rightly rejects this.

22. יוֹצִיא. Sellin (7) translates 'er soll kundtun', Volz, 'Recht hinaustragen'. But there is no reference to missionary activities, as the latter assumes.

23. לֶאֱמֶת. Sellin (7), p. 188, translates 'wirklich, ganz gewiss'. Begrich (2), p. 163, rightly rejects this, but decides on 'das Urteil als Wahrheit bekanntmachen'. There is no doubt that the AV is right, 'unto', that is 'according to' truth, see Brown–Driver–Briggs, p. 516a, (i) b.

24. tōrā^h. There are recent discussions of the meaning in Elliger and Begrich. The term can never be exactly defined, and the precise nuance of meaning does not affect the present purpose. But it is important to note that this tōrā^h can only be imposed by a man of courage and resolution; the emendation יָרוּץ., which is ancient, does not affect this point.

Page 55.

25. For a useful discussion of the meaning see Hertzberg, *Die Entwicklung des Begriffes* מִשְׁפָּט *im AT*, in ZATW, xli (1923), pp. 16–76, especially pp. 34, 39–42.

26. Begrich (2), pp. 136, 163–4, who extends this symbolism also to the verbs of verse 2.

27. See San Nicolo, *Die Schlussklauseln der altbabylonischen Kauf- und Tauschverträge*, pp. 24–5, note 44; R. Clay, *The Tenure of Land in Babylonia and Assyria* (University of London, Institute of Archaeology, Occasional Paper no. 1), 1938, pp. 13–14.

28. See the passage in the prayer to Ishtar published by L. W. King, *Seven Tablets of Creation*, ii, plates LXXV ff., translated in i, pp. 222 ff., lines 87–8:

> eṭū šurū   limmer kinuni
> biliti linnapih dipari

'It is dark, it is black; let my charcoal-stove lighten: let my torch, that was out, flame up again.'

Thureau-Dangin, RA, x, pp. 93–7, and *Archiv Orientalní*, i, pp. 271–2, has explained Sumerian, IBILA, 'heir', as a compound word, IA or I, 'oil', and BIL, BI.LA, 'to burn', and refers it to a worship of ancestors; only free men have ancestors. Koschaker brings this derivation into connexion with the expressions *ša kinunšu bilu*, 'whose charcoal-stove is extinguished', in Ungnad, *Babylonische Briefe*, no. 229, and *ša kinunim bilim*, in Koschaker und Ungnad, *Hammurabi's Gesetz*, no. 1741. I think it more probable that these expressions mean that the families have lost their civil rights, than that there were no heirs to the property.

Page 56.

29. Begrich (2), pp. 163–4.

30. So Sellin (7), p. 188, assuming that the passage means that the 'servant', whom he identifies with the prophet, is no longer allowed to preach in public.

31. W. E. Barnes, pp. 35–6.

32. Marcus says that [קול] נשׂא in 78 per cent. of occurrences means 'to raise the voice in distress', צעק in 97 per cent., 'to cry for help in need'. The reasoning should be extended to the Hiph'il of שׁמע, regularly used of proclaiming publicly. Marcus translates, 'A crushed reed he may be but he shall not break . . .'; this is strained and due to his identification of the 'servant' as the reed.

Page 58.

33. H. S. Nyberg, *Cosmogonie et Cosmologie Mazdéennes* in JA, ccxix, juillet–septembre, 1931, p. 16, note 1.

Page 59.

34. So Gressmann (3), pp. 293–4.

Page 61.

34 a. A good example of such different senses may be found in the use of תהו in xli, 29 and xlix, 4. In the first instance רוח ותהו exactly describe the composition of a hollow-cast figure made of a cheap alloy; in the second, תהו והבל, the phrase is a figure. The argument that there is a constant change of *nuance* in the use of words in these chapters was employed by Caspari to prove plurality of authorship. Such change is due rather to multiplicity of occasions. The opposite extreme, the effort to tie a phrase or word down to a single meaning, is a striving after consistency such as ancient authors, especially speakers, never attempted.

Page 62.

35. Cheyne in *Encyclopaedia Biblica*, iv, col. 4344, characteristically avoided the identification with Petra by taking the word as collective. There is no really sound reason for denying that Sela' may be Petra. It is, of course, impossible to prove it,

because, unfortunately, though the wording might be understood to imply that Sela' was in Qedar, it is ambiguous. Qedar was one of the *ḥāṣōr*-kingdoms attacked by Nebuchadrezzar II, presumably before his war with Amasis, Jeremiah, xlix, 28, and the *ḥāṣor*-kingdoms may possibly be the lands where semi-nomads with sheep and goats build just such camps, *ḥaṣērīm*, ἐπαύλεις, as armies use, see Musil, *Arabia Deserta*, 490, 495. H. M. Oblinsky in *Journal of the American Oriental Society*, lix (1939), p. 22, points out that the present passage does not prove that חָצֵר and עִיר are interchangeable in II Kings, xx, 4; it may be added that the supposed parallelism here, in xlii, 11, may rather be an opposition. In that case, the first double-verse may distinguish three parts of Qedar, the *miḏbār*, the cities, and the camps; that would suit very well the known location of Qedar, Lecture II, p. 37, and what is known of the geographical sense of *miḏbār*, Lecture III, p. 65, but the looseness in the appositions of xlii, 11 prevents any certainty. In any case, there may have been a 'city' or 'settlement' at Petra, though no trace of early occupation has yet been found there, or is likely to be; not many sites in that area are fit for habitation, and Petra would not be left vacant. Levy, translating 'cliff', thinks of the 'cliffs', '*Iraq*, or alternatively of the Zagros; the immediate sense is thus lost, and Qedar is referred to any Badawin. Yet when uttered, Qedar can only have meant the tribe of that name, and Sela' must be some specific place.

Page 64.

36. Gressmann, *Eschatologie*, pp. 216–17, claims that Israelite eschatology is characterized by the abundance of its different schemes, an observation which arises directly from his interpretation of xlii, 15–16 and xliii, 19–20; but that interpretation does not fulfil Gressmann's own precept, p. 219, 'We have no right to an allegorical explanation; we must take the words as they stand.'

There is one passage which unquestionably is a forerunner of one specific feature of the concrete description of the heavenly Jerusalem, namely, liv, 11–12. It seems possible that this is the earliest description of floor mosaics, previously unknown in Palestine. The inlay of black and white stones in geometrical patterns on floors and walls seems to have arisen in Urarṭu, see Lehmann-Haupt, *Armenien Einst und Jetzt*, ii, 2. Hälfte, pp. 551 ff.; it was doubtless a substitute for painted decoration, just as painted decoration replaced the mosaics of the early Sumerian period.

The mosaic floors of an Achaemenean palace are mentioned in Esther, i, 6; for such floors at Pasargadae see Wachtsmuth in A. U. Pope and Phyllis Ackerman, *A Survey of Persian Art*, i, p. 310, at Susa see de Mecquenem, *ibid.*, p. 326. The prophet of these chapters, a man of exceptional information about Persia as well as Babylonia, may have seen or heard of mosaic floors, and therefore mentioned them as a glory of Jerusalem restored. But it is most improbable that this was a fixed feature of an eschatological picture of the new Jerusalem before 550, and that it appears in liv, 11–12, because it was well known in that relation. Yet it is this assumption that Begrich's argument requires. The truth is, then, most probably, that this feature in the late eschatological picture was borrowed from the prophet.

37. For the distinction of 'My messengers' from the prophet, 'My servant', see xliv, 26, which most editors emend. An elaborate interpretation, favoured by some modern critics, finds in xl, 1–8 a vision, assumes the presence of 'angels', and depicts the prophet as overhearing the orders of God.

38. The meaning of נַחֲמוּ is not adequately rendered by 'comfort' here, if Caspari (3), p. 72, is right in saying: '"To comfort" is in other cases an action of those friends who cannot really help. Now God will be a comforter. His comfort is a declaration of preparedness for active help, li, 12. The root of the divine address, xl, 1, may therefore be assumed to be in the usual invitations to participation in mourning ceremonies, yet the formula in xl, 1 shows that it is already free of association with such arrangements.' But נַחֲמוּ has no such 'root', and though it generally means ' to console', the use of the Hithpa‘el in Ezekiel, v, 13 and Genesis, xxvii, 42 shows that נַחֲמוּ in combination with דַּבְּרוּ עַל לֵב must be something like 'to put in good heart'. In li, 12 this nuance of the Pi‘el is indicated quite clearly, 'I, I am he that encourages you, מְנַחֶמְכֶם: who are you, that you fear a mortal man, or sons of men that will be made as grass?'

39. The translation is not certain. Ordinarily צָבָא is masculine; the verb is feminine. Volz takes Jerusalem as the subject, צָבָא as the object. The difficulty about this rendering is that formal parallelism is lost, so that Cheyne and others assume that צָבָא is feminine here. The variations in translation are not inconsiderable. LXX has ἡ ταπείνωσις αὐτῆς. For an elaborate explanation see Ziegler, p. 123. The matter may be more simple. ταπείνωσις is used, e.g. by Diodorus, as parallel to δουλεία, and may well have been a common term for forced military service which was

in fact most often *corvée*. The Vulgate *malitia* is a literal translation of the LXX.

40. The punishment is Israel's sacrifice to God, cf. Leviticus i, 4; xxii, 25.

Page 65.

41. This clause is nearly always interpreted as causal. LXX could be so interpreted, but need not be. The Hebrew is against this. The three כי-clauses, when delivered aloud, must inevitably be taken as parallel. Caspari (3), p. 77, says: 'He (the prophet) gives them (his fellow believers) three themes to illustrate God's comfort; all three may be derived from legal conceptions— liberation, amnesty, compensation; all are of immediate concern for the hearers and prepare them for tasks. *ki* in xl, 2 is, there- fore, incorrectly treated as causal. Itkonen, p. 8, obtains the meaning 'because' only by excising the *verbum dicendi*, cf. Köhler, p. 73. The two first themes belong together in content without being identical. One Hebrew MS. omits the third *ki*; several Greek the second. Praetorius too considers the second theme a gloss on the first—arbitrarily.' This is clearly right. Contrast Köhler's views, Lecture I, note 79.

42. The wording implies that the three clauses are not put into YHWH's mouth. There is indeed no reason why they should be, though Köhler and others correct to 'from My hand'. Cas- pari (3), p. 76, has seized this point, and makes everything from דברו an utterance of the prophet, rightly.

43. Köhler (2), p. 142, says: 'Finally there remains still another characteristic of the Second Isaiah's style to be men- tioned; occasionally he exaggerates his utterances and makes them grotesque. Israel has received from Jahve double punish- ment for his sins. This sentence, a monstrosity for a theologian or Puritan, is very intelligible humanly.' Such a statement would be impious, however intelligible. Similarly Torrey speaks of 'rhetorical exaggeration'. This is due to a misunderstanding of the sense of מיד יהוה, for which see xlvii, 6 וְאֶתְּנֵם בְּיָדֵךְ. Babylon was the agent, the 'hand', of YHWH, as Assyria was His rod. In xli, 10, the 'righteous right hand' is Cyrus.

44. The English 'shall' forms in RV might be taken as strong affirmation, but are really hortative; this sense cannot be avoided in the context. Volz translates as futures, because he interprets the verse as an eschatological picture; Köhler, better, 'soll'.

44a. On the correct translation see Snaith.

45. Almost a characteristic word in the book of Isaiah, see vii, 3, מְסִלַּת שְׂדֵה כוֹבֵס; xi, 16, 'there shall be a highway for the remnant of his people, which shall be left, from Assyria'; xix, 23, 'In that day shall there be a highway out of Egypt to Assyria'; xxxiii, 8, 'the highways lie waste'; xlix, 11, 'And I will make all My mountains a way and My highways shall be raised'; lix, 7, 'wasting and destruction are in their highways'; lxii, 10, 'pile up, pile up the highway'. The earliest passage, vii, 3, is a reference to the practice of making raised paths in the 'fuller's field' and does not affect the question. In xi, 16, xix, 23, xxxiii, 8 the allusion is to the natural main routes followed by Assyrian armies for centuries. The passages lix, 7 and more especially lxii, 10 are imitations of the phraseology of xl, as is xxxv, 8, maslūl. Actually then mᵉsillāʰ is first applied to an artificially raised road along a depression in these chapters.

46. The earliest use of ʿarābāʰ designates (a) the arid steppe west of the Dead Sea in southern Judah, and also, Amos, vi, 14, east of that sea; (b) the Jordan valley, either west or east of the river. Later it also came to be used of the *Wadi ʿArabāʰ*, from the Dead Sea to the Gulf of ʿAqaba. Brown–Driver–Briggs make a special entry for Isaiah xl, 3 and xli, 19, 'apparently the North Arabian desert', but there is no justification for this, other than a mistaken exegesis. It is more likely that the *Wadi ʿArabāʰ* is meant in both passages than the Jordan valley, because the *miḏbār* must be contiguous. xli, 19 is particularly instructive in showing the occasional fertility of both *miḏbār* and *ʿarābāʰ*; neither, therefore, can be located in the desert between Palestine and Euphrates south of Palmyrene. The strange idea that the festival road of Marduk in Babylon suggested the figure of a highway across the Syrian desert is a modern fancy first advanced, apparently, by Gressmann, *Eschatologie*, p. 223.

Page 66.

46 a. This translation, to which there are also objections, is chosen in preference to 'for ever', because that can imply a reference to an eternal future, and to apocalyptic conceptions, not necessarily intended in the Hebrew. The Septuagint translation, εἰς τὸν αἰῶνα, once the astrological accretions of the Hellenistic age were associated with αἰών, has led to the association of late ideas with this passage, and some talk of 'Urzeit und Endzeit', which is not in place. There are some wise remarks on עוֹלָם and αἰών by Professor Cadoux in *The Expository Times*, vol. xlii, no. 10, p. 380.

46b. On the sense of חסד see Snaith.

47. This interpretation is made almost certain by li, 12, which must refer back to this passage: 'I, I am he that encourages you; who are you, that you should fear a mortal, or sons of men that will be made grass?' where 'sons of men' can only mean the Babylonians, who are no more than mortals.

48. For an eccentric interpretation, see Caspari (3), pp. 96–8; 'If these various possibilities are considered, Isaiah xl, 9 must be addressed to real women, on the march, who are exhorted to go up a mountain that has to be passed on the way, though the ascent is difficult for them. (While mounting the hill they are also to cry aloud to people far off.)' Volz, p. 6, considers the question of objective and subjective genitive, rightly deciding that Jerusalem is to announce. Torrey, pp. 306–7, has an amusing and just criticism of Duhm.

Page 67.

49. See Begrich (2), p. 53, as against Volz, on the basis of Ezekiel xxix, 18–20.

50. The technique of making divine figures is dealt with in xl, 18–20; xliv, 9–20; xlvi, 5–8. xli, 6–7 is often, wrongly, classed with these. The three passages differ from the mention of idol-worship in xli, 29; xlii, 17; xlv, 20; xlvi, 1–2, in that they mention details of technique; but to say, as Elliger, p. 226, does, that the content of the two sets of passages is opposed, in that the purpose of the first set is to make the manufacture of gods ridiculous, while the other references do not go into the folly of such idolatry, goes beyond the facts, for xli, 29 אָוֶן רוּחַ וָתֹהוּ · · · very clearly has this intention. As to Elliger's other contention, that the language does not belong to either his 'Deutero-Isaiah' or his 'Trito-Isaiah', the answer must be that no man can use ordinary language in technical matters, nor technical language in ordinary matters; the application of the percentage method to these passages is a *reductio ad absurdum*. The positive argument for believing that the three passages were written about 555–540 must rest on historical grounds. There were two periods after the fall of Jerusalem, before the Roman conquest, when pagan religion constituted a serious menace for Jewry. One was during the Seleucid period, and culminated in the Maccabaean revolt. The other was towards the end of the exile, when some Jews had lost their faith. The open denunciation of the worship of images was only possible owing to the Persian attitude to religion; it was

necessary because Babylonian magic found widespread acceptance. The three passages cannot possibly be so late as the
Maccabaean period. There would be no compelling need to
speak or write against idolatry in Palestinian Jewry during the
5th or 4th centuries. There is, then, *a priori* reason for dating
these passages in the 6th century, and no sound reason against
believing that they belong in their present contexts.

The passage in xl, 19–20 is, however, frequently condemned as
corrupt. There is a difficulty in the wording of verse 19, though
the meaning is clear. On a metal figure, פֶּסֶל, cast by the
'artificer', חָרָשׁ, the gold- and silver-smith, צָרַף, proceeds to
hammer a gold overlay, בַּזָּהָב יְרַקְּעֶנּוּ, 'smelting bonds of silver',
that is pouring molten silver alloy into sockets to hold the
figure upright, רְתֻקוֹת כֶּסֶף צוֹרֵף. The repetition צָרַף and צוֹרֵף
in parallel clauses with different meanings is unquestionably
clumsy, and the syntax of the participle unusual, to say the least.
But whether clumsiness and unusual syntax justify the violent
emendations proposed, it is permissible to doubt. Elliger himself
admits, p. 245, that the elimination of repetitions is not a sound
method. The use of silver as solder must have been unusual;
I can quote no examples. Perhaps silver is here confused with
lead.

There is a different, and simpler, problem in verse 20. The
essential difficulty lies in the first two words, הַמְסֻכָּן תְּרוּמָה. If
they be omitted, as LXX omits them, the verse is intelligible,
with a single alteration in the order of words. The 'wise artificer',
a workman superior to the 'artificer' of 19, selects a piece of
wood that will not rot, and seeks to fix to it a cast figure, פֶּסֶל,
in such a way that the figure will not tumble. It is, then, a
question of a different kind of base from that in verse 19, where
the silver solder points to a metal base. This interpretation
requires the transference of לוֹ from its present position after
יְבַקֶּשׁ to a position after לְהָכִין; once the passage was misunderstood, the transposition might seem natural, even necessary.
Presumably the LXX took לוֹ to mean 'to it', for σοφῶς ζητήσει
πῶς στήσει αὐτοῦ εἰκόνα shows that the imperishable wood was to
be used for a basis, and αὐτοῦ must render לוֹ.

Now הַמְסֻכָּן 'AMSUCHAN', Jerome says, was a kind of wood;
he therefore took the word as grammatically in apposition to
עֵץ לֹא יִרְקַב. He obviously knew a tradition which connected
הַמְסֻכָּן with *musukkanu* of the Assyrians, Sumerian GIŠ.MIS.

MA.KAN.NA, 'wood of the land Magan', which Dr. Campbell Thompson, *The Assyrian Herbal*, p. 181, identified as mulberry. In the inscription of Darius concerning the building of Susa published by Père Scheil in *Mémoires de la Mission Archéologique de Perse*, tome xxi, *Inscriptions des Achéménides à Suse*, it is stated that MIS.MA.KAN.NA came from Gandara and a land which Herzfeld, AMI, iii, p. 36, almost certainly rightly, restores as [K]irman. This is decisive in favour of mulberry, for Arab geographers specially mention the mulberry trees, توت, of the Kirman plateau, see G. Le Strange, *Lands of the Eastern Caliphate*, p. 308, and the references there. The Assyrians used this wood for making doors, and frequently demanded it as tribute; if it was tribute, it is likely also to have been required as an 'offering', תְּרוּמָה, for pagan temples. Wood thus dedicated would be suitable for bases of divine figures, though perhaps not for the figures themselves, since according to xliv, 13–16 cedar, cypress, and oak were the hard woods used for this purpose; Jerome's statement, *genus ligni . . . quo vel maxima idola fiunt*, must be an exaggeration. If then verse 20 be translated 'The wise artificer chooses mulberry of the offering, a wood that will not rot; he seeks to secure to it the cast figure, so that it will not tumble', there is no need to assume far-reaching corruption. This rendering is, of course, subject to the sweeping, but baseless, condemnation by Torrey of 'the fantastic Jewish exegesis of the (corrupt) passage adopted by Jerome . . . (which) does not deserve any serious attention'. The explanation of המסכן was first suggested by H. Zimmern, in ZA, ix (1894), pp. 111–12, but he identified the wood wrongly as palm, treated ה as the article, and regarded תרומה as an insertion. There is no reason why the Hebrew form should correspond exactly to the Akkadian, and if the construction is construct with genitive of identity, there is no difficulty. Sa'adya thought the wood was holm-oak, see Levy, *ad loc.*

Those who alter הַמְסֻכָּן to הַמְּסֻכָּן have either to emend and excise, as Volz does, or abandon as corrupt, for המסכן תרומה cannot then be explained. They also lose the parallelism of verses 19 and 20, which describe two different ways of making cast figures stand, and impose on the text an improbable idea, that wooden figures, made by a 'cunning craftsman', were cheaper than metal and could be purchased by the poor in Babylonia. Good wooden statuettes were probably more expensive than bronze, and there is no archaeological evidence that wood was commonly used for carving in Babylonia or Palestine.

The case for regarding these verses as intrusive and hopelessly corrupt is not well based. The sense is, 'How can God be compared with gods whose images can only be made to stand up by some special device of a craftsman?'.

51. For a description of this statue see the verse account, i, 19–32. This is an indignant report of the form the statue took, rather than of the technique. The emphasis, however, shows that this particular statue was, at the time, of peculiar importance, and a memory of it may perhaps be found in Daniel iii, 1. Baumgartner's objection, in ZATW (NF), iii (1926), p. 47, that the making of new statues was fairly common, misses the point. Even though many figures of gods were made every day, the exceptional and historical importance of the figure described in the verse account puts it in a different class from others, and the same is true of the statue in Daniel iii. If the attention to the technique in cc. xl–lv is not due to this particular case, then it may arise from the extensive use of hollow-casting for making large figures in the 6th century, as opposed to the earlier practice for small figures, the *cire-perdue* process. Sennacherib initiated the new procedure, see L. W. King, *Cuneiform Texts*, Part 26, p. 25, col. vi, 80–col. vii, 8.

Page 68.

52. For the emphasis on the stars see p. 58, and note 33.

53. נְעָרִים, see Genesis xiv, 24; 1 Samuel xxv, 5 ff.; 2 Samuel ii, 14 ff.; 1 Kings xx, 14 ff.; 2 Kings xix, 6.

54. בַּחוּרִים 2 Kings viii, 12; 2 Chronicles xxxvi, 17; Isaiah ix, 17, xxxi, 8.

55. Torrey, rightly insisting that the sense given by AV must be correct, takes אֵבֶר as adverbial accusative, but translates 'on pinions', which is instrumental; if the adverbial accusative is possible, then manner is indicated, and a natural figure results. Volz says: 'Die genaue Übersetzung ist nicht: sie treiben Schwingen, wie Adler Schwingen treiben; sondern, sie treiben "Adlerschwingen": כ entspricht unseren Anführungszeichen.' This is forcing the syntax; but in either case the phrase is an unusual construction.

56. The emendation רִמַּת, 'worm', for מתי, to secure absolute parallelism, is pedagogic; the word in the text is contemptuous.

57. מוֹרַג. For the construction and operation of the threshing sled see G. Dalman, *Arbeit und Sitte in Palästina*, iii, pp. 85 ff.; it is rare in Palestine, and is called *nawrag* in Egypt. It was

apparently used in the Near East as early as the 14th century, see RA, xxii (1925), p. 67, note xix. But these sleds do not thresh stone, and Levy is not justified in saying that the mountains stand for enemies. What the sled does to corn, the men of Israel must do to the mountains.

Page 69.

58. e.g. xlv, 9 ff.; xlvi, 12; xlviii, 1–11; l, 1–3.

59. The MSS. are divided, most favouring לֹא, but there is also good evidence for לוֹ. Many scholars consider that the text is in disorder, and remodel the passage by transferring clauses. Yet, whichever reading is correct, the sense of the passage as it stands is clear. The new oracle, given in verse 6, means that the prophet will succeed in the purpose here specified, where previously he failed, and will achieve yet more. If any emendation is required, the easiest is that suggested by Professor Robertson in *Journal of Near Eastern Studies*, ii, 38, לוֹ לְאֵסֹף, 'to gather to him'.

Page 70.

60. לְהָקִים אֶת־שִׁבְטֵי יַעֲקֹב, cf. Ruth iv, 5, 10 for הקים, in a different context, of re-establishing a person's lost rights. That the specific reference is to re-establishing national organization of the land according to the old tribal divisions, obliterated by the foreign régime, seems a natural deduction from the wording; it is put beyond doubt by the echo in xlix, 8, 'I give you for a covenant of the people, to establish the land and to allot wasted inheritances.' This aspiration for the restoration of rights to land on the model of the old native administration, which Nebuchadrezzar had swept away when he introduced new settlers, is of a kind constantly found among conquered peoples. It was not, of course, realized, and could not be, owing to practical difficulties; see Nehemiah, v, 1–13, for the complaints of those who returned, and of those who had come into possession of land during the exile, when a resettlement, though not one on the old lines, was actually effected.

61. Not because he was in any way to supplant the Persian, but because, for the fulfilment of YHWH's plan through Cyrus, a Jewish leader must appear, who would support in action the revolt of the western provinces, and so reveal Israel's true position in the new dispensation. This view is diametrically opposed to the position of Haller and Hempel. The prophet uses the same epithets for Cyrus and himself, not because he is to take

the place of Cyrus, not because he has lost faith in him and the
message previously proclaimed, but because his own activities
and those of Cyrus become indistinguishable.

62. לִמּוּדִים. The double occurrence of the word has been
regarded as suspicious, but is not objectionable, precisely because the meaning of this passage depends on the emphasis on
this idea. The meaning is now often rendered 'pupil', 'disciple',
but this is not the true use. Volz says: '*limmud* heisst der
Geschulte, aber nicht im Sinn des Fertigen, jedenfalls hier nicht,
vgl. 4*b*β, sondern des in der Schule stehenden, durch die Schule
Geübten'. He proceeds to say of the prophet, he is 'ein Jünger
Gottes, ein Immerlernender'. The word cannot be twisted thus.
The prophet has been enabled to speak and to understand spoken
words as one 'instructed' would; instructed men do not use
ordinary speech, but have a language intelligible to themselves.
This is true whether the 'instructed' are skilled craftsmen, priests,
or, as in the present case, conspirators. Such seems a plain interpretation of the words, without violation to the sense of *limmūdim*.
Torrey distinguishes between the two occurrences; for the first
he compares Ben Sira li, 28 and translates 'teaching, instruction',
the second 'like pupils'.

63. לדעת לעות את־יעף דבר. LXX paraphrased, . . . γλῶσ-
σαν τοῦ γνῶναι ἡνίκα Δεῖ εἰπεῖν λόγον; לעות is interpreted as ' to
utter at an appropriate time', and את־יעף omitted. Hempel in
his special glossary translated עות 'unterstützen'. Praetorius (3)
took the infinitive לְעֻוֹּת passively, and translated את 'with'.
Caspari (3), p. 36, says that *lā'ūṯ* defies explanation, and that
lāda'aṯ must be excised as a doublet. Torrey also speaks of an
'obvious doublet, shown to be such by the meter', and proceeds
to follow the methods he parodies so well, (1), pp. 180–2, by
excising לדעת and interpreting עות as Aramaic. Volz compares
עות with Talmudic and removes לדעת דבר after verse 5*a*.
Grätz conjectured לענית חנף, ' to answer the heathen', and Levy
לְעוֹת זְעֵף דָּבָר, 'to silence the vexed with a word', if that is
Hebrew.

' To twist speech ' must have meant as many different things
in ancient languages as it does in modern. In an inscription of
Hammurabi, published in Gadd and Legrain, *Royal Inscriptions
from Ur*, no. 146, p. 45, it is said of the inhabitants of Gutium
and Subartu, men of the eastern and northern hills, *lišanšunu
egru*, 'their tongue is twisted', which means, probably, that they
spoke incomprehensible dialects. In the Qur'ān, Sūra 4, verse 46,

Muḥammad accused some Jews; they 'move the words furtively from their places . . . by twisting with their tongues and abusing the faith'. This may refer to deliberate mispronunciation or misinterpretation by Jews who pretended to accept the faith but had mental reservations. There is no reason why 'to twist the word' should not mean, to employ speech not understood by all, to give words special senses they do not ordinarily bear. The LXX interpreted the word similarly, but applied it not to the manner of speech, but to the choice of appropriate occasions. The difficulty lies, not in לעות, but in the order of the words, unless that order is due to exceptional emphasis on דבר. The LXX solved this difficulty by excision; rightly?

Page 71.

64. That the clauses אשר· · ·לו refer to עבדו, and that the subject of יבטח מי is seems clear, but some commentators combine otherwise. The passage provides an interesting example of a principle which the present study seeks to establish, affecting exegesis. Syntax does not necessarily compel the connexion of אשר הלך with עבדו; the relative could, theoretically, refer to ירא and שומע. Any reader might come to that conclusion, and the passage has, therefore, been so interpreted. But if the words are read aloud, the hearer inevitably connects אשר with עבדו; the sense must accord with the first impression given by the spoken words, if this is prophecy. Apart from the clear indication in l, 10, that the prophet was in hiding, which is avoided by those who, like Elliger, p. 37, attribute the passage to the compiler, there is another such in xlix, 2, where Elliger, p. 92, recognizes it: 'Es scheint in den Sätzen "Im Schatten seiner Hand barg er mich" und "In seinem Köcher versteckte er mich", auch der Gedanke mitherein zu spielen, dass Jahwe einst den Knecht wirklich deckte und schützte. Die Frage liegt nahe, warum das ausdrücklich betont wird.' If the prophet was in hiding from time to time, he cannot always have issued his utterances from the same place.

The discussion as to where the author of these chapters spoke or wrote has turned on assertion and counter-assertion rather than reasoning, for there is no conclusive proof. Duhm thought the prophet lived in the Lebanon, Marti and G. Hölscher in Egypt, Kittel, Gressmann, and Volz in Babylonia, Maynard, Buttenwieser, and Mowinckel in Palestine, while Staerk divided the chapters into two parts, xl–xlviii written in Babylonia, xlix–liv in Palestine. Caspari (3), pp. 241–2, also considers that the various authors he assumes lived in Babylonia, at any rate most of them. Abraham Lévy, *The Song of Moses*, maintained that some of the many authors of these chapters lived in Elam. The arguments are unconvincing. Caspari says, 'Deutero-Isaiah speaks of Palestine as the desired but distant goal'; that is sub-jective. Mowinckel argues that the complete misunderstanding of the position of the exiles in Babylonia shown in li, 13–14, or, still more, in xlii, 22, could only have arisen in Palestine. The words are figurative, and there is no reason to doubt that some, though not all, of the exiles in Babylonia were living in the conditions the prophet pictured. Pfeiffer, p. 470, says that Jeremiah xxix, 5–7 shows that the original exiles were allowed 'free economic and social development'; the passage actually urges the Jews to make the best use of the conditions in which slaves in Babylonia lived, and proves that many did not, because they refused marriage with non-Jews. The commercial activity of certain Jews in Babylonia under Artaxerxes I and Darius II, for which see E. Ebeling, *Aus dem Leben der jüdischen Exulanten*, does not affect the position before 540 B.C. But xlii, 22 could be understood of, and may originally have referred to, the peasants in Palestine. Kittel argued that similarities in expression between xlv, 1 ff., and the Cyrus cylinder pointed to residence in Baby-lonia; they merely prove that the writer was well informed about the language and ceremonies of the Babylonians, as is further demonstrated by Stummer. But then he shows exceptional information about Persia, the western provinces, and Egypt too. (A striking instance in the case of Egypt may be found in xliv, 5; see Guillaume in *The Expository Times*, xxxii, 377–9.) Another argument, that lii, 11 and xlviii, 20 point to the prophet being outside Babylon, has been countered by the assumption that he was in some other town in Babylonia. Haller's view, that the prophet's close connexion with Cyrus would be best explained if he were, at any rate for a time, in the Persian camp, has been answered, characteristically, by Volz, p. xvi, note: 'The relation of Jahwe to Cyrus and of Cyrus to Jahwe can in no way be explained by rational considerations; they belong to the super-abundance and the supra-rational element of faith.' It has also been sharply attacked by Mowinckel, who says, 'This is only an example of the fact that learned work on traditional texts can also become an element in the formation of legends.' But this, carried to a logical conclusion, would mean that the Cyrus of cc. xl–lv is also a legend. That the prophet was in communica-tion with Cyrus is an inevitable conclusion, if his preaching was contemporary with the events of 545–538. But Haller's deduction is not necessary. Inferences made here point to Palestine as the prophet's head-quarters, but not his permanent residence; but the inferences provide no proof.

65. Reading בריחם for בריחים, which AV rendered 'nobles' and RV 'as fugitives'. Most commentators interpret the word as meaning 'bolts' and this has led to strange emendations. Thus Volz emends from הורדתי to וְהָרַסְתִּי בְּרִיחֵי כִלְאֲכֶם, and before רְנָּתָם he inserts יֵאָסְרוּ אַיֵּה: '(ich) zerbreche die Riegel eurer Haft; die Chaldäer werden auf den Schiffen gebunden, wo ist ihr Lärm?' Oesterley and Robinson, p. 265, emend

וְהוֹרַדְתִּי בְרִיחֵי כֶלֶא וְכַשְׂדִּים וְהִשְׁבַּתִּי בַּאֲנִיּוֹת רִנָּתָם

'I will bring down the bars of the prison-house (Babylon); and as for the Chaldaeans, I will still their shouting with sighs.' This seems very questionable Hebrew. The emendation בריהם, suggested by Caspari (3), p. 25, note 3, and accepted in the translation, is plausible only if it is admitted that in xlvii, 13 הברו שמים the first word is to be read without ה, as a Babylonian loan-word, baru, so that the words mean 'those who divine from the appearance of the night-sky', as suggested by Caspari (3), p. 7, note 3. In any case the corruption in xliii, 14 is more likely to lie in this word than in the rest of the verse.

66. Does the following clause delimit the Chaldaeans meant? If the question be asked, with regard to this verse, whether there is any evidence that the Jews assisted in an attack on Nabonidus at Tema', the answer must be, there is none. Those who require other evidence before using Old Testament documents as historical sources will continue to regard the text as corrupt. The historian must be allowed to use all the sources that exist.

67. רִנָּה is regularly used of joy; there is nothing to show that it could mean a battle-cry. Perhaps then the meaning is, ' who exult in their ships', rejoice in seafaring. These must be men from the marshes, the Chaldaean tribesmen long settled in the Sea-Land. But a special application would be more suitable; the cry of joy may be due to the opportunity the ships offer for escape.

Page 72.

68. See e.g. Ezekiel xxi, 26 (21); or the inscription of Ashurna-ṣirpal in Budge and King, *Annals of the Kings of Assyria*, i, p. 351, (m)*Bel-aplu-iddina* (amel)*baru alik pan ummanatišu*, 'the diviner who leads his armies'.

69. The South Arabians are not in general a tall or powerfully built race, so that the description does not seem to fit. Winckler, *Altorientalische Forschungen*, Reihe I, Heft II, p. 194, suggested that מִדָּה here means 'tribute', as in Nehemiah v, 4. This may be right. The LXX interpreted the passage as referring to slaves, presumably because of the parallelism of men and goods. If that is the true sense, perhaps 'Sabaeans' means slaves from Africa sent north from Saba. That would accord with xliii, 3, where Egypt, Nubia, and Saba are called the ransom, כֹּפֶר, of Israel, because from trade with those lands will come the means for remitting tribute. Caspari (3), p. 93, Anm. 3, is inclined to think that סְבָאִים is genitive, parallel to כוּש; if this is correct, the Saba meant must be in Africa, south of Nubia. Is that possibly due to some temporary supremacy of the Sabaeans on the west coast of the Red Sea, such as they established later? Elliger, p. 246, Anm. 1, emends the beginning of the verse, יְגִיעַ מִצְרַיִם וְסֹחֲרֵי כוּשׁ 'the workers of Egypt and the tradesmen of Nubia and the tall Sabaeans', which reads smoothly, too smoothly perhaps to be correct. Volz emends by transferring the opening to verse 13, much too violent a method. The difficulty in the verse is due to just such a failure in clarity or false parallelism as may occur in all speakers and writers. The uncertainty of interpretation is unfortunate; for if the Sabaeans of this verse were certainly men of South Arabia, the passage would provide some proof that Nabonidus not only prevented the diversion of South Arabian trade westwards, but even stopped the traffic to Palestine (see p. 39).

70. This is intelligible if slaves are meant. Might the word זִקִּים mean in this context, not fetters, but heavy anklets worn to enhance dignity?

70a. See T. H. Gaster in *Ancient Egypt*, 1932, Pt. iii, p. 68.

Page 73.

71. Thus Sennacherib says of Mushezib-Marduk (Shuzubu), the rebel king of Babylonia, *ina abulli qabal ali ša Ninua arkussu dabueš*, 'I bound him in the great gate before the city of Nineveh like a bear', see Luckenbill, ii, art. 354. On this custom see Landsberger, *Die Fauna des alten Mesopotamiens* (*Abhandlungen der phil.-hist. Klasse der sächsischen Akademie der Wiss.*, Bd. xlii), Leipzig, 1934, pp. 80-3.

72. M. Streck, *Assurbanipal*, Teil ii, p. 54, lines 65-9, (*iṣ*)*qišati pazrati* . . . . (*amel*)*ṣabe tahazia* . . . . . *emuru puzrašin.*

73. Herodotus, i, 187.

74. Herodotus, i, 183.

75. JRAS, 1928, pp. 849 ff.

76. R. Kittel, *Cyrus und Deuterojesaja*, in ZATW, xviii (1898), pp. 149–62, pointed out several parallelisms between the language employed in cc. xl–lv and the clay cylinder, especially between this phrase and the cylinder line 12, *ište'ema malki išaru bibil libbi ša ittamah qatussu*, '(Marduk) sought out a righteous king as his favourite, whose hand he would grasp'. Out of these resemblances Gressmann constructed, first in his *Ursprung der israelitisch-jüdischen Eschatologie*, and later in the essay (3), pp. 59–63, his theory of 'the court style'. This is unquestionably an exaggeration, and has been roundly condemned by Torrey, p. 26, note, and modified by Caspari (3), p. 181, Anm. 4. But there is in it this much truth, that this prophet was exceptionally well informed, and could, when need was, use the international language of the time, though it involved acquaintance with pagan ritual and foreign customs. See Stummer, pp. 177–8. The clear implication of the words, a proclamation of Cyrus as king, is that Cyrus had finally conquered Babylon. Begrich's assertion to the contrary, (2), p. 64, 'the words of Deutero-Isaiah know no allusion to the capture of Babylon in 539', is not more than a paradox.

Page 74.

77. Begrich, p. 127.

78. Why are the mountains mentioned here? Is it because a single express messenger was sent from the Euphrates to Palestine across the desert, by way of Jawf and Amman?

79. In this context the historical content of this phrase cannot be doubted; the prophet meant that the old theocratic kingdom of Judah was to be restored in a new form. Mowinckel (2) argues that the words derive from the language of Psalms 93–100 and his assumed *Thronbesteigungsfest*; this tears the words from the historical setting and the immediate context. See Lecture I, note 103.

Page 75.

80. Gressmann (3), pp. 318–19, attempted to state a case against this explanation of c. liii: 'As we know, prophets from time to time came to die for their calling; in the circles of their disciples they may well have been considered innocent martyrs. But their deaths could not be treated as a great mystery; at any rate they could not have been thought to be marked by God

and branded as criminals, so that afterwards the idea could arise that they had taken the sins of Israel on themselves.' The argument is unconvincing, partly owing to the dogma that there is some 'mystery' in the events referred to in c. liii. That is due to the confusion between the incidents to which the words immediately refer, and the religious beliefs implied in the words used; the 'mystery' is in the religious interpretation of an historical event, not in a ritual act, as Gressmann argued.

81. The account of the return in the time of Cyrus under Sheshbazzar in Ezra i does not necessarily imply that the totals given in Ezra ii, 64 ff. apply to that return alone. There is a lack of clarity in the Chronicler's statements, and there may be wrong interpretation of sources, though the errors can be no greater than are to be found in any account of confused periods. The account seems to show that there was a series of efforts, mostly failures, over a number of years. If the prophet perished while attempting to lead exiles to return, the driving power was lost, and not fully recovered till Ezra and Nehemiah took up the task.

Begrich (2), p. 66, says: 'As to the dating of cc. xl ff., the presumption of the existence of an edict of Cyrus permitting the return is not a sufficient basis for it. Was such an edict promulgated in 538? Did multitudes of exiles undertake to return home? There are important reasons against an affirmative answer. We are compelled to look for other possibilities in dating.' This point of view is unhistorical. The question of the number of exiles who returned under Sheshbazzar does not affect the certainty that Cyrus issued an edict of which the tenor is known, nor the equal certainty that lii, 11–12 can only have been written or spoken when Cyrus's edict was known. Similarly xlv, 11–13 and lv, 12–13 can only be understood as addressed to exiles after the fall of Babylon.

82. The important problem of the relation of the prophetic mission to the political activity of the individual prophet has been dicusssed most recently by J. Hempel (3). He has not brought out the close relation of Isaiah the son of 'Amoṣ and of the prophet of cc. xl–lv in their political attitude. Each was determined to preserve the theocratic state in Judah, the one by steering a course through the conflict between Assyria and Egypt which took no account of the interests or desires of the king, the other by resolute support of the only power likely to grant a restoration of national life, a support that involved abandoning dreams based on the dynasty of David. Both had a tenacious hold on principles which

went back to the time of Samuel, yet both were firmly convinced
that the religious life of their people must be centred on Jerusalem
(though this of course can be denied by the critics who refuse to
accept Isaiah xxxi, 6–9 as an utterance of the son of 'Amoṣ, and
deny the biographical record, xxxvii, 6–7, 22–35, validity because
these passages do not fit their own conceptions). The struggle
did not end with the prophet of cc. xl–lv; the same ideas can be
dimly discerned in the later Persian period, and were active in
the time of the Maccabees.

ADDENDA

Page 64, lines 22–3.

'the details, however fantastic, cannot vary much.' This is
true, of course, of all myth, not merely of eschatological vision,
which is a special kind of myth. Compare what is said by
C. S. Lewis, *A Preface to Paradise Lost*, p. 56: 'There is . . . a
special reason why mythical poetry ought not to attempt novelty
in respect of its ingredients. What it does with the ingredients
may be as novel as you please.' xliii, 20 is a reference to traditional history, Exodus xvii, 5–7, not to the future, and a promise
for the present.

Page 160, note 8.

On Persian scale armour see Herodotus, vii, 61 : ix, 22 : i, 135
and Lawrence, pp. 562–3. The comparison to fish-scales is interesting as the Hebrew word applies to the scales both of fish
and of armour. Iron and bronze scales were found at Persepolis,
and some were plated with gold, see E. F. Schmidt, *The Treasurv
of Persepolis*, p. 44 and fig. 27. For a full discussion of all earlier
evidence see now B. Thordeman, *Armour from the Battle of Wisby*
(Stockholm, 1939), vol. i, pp. 270–80, 446–8.

Page 167, note 36.

The archaeological evidence has been discussed, with full
bibliographical references, by Valentin Muller, *The Origin of
Mosaic*, in *Journal of the American Oriental Society*, lix (1939),
pp. 247–50.

CHRONOLOGICAL ARRANGEMENT AND ANALYSIS OF THE PROPHECIES

Time:

After the outbreak of hostilities between Cyrus and Nabonidus, shortly before the attack on the Babylonian governors in North Syria.

Prophecies:

xli, 1–13.

The victory of Cyrus, planned by YHWH, may cause others, but need not cause Israel, fear.

Formal analysis:

1 *a.* YHWH summons 'isles and nations' to audience.
1 *b.* Exhortation by the prophet to the audience.
2–4. YHWH addresses the 'isles and nations'.
5–7. Prophet's description of events.
8–13. YHWH addresses Israel.

Summary of argument:

The pagan gods cannot disprove the claim that YHWH brought Cyrus victory (1–4). The cities of the coast and of the north have cause to fear war and are arming (5–7), but Israel need not fear, for YHWH will support His servant (8–13).

xli, 14–xlii, 9.

The first call to revolt in favour of Cyrus.

Formal analysis:

14–20. YHWH addresses Israel.
21–24. YHWH challenges the pagan gods.
25–26. YHWH proclaims the attack of Cyrus and the truth of His oracles.
27–29. Letter of YHWH to Jerusalem.

Summary of argument:

YHWH will enable an insignificant nation to perform a mighty task, the reduction of mountains; He will provide oases in the barren land (14–20). The pagan gods cannot predict events immediately forthcoming, as YHWH has done through His prophet; their failure is denounced (21–4). Cyrus will attack

Syria, for YHWH has already inspired him to do so; the pagan gods know nothing of this, for they are but cast metal (25–9). The law of YHWH will be restored in Palestine through Cyrus (1–4). The universal Creator supports Cyrus in order to release the exiles (5–7), and promises the Jews that no concession shall be made to idol-worship (8); they are reminded that as past prophecies came true, so will the new message (9).

[These two prophecies may be parts of one whole.]

PERIOD II

Time:

After the adhesion of Phoenicia to Cyrus and the invasion of the lands east of Jordan.

Prophecies:

xlii, 10–25.

The second call to revolt by aiding Cyrus in the Arabian war.

Formal analysis:

10–12. Address by the prophet to Phoenicia and Qedar.
   13. Proclamation of the war of YHWH on His enemies by the prophet.
14–17. General proclamation by YHWH.
18–19. YHWH addresses the 'blind'.
  20 *a*. YHWH addresses His servant.
  20 *b*. Statement concerning the servant.
   21. Comment by prophet on the intention of YHWH.
22–23. The prophet challenges other national leaders.
24–25. The prophet reflects on past history.

Summary of argument:

There is cause for rejoicing in Phoenicia and Qedar, for God has marched against His enemies and He will drive them back (10–17). [A passage that is partly corrupt and not fully intelligible seems to mean that there have been men who would not hear the prophet's message, though they profess to serve YHWH (18–20).] YHWH will rejoice in the re-establishment of His law (21). The present condition of the people is desperate, and someone must hear so as to bring future redress (22–3). The punishment has been inflicted for past sin, and yet the sufferer has not realized the cause (24–5).

xl, 1–31.

The third call to revolt by aiding Cyrus.

Formal analysis:

1. Instruction of YHWH to His messengers.
2. Exhortation of the prophet to the messengers.
3–5. An order communicated by a herald.
6–8. Communication of a message to be proclaimed.
9–11. Order to Jerusalem to announce good news.
12–24. The prophet addresses Israel.
25. YHWH's question.
26–31. Continuation of prophet's address.

Summary of argument:

Israel is to be of good heart, for tribulation is at an end (1–2). A high road is to be built in the desert and through the mountains (3–5), for Babylon is weak and about to fall (6–8). The Jews in Palestine are to be told that the exiles will return (9–11). No one can estimate, and no one must question, God's creations and His demands (12–17), for He is not as one of the idols that are only kept upright through being fixed to bases (18–20). The Creator who governs the universe can dispose of kingdoms and empires; He is incomparable (21–6). Israel has despaired without reason, for confidence in YHWH will bring success (27–31).

xliii, 16–xliv, 23.

The fourth call to revolt, in the assurance of success.

Formal analysis:

xliii, 16–xliv, 22. YHWH addresses Israel.
     xliv, 23. Prophet's hymn of praise.

Summary of argument:

The God who rescued Israel from Egypt orders His people to turn their thoughts to the new dispensation actually developing (16–18). He will make a road and oases in the land east of Jordan though Israel has not persisted in worshipping Him (19–22). He has not even received the sacrifices due to pagan gods; however, He demands not material sacrifices but obedience to His will (23–5). The punishment inflicted on the nation has been imposed because the leaders of the people disobeyed God (26–8). But now God has assured Israel of His support, and the young generation shall not thirst, but will multiply (1–4). Individuals should now declare themselves

God's followers (5). God has ordered what is to come as He ordered what is past, and no other but God can reveal what is happening (6–7). There is no cause for fear, for the idols of the pagans are ridiculous (8–20). God has redeemed, not forgotten, Israel (21–3).

PERIOD III

Time:

The commencement of the Babylonian withdrawal from Palestine.

Prophecies:

xlix, 1–26.

Justification of the prophet: Palestine will be freed and the exiles return.

Formal analysis:

1–6. Prophet's autobiography.
7–12. Oracles of YHWH addressed to the prophet.
13. Prophet's hymn of praise.
14–26. Address of YHWH to Jerusalem.

Summary of argument:

Foreigners and Jews in distant settlements are told that the prophet's mission has caused dissension, but God has protected him. At one time the prophet despaired of fulfilling his mission, that is of restoring the ancient land rights and bringing back the exiles; but God has assured him that success will be achieved by turning to other nations, whom the prophet is to enlighten (1–6). God will save the prophet, and will release the Jews from their bondage and bring them, by means of oases and high roads, from all quarters (7–12). Natural creation is called upon to praise God (13). The doubts that have been openly expressed are specifically answered by the promise that God will remember Zion; 'the destroyers shall go forth'. Palestine, now desolate, shall again be populous (14–21). Judah will regain a position among the nations; the exiles will return and vengeance will be taken on the oppressors (22–6).

li, 9–16.

God orders the prophet to persevere in confidence.

Formal analysis:

9–11. Summons by the prophet to the 'arm of YHWH'.
12–16. YHWH replies to the prophet.

Summary of argument:

The prophet calls for divine intervention through human agency as mighty as that of the past (9–10), so that the exiles may return (11). There is no reason to fear the Babylonians nor to forget that God the Creator will relieve Israel from the oppressor (12–13). The urgent desire of the exiles for release must be accommodated to God's order (14–15). The message of the prophet is from God, who has protected him (15–16).

li, 17–lii, 6.

The call to reconstruct Jerusalem.

Form:

Address of YHWH to Jerusalem.

Summary of argument:

The punishment is at an end and will not be imposed again (17–22); but those who have joined the oppressors shall endure God's fury (23). The city must arise from its dust (1–3). Because the foreign rulers have abused YHWH, He will again reveal Himself as formerly in the release from Egypt, or when the Assyrians attacked Judah (4–6).

PERIOD IV

Time:

After Palestine had been freed, before the Babylonian withdrawal from Taima.

Prophecies:

li, 1–8.

Call to return to ancient ways, to obey the divine law imposed by Cyrus, and to disregard opposition.

Formal analysis:

1–3. Address by the prophet to his followers.
4–8. Address by YHWH to His own people.

Summary of argument:

Israel must turn back to ancient ways, for Palestine, now free, will be restored (1–3). Law will be imposed by Cyrus; and God's law will abide even though the natural universe should not prove permanent (4–6). The prophet's followers are not to shrink from the abuse of the elders, for the elders are subject to corruption through inertia, whereas the righteousness of God abides (7–8).

liv, 1–17.

The future of Jerusalem.

Formal analysis:

1–6. Address by prophet to Jerusalem.
7–17. Address by YHWH to Jerusalem.

Summary of argument:

Jerusalem must be prepared for a great re-settlement (1–3).
There is no cause for fear, for the Babylonians, who have
desecrated the city during the time it was deprived of YHWH's
protection, have held power only a short time (4–8). God's
favour, now restored, will be permanent; He will protect His
servant from all attacks (9–17).

xliii, 1–13.

Reassurance that in spite of dangers Israel will be saved and the exiles will return.

Form:

Address by YHWH to Israel.

Summary of argument:

There is no cause for fear, for God will provide protection
through every danger (1–2). The victory, which has opened the
routes to Egypt, Nubia, and the Sabaeans for Cyrus, has freed
Palestine (3). Others will suffer, Israel will be preserved (4).
There is no cause for fear; the exiles will return (5–7). Those
who have persisted in disbelieving the prophecies and in refusing to acknowledge the true course of events must now see
that no one else has been right, and that God is the only Saviour
(8–11). The prophecies which have been revealed 'when no
stranger was among you' have been proved true by the event,
and Israel is a witness that God is the only deliverer (12–13).

PERIOD V

Time:

After the Babylonian withdrawal from Taima.

Prophecy:

xliii, 14–15.

Announcement of the withdrawal by sea.

Form:

Announcement by YHWH.

Argument:

The measures preliminary to a withdrawal by the Babylonians from the Red Sea have been taken (14). God the Creator is King of Israel (15).

PERIOD VI

Time:

Before the siege of Babylon.

Prophecy:

l, 1–11.

First rebuke, to those who persecute the prophet.

Formal analysis:

1–3. Address by YHWH to those who complain against Him and refuse obedience.

4–9. Autobiography of the prophet.

10. Call of the prophet for followers.

11. Threat by YHWH to those who stir up dissension.

Summary of argument:

There are those who say that God disregards and neglects His people. All was in the past and still is due to Israel's sin; God is the all-powerful Creator (1–3). The prophet was instructed by God in the way to deliver His message, and it has been delivered without flinching, though he endured persecution from those he addressed. Final justification is assured; opposition will disappear in the course of time (4–9). Individuals are called to assist the prophet while he is in hiding (10). His opponents are warned that their activities will lead to their destruction (11).

PERIOD VII

Time:

During the siege of Babylon.

Prophecy:

xlvii, 1–15.

Railing song against Babylon.

Form:

Address of YHWH to Babylon.

Summary of argument:

The imperial city will be reduced to the position of its own most despised vassals. Magical religion will prove no protection.

PERIOD VIII

Time:

After the fall of Babylon.

Prophecies:

xlvi, 1–2.

Announcement of the fall.

Form:

Message of the prophet to his followers.

Argument:

The gods of Babylon are now captive; they had been loaded on pack animals in the attempt to escape, but the burden proved too heavy. The heathen gods were unable to deliver themselves.

xliv, 24–xlv, 8.

The appointment of Cyrus.

Formal analysis:

24–8. Protocol of YHWH.

1–7. Address by YHWH to Cyrus.

8. Invocation by the Creator to His creation.

Summary of argument:

The Creator of all—who has confounded the magicians of Babylon, who ordered the repopulation of Jerusalem and the rebuilding of the cities of Judah, the God who caused a drought, who announced that He appointed Cyrus shepherd of the people to do His will, who commanded the rebuilding of Jerusalem and the Temple, the God who redeemed, as He created, Israel—has not only appointed Cyrus to rule over the pagan nations in accordance with their religious rites, but has anointed him to rule over Judah. All the wealth of Babylon now belongs to Cyrus. Favour has been shown to him so that all may know that the God of Israel is the Creator. 'Right' shall bring forth 'righteousness'.

lii, 7–10.

News of peace.

Form:

Message from the prophet to Jerusalem.

Argument:

The messenger who is approaching Palestine across mountains brings news of peace; that means, Israel is saved. Summons to rejoice. All will recognize the 'holy arm' of YHWH.

lv, 1–13.

First order to exiles in Babylonia.

Form:

Address by the prophet to the Jews.

Argument:

Call to abandon daily occupations and return to the Covenant (1–3). Cyrus is the witness of the new Covenant, and the Persians are Israel's allies in it (4–5). God's plan must not be questioned (6–11). There will be a glorious return to a fruitful land (12–13).

lii, 11–12.

Second order to exiles in Babylonia.

Form:

Message of the prophet to the Jews.

Argument:

The exiles are to leave Babylonia, taking all that came to Babylon from the old Temple in Jerusalem.

xlvi, 3–13.

Second* rebuke, to the disobedient.

Form:

YHWH addresses the Jews.

Summary of argument:

God has supported Israel from the beginning and will do so to the end. He is no heathen god made of precious metal but not endowed with the power to help (3–7). Sinners should call to mind the declared will of God. His plan is to be executed by Cyrus; resistance is sin. The plan includes the coming re-institution of worship in Jerusalem and is near realization (8–13).

* For the first, see Period VI.

xlviii, 1–22.

Third rebuke, to those who dispute the appointment of Cyrus. Renewed order to the exiles to leave Babylonia.

Form:

Address by YHWH to Israel.

Summary of argument:

The new things that have come to pass were predicted, but the Jewish unbelievers paid no attention (1–4). In spite of the prediction, intended to prevent Israel's persistence in disbelief and disobedience, Israel did not hear the call (5–8). God will refrain from destroying the nation (9), but, since there is still bad alloy in Israel, He will purify the people for His name's sake (10–11). The Creator appointed Cyrus to perform the task that he is carrying out, the destruction of the Babylonian Empire (12–15). There has been no secret in the prophesying of this event (16). The acceptance of God's will is Israel's duty (17). Had there been obedience in the past, Israel would by now be innumerable (18–19). The exiles are to leave Babylonia and return to Palestine. Israel is now redeemed as it was of old (20–2).

xlv, 9–25.

Fourth rebuke, to opponents, and last words to the exiles.

Formal analysis:

9–10. Denunciation of opponents by the prophet.

11–13. Oracle of YHWH concerning Cyrus.

14–17. Oracle of YHWH concerning Palestine.

18–19. Oracle of YHWH confirming His prophet.

20–25. Address of YHWH to those who have escaped from the unbelievers.

Summary of argument:

The thing created cannot oppose its creator (9–10). The Creator, YHWH, is willing to reveal the future that He plans for Israel (11–12). Cyrus, who has been directed by YHWH, is to rebuild Jerusalem and free all exiles (13). Trade will return to Palestine; the southern countries, too, Egypt, Nubia, and the Sabaeans, will acknowledge the greatness of the Only God (14–17). There has been no mystery about the prophecies in the immediate past and they have proved right (18–19). The exiles now freed know that pagan religion is futile; God is the only help and His decree is immutable (20–3). Those who resist His will will suffer; but Israel's future generations will benefit (24–5).

PERIOD IX

Time:

After the death of the prophet.

Prophecy:

lii, 13–liii, 12.

Recognition of the prophet's mission and achievement.

Formal analysis:

13–15. Oracle of YHWH addressed to Israel.

1–10. Lament for the 'servant of YHWH' by members of a community to which he belonged.

11–12. Utterance of YHWH concerning the 'servant'.

Summary of argument:

YHWH proclaims that His 'servant', because of his foresight, shall be raised (from the condemnation he has suffered) (13). Many people in many places have been shocked by the disfiguration of his body; for that reason his blood shall be as it were a ritual means of purifying sinners and bringing reconciliation among many peoples (14–15). Kings will chatter with dismay when they see and reflect on results of actions they had not been told about (15). The speakers had known the prophet when he was brought as a child to serve YHWH. Because he was inconspicuous he was despised; when he was despised he was not understood (1–3). His sorrows were brought on him by the sins of the nation, not as his fellows thought, by God as a punishment of his own sins (4–5). The nation was redeemed through his sufferings (5–6). When he was condemned to death, he endured in silence and was treated as a felon, because he would not deny his words (7–9). What has happened was God's will, and God will restore him to his lost rights (10). God Himself has declared that the prophet by bearing the sins of others has justified the greater part of Israel. The prophet's part in the booty of Cyrus is to be the exiles whom he redeemed (11–12).

REFERENCES TO BIBLICAL PASSAGES

[Numerals in roman type indicate pages; italics give the relevant note]

(1) cc. xl–lv

xl. 5; 6; 11–14; 55; 61; 64–8; 86, 7; 90–1, 38; 92, 46; 93–4, 48; 94, 49, 54, 56, 58, 60; 95, 65, 68; 96, 77, 78; 98, 90; 103, 105; 104, 113; 111–12, 140; 112, 142; 124, 36; 158, 2; 159–60, 8; 161, 11; 167, 37, 38; 169, 46; 170–2, 48, 50; 185.

xli. 49–51; 53–4; 68–9; 86, 7; 87, 11; 91, 39; 93, 46, 48; 94, 48a, 50, 55; 95, 63, 64; 104, 113; 107, 116; 108, 124; 110–11, 135; 112, 141; 158, 1; 159–60, 8; 161–2, 11; 162, 13, 14; 163, 18; 163–4, 21; 165, 34a; 168, 43; 169, 46; 170, 47, 50; 183.

xlii. 19; 20; 52; 54–63; 91, 39; 93, 46; 94, 52, 56, 60; 95, 63, 70; 96, 78; 98, 93; 100, 99; 103, 107; 107–8, 124; 110–11, 135; 158, 1; 163, 19; 164, 21; 166, 35; 166–7, 36; 170, 50; 177, 64; 183–4.

xliii. 13; 16; 40; 52; 63–4; 71–2; 86, 7; 92, 41; 94, 50, 52, 55; 95, 63, 64; 110, 134; 158, 1; 159, 7; 166–7, 36; 178, 65; 179, 69; 185; 188.

xliv. 13; 72; 86, 7, 9; 92, 41; 93, 46; 94, 53, 55; 95, 63, 64, 65, 67, 70; 96, 78; 111, 136; 158, 1; 159, 7; 162, 15; 167, 37; 170–2, 50: 177, 64; 185; 190.

xlv. 10; 19; 52; 53; 58; 72–3; 86, 7; 89, 19; 91, 40; 92, 46; 94, 52, 55, 56; 95, 63, 65; 96, 78; 158, 1, 3; 161–2, 11; 162, 13, 16; 163–4, 21; 170, 50; 174, 58; 177, 64; 190; 192.

xlvi. 86, 7, 8; 93, 46; 94, 54, 59; 95, 63, 65; 158, 1; 170, 50; 174, 58; 190; 191.

xlvii. 14; 86, 7; 88–9, 18; 94, 59; 95, 74; 98, 90; 101, 100; 123, 36; 168, 43; 178, 65; 189.

xlviii. 86, 7, 9; 93, 46; 94, 52, 53, 55; 95, 63, 64, 65, 66; 104, 113; 158, 1; 159, 7; 174, 58; 177, 64; 191–2.

xlix. 10; 19; 69–70; 93, 46; 94, 50, 54; 95, 63, 71, 72; 96, 78; 100, 98, 100; 104, 113; 111, 140; 165, 34a; 169, 45; 174, 60; 176, 64; 181, 81; 186.

l. 19; 70–1; 94, 52, 53; 95, 64, 65, 71; 96, 78; 100, 98; 174, 58; 176, 64; 189.

li. 60; 93, 46; 94, 50, 54, 57; 95, 63, 71; 96, 78; 112, 141; 167, 38; 170, 47; 177, 64; 186–7.

lii. 17; 19–20: 74; 90, 30; 93, 46; 94, 58; 95, 66, 73; 96, 78; 103, 105; 105, 114; 177, 64; 181, 81; 187; 190; 191; 192–3.

liii. 17; 19–20; 87, 13; 94, 50; 99, 94, 98; 102–3, 105; 180–1, 80; 192–3.

liv. 13; 86, 9; 93, 46; 94, 54; 95, 63, 66; 107, 115; 158, 1; 166–7, 36; 188.

lv. 13; 94, 53, 54, 56; 95, 63, 67, 69; 96, 78; 104, 112, 113; 112, 142; 181, 81; 191.

GENERAL INDEX

(*continued from p.* 157)

Posener, *La Première Domination Perse en Égypte*, pp. 70, 186, Pl. VI, no. 21, is probably right in assuming that *ť ṭmḥw*, *Ta Temeḥu*, in the hieroglyphic list on the stele from Kabrit, corresponded to *Putaya* in the cuneiform. The land so designated may not be Libya or even the western Delta, as in earlier usage. In the sixth century the eastern Delta and its border were garrisoned by Libyan colonists. Since Amasis was fighting Greeks in 568 B.C., Breasted, *Ancient Records*, IV, §§ 1002–7, the 'city *Puṭu-Yaman*' can hardly be Cyrene, the only natural interpretation if *Puṭu* is Libya. In the reign of Amasis enemy territory across the eastern frontier was called *ť pd.t*, *Ta Peṭe*(t), Breasted, AR, § 1014 (not Nubia); Posener admits the probability of a connexion between *Putaya* and *pdt*, and the land meant may be the Babylonian *Puṭu*, *Biblical Pūṭ*, which is derived from the official Aramaic form used in the Achaemenean Empire. The LXX translations render *Pūṭ* by 'Libyans' because the official hieroglyphic lists introduced a distinction between Egyptian and Persian terminology. But even if *Puṭu-Yaman* could be proved to be Libya, or rather Cyrene, the war of 568 took place round the northern end of the Red Sea.

Page 152, note 139.

For a discussion of the site at Tall 'Umar see Clark Hopkins, *A Bird's-eye View of Opis and Seleucia* in *Antiquity*, xiii (1939), pp. 447–8. The site of Opis has not been found, 'it may still lie beneath Seleucia or it may lie some distance away, presumably towards the north'. Dr. Jacobsen has considered the relation of *Akšak* and *Upi*, Opis, in *Atti del XIX Congresso Internazionale degli Orientalisti* (Rome, 1938), pp. 92 ff. The opinion that the ideographic writing when it refers to early periods is to be read *Akšak*, and that *Upi* is the later name, has been disproved by two documents from Iščali which belong to the time of the First Dynasty of Babylon, see S. L. Feigin in JAOS, lix (1939), pp. 106–7. One of these mentions the transport of bitumen, the other of beams, from *Upi*. The reasonable inference that the place was a suitable unloading place for distribution in the *Ešnunna* area would point to a location near the juncture of the Euphrates and Diyalah, to which bitumen could easily be brought from Hit by canal. The evidence, still unpublished, from Tall 'Umar may prove inconclusive.